Five O'Clock Lightning

To John
   What a catcher!
Congratulations for en-
joying the tools of
ignorance! I'm kidding
I've admired every catcher
I ever saw — I couldn't
do that position — — No How —
         Best Wishes
   Tommy Henrich

Hope you enjoy this.

FIVE O'CLOCK
LIGHTNING

Ruth, Gehrig, DiMaggio, Mantle and the Glory Years of the NY Yankees

by Tommy Henrich
with Bill Gilbert

A BIRCH LANE PRESS BOOK
Published by Carol Publishing Group

A Birch Lane Press Book
Published by Carol Publishing Group
Birch Lane Press is a registered trademark of
Carol Communications, Inc.

Editorial Offices   Sales & Distribution Offices
600 Madison Avenue   120 Enterprise Avenue
New York, NY 10022   Secaucus, NJ 07094

In Canada: Canadian Manda Group
P.O. Box 920, Station U
Toronto, Ontario M8Z 5P9

Manufactured in the United States of America
10 9 8 7 6 5 4 3 2 1

ISBN 1-55972-101-4
Publication data for this title may be obtained from
the Library of Congress.

Carol Publishing Group books are available at special discounts
for bulk purchases, for sales promotions, fund raising, or
educational purposes. Special editions can also be created to
specifications. For details contact: Special Sales Department,
Carol Publishing Group, 120 Enterprise Ave., Secaucus, NJ 07094

To Eileen—although not a fan, she has never interfered with my passion for baseball over fifty years. When she asks me, as she has a thousand times, "Don't you ever get tired of talking baseball?" and I answer simply, "No," she accepts my answer gladly. All of which proves there's more to marriage than a love of baseball. She's been a perfect balance for me.

To our five children—Patricia, Ann, Tom, Mary Louise and Paul—who made everything worthwhile for both Eileen and me.

To the people of New York, who always welcomed us and made our lives fun.

And to Yankee fans and baseball fans everywhere, for their own role in making baseball a special part of life in America.

Contents

Acknowledgments

There is considerable emphasis in this book on teamwork and the need for each player to have a strong team attitude. The same is true of writing a book, which is never the product only of one or two names on the cover.

We want to pay special tribute to the other members of the team that helped us produce this book:

—Our editor at Birch Lane Press, Alan Wilson, and our production editor, David Goodnough.

—Bill Deane, the senior research associate at the National Baseball Library at the Hall of Fame, and Pat Kelly, the manager of the photo collection there.

—Lillian Gilbert and Dave Gilbert for their preliminary editing and administrative services.

—Our mutual friend, Ed Liberatore, who found that one baseball book sometimes leads to another.

—And to our agent, Russell Galen, a vice president at the Scott

Meredith Literary Agency in New York, who, as always, found the right publisher for the right book.

Tommy Henrich and Bill Gilbert
February 1992

Five O'Clock Lightning

_____

One

Of Pinstripes and Legends

When I walked onto the diamond at Yankee Stadium on Opening Day of the 1937 season and looked around, there they were—Lou Gehrig, Joe DiMaggio, Red Ruffing, Lefty Gomez, Bill Dickey, Tony Lazzeri, Joe McCarthy, and so many other legends from the boyhood of a rookie from Massillon, Ohio.

When the end neared and I walked onto that same diamond thirteen years and one war later and looked around, there they were—new and future legends like Phil Rizzuto, Eddie Lopat, Allie Reynolds, Vic Raschi, Yogi Berra, Whitey Ford, Billy Martin, and the enduring one, the man Ernest Hemingway called simply and grandly "the great DiMaggio."

In between, there were eleven seasons as a member of the New York Yankees during one of their golden ages—eight World Series teams and a winner every time except the year I entered the Coast Guard, the only player in baseball history so blessed I can look back on a key role in the most famous third strike in·Series history, a classic pennant race in 1949, and a home run in every Series I played in, including a dramatic game-winner off Don Newcombe in '49.

As the historic and not-so-historic events unfolded, I also had an eyewitness view of some of baseball's most fabled moments: the tearful goodbyes for Lou Gehrig and Babe Ruth, the .406 season of Ted Williams, Joe DiMaggio's 56-game hitting streak, the drama that was Joe Page, the almost-a-no-hitter by Bill Bevens in the 1947 World Series, and the classic catch by Al Gionfriddo. As if that weren't enough, I shared the laughs, lives, and times of young men with names like Scooter, The Crow, Poosh 'Em Up, Twinkletoes, Spud, King Kong, Flash, The Springfield Rifle, Spec, Bobo, Superchief and so many other teammates, plus our leaders, Joe, Bucky, and Casey.

On my first day in New York, I checked into the New Yorker Hotel, where a room had been reserved for me by the Yankees. The bellhop stared at me on the elevator and said after what seemed like a long time, "You're Henrich, aren't you?"

Then, almost without waiting for my answer, he went on: "Geez, I wouldn't want to be in your shoes."

When I asked why, he told me something I already knew: The Yankees had a bumper crop of good outfielders—DiMaggio, Jake Powell, George Selkirk, Roy Johnson, and Myril Hoag. To make sure I got his message, the bellhop added free of charge, "I wouldn't want to try to break in there."

Then, with the confidence of the young, I said, "Yeah, but you haven't seen me play."

I wasn't the only young man in America excited to be starting that week on what I hoped would be the road to success. There was a special election held in Texas that week to fill the unexpired term of the late James P. Buchanan to represent the state's Tenth Congressional District. The name of the young man who won the election was Lyndon Johnson. Unlike Congressman-elect Johnson's, my path took an early detour.

My long road to New York and our team of glory began with softball more than baseball back in Ohio and seemed to include experiences of every kind, even a declaration by the first commissioner of baseball, Judge Kenesaw Mountain Landis, making me the first free agent in history, thirty-seven years before the court rulings on Dave McNally and Andy Messersmith.

Long before it ended for me after our 1950 World Series victory

over the Philadelphia Phillies "Whiz Kids," I was telling people
there was only a one-word difference between the title of the Lou
Gehrig movie and my feeling about my baseball career. Lou's
story, starring Gary Cooper and Teresa Wright, was *Pride of the
Yankees*. My baseball career was a story of pride *in* the Yankees.

The chain of events that made me a Yankee started back home
in Massillon, a town more famous for football as the launching
pad for the career of Paul Brown, where I thrilled to Babe Ruth's
home runs through the magic of radio in its infancy in the 1920s
and began to dream of someday playing for the New York Yankees.

I was seven years old when the Babe hit New York in 1920
after being traded by the Boston Red Sox. The country was going
crazy over all those home runs he was hitting that summer, just
in time to shore up the nation's faith in the game and fire up its
enthusiasm after the Chicago "Black Sox" gambling scandal involving the 1919 World Series.

The owners were alarmed when eight members of the White
Sox were charged with criminal violations for allegedly fixing the
Series, won by the Cincinnati Reds. As soon as the owners appointed Judge Landis, he banned the players from baseball for life
even though they were cleared of the charges.

But that's not what brought the fans streaming into the major-
league ballparks. Babe Ruth did. He led the American League in
home runs in his first year as a Yankee with 54, almost quadruple
the 15 by Cy Williams that led the National League.

Ruth was even better the next season. My eight-year-old eyes
kept popping all season long with the news that my hero, the flashy
Babe, hit still another one that day. By the end of the 1921 season,
Ruth had 59 home runs, a staggering amount that had been beyond anyone's ability to imagine.

As one who was also privileged to wear the Yankee pinstripes,
I can say with pride that Babe Ruth was not only the greatest
thing to happen to baseball in those years—he was the greatest
thing that ever happened to any sport in any year. Today he re-
mains the all-time sports idol of America. Seventy years after he
arrived in New York, his is the Number One name in any conversation about sports heroes. You'll hear mention of Jim Thorpe,

Magic Johnson, Bobby Jones, Joe Louis, Muhammad Ali, and Babe Didrickson Zaharias, but no one else gets the acclaim that the supreme athlete, Babe Ruth, still commands.

In football-crazy Massillon, I was a baseball fan, so from the start I showed an independent streak. But after one year of playing baseball in the fourth grade at St. Mary's Grade School on the corner of Mill and Cherry Streets, I switched to softball. One reason was something that every baseball player can relate to: That big softball was easier to hit.

I kept hitting softballs instead of baseballs until my senior year at St. John's High School in Canton, another town more famous for football as the home of the Pro Football Hall of Fame. Then, with a growing ambition to test my skills at higher levels, I returned to baseball at the semi-pro level. As an outfielder for Acme Dairy, I caught the eye of a major-league scout who had never even heard of me.

Billy Doyle was a scout for the Detroit Tigers who came to an Acme Dairy game to evaluate a pitcher. I got two hits off that pitcher, so Doyle forgot about him and started talking to me. Another scout, Bill Bradley of the Cleveland Indians, a major-league third baseman for fourteen seasons, mostly with the Indians, also began following me around. After the 1933 season, he invited me to go to Cleveland to meet with the general manager, Billy Evans, a legendary figure over the years as a great umpire, later the president of the Southern Association, and today a member of the Hall of Fame.

I started on the road that led me to New York by signing with the Indians and being assigned to their farm team in Zanesville, Ohio, for the start of the 1934 season. I barely had time to unpack. After one week, I was moved to the Indians' team in Monessen, Pennsylvania, where my living expenses included six dollars a week for my room at the Grand Hotel and five dollars for a book of dinner tickets for the week. On a salary of $80 a month, a hotel room costing less than a dollar a night was almost beyond my means.

But professional ballplayers at every level in those years were playing because of their love of the sport. Eighty dollars a month? Even by Depression standards it wasn't much, and it certainly wasn't fair, but so what? We were doing what we loved to do. I managed to hit .326, so my living conditions must not have been too bad.

In the minor leagues you can learn more than you ever dreamed possible about how to play baseball. If you're lucky, you can also learn about life and what it takes to win. That was my good fortune at Zanesville after the Indians returned me there for the 1935 season, at a salary of $120 a month. It was a raise of $40 a month, hardly enough to cause me any tax problems.

Our general manager, Buzz Wetzel, was quoted in the paper late in the season as saying, "If my ballplayers cared as much about winning as they do about their individual averages, we'd be doing a lot better."

The quote was the subject of discussion in our dressing room as we prepared for our game that day. John "Shine" Cortazzo, who was almost thirty-one at that point and had been up with the White Sox for one time at bat in 1923, asked the obvious question: "Well, who *is* leading our team in hitting?"

With that, Bill McIntyre, one of our leaders in batting average, home runs, and runs batted in, spoke up. Bill used to hit like Ducky Medwick, getting his full chest into his swing and hitting four-hundred-foot home runs even though we were in a Class C League where you're not used to seeing ability like that. McIntyre reached into his back pocket, pulled out his wallet, and proceeded to recite the names of the three players who led our team in each of those offensive categories.

I was stunned that anyone would be so hung up on that subject that he'd be carrying his own list in his wallet. But then, to my even greater shock, one of our other players, Jimmy Wasdell, did the same thing. Wasdell later played in the majors for eleven years, breaking in with the Washington Senators in 1937 when I was a rookie with the Yankees.

Wasdell didn't just have a copy of McIntyre's list. He had his own, with different figures. Here were two players who seemed to place their individual performances above the good of their team to such an extent that they kept their own statistics—and even carried the stats around with them.

Cortazzo looked at me and said, "I guess Buzz knows what he's talking about." That's what was wrong with our team.

It was a valuable lesson for me to learn about life in general and baseball in particular. It didn't take me long as a Yankee to learn that our manager, Joe McCarthy, agreed with the Buzz Wetzel philosophy. When you look at the Yankees' individual stats, you see that we didn't always have overpowering numbers— but we won. Joe insisted we play as a team. That's how we became a well-knit, tough ball club, with some great individual stars like DiMaggio and a unit of strong team players, each with a winning attitude.

McCarthy used to point to Joe Gordon as the best example of his philosophy. We were on the field during batting practice at Yankee Stadium one day when one of the writers asked McCarthy why he liked Gordon so much.

McCarthy turned to the infield and hollered, "Joe! C'mere!"

When Gordon reached the group, McCarthy asked him, "Joe, what's your batting average?"

Gordon said, "I don't know."

"Well then, what's your fielding average?"

"I don't know that either."

McCarthy turned to the writer with a big grin on his lantern-jawed face and said, "That's what I mean. All he cares about is beating you."

McCarthy's demand that you play for the team first instead of for yourself led directly to my arrival in New York. The Yankees had Roy Johnson on their roster as one of the outfielders that the bellhop at the Commodore was talking about. Johnson overheard McCarthy complaining one afternoon in Detroit that the Yanks had played two bad games in a row.

Johnson said to one of his teammates, "What does that guy expect to do—win every game?"

As a matter of fact, that's *exactly* what McCarthy expected. He overheard the remark and headed straight to the nearest telephone. He called Ed Barrow, the Yankees' general manager, in New York and told him, "Get Johnson off this ball club."

Barrow said he'd see what player he might be able to get in a trade, but McCarthy told him in words of one syllable, "I don't care who you get. Just get him out of here. And then get me that kid at Newark."

I was "that kid."

Two

The Judge's Shocker

My effort to make it to the big leagues took three years. It would have taken far longer if the independent streak in me had not surfaced at that point and set in motion a series of events felt at the very foundation of major-league baseball.

The Indians, for reasons that teams didn't have to explain to their players in 1935, shifted me back to Zanesville, where I succeeded in hitting .337 even though I didn't carry my own batting average in my hip pocket like those two teammates. In September, with the end of the season approaching, the Indians transferred me again, this time to their farm team in New Orleans, where I enjoyed another strong year. After three seasons in the minor leagues, I could point to batting averages of .326, .337, and .346.

Then a funny thing happened: New Orleans sold me to Milwaukee, then a minor-league team in the American Association. The Brewers were independently owned, but they had a working relationship with the Indians, and that was where the fun began.

During the winter before the 1937 season, while casually reading the newspaper one evening, I spotted an article saying Milwaukee was planning to sell me to the Boston Braves. But then there was another article saying the *Indians* were going to trade me to the St. Louis Browns. Two teams selling or trading the same player?

For a kid not long out of high school, this was confusing, and for anyone of any age, even an experienced lawyer, these reports raised obvious questions: Which team did I belong to? Which trade or sale should I obey and which should I ignore? In other words, just which team was I playing for anyway?

I took the direct approach, a tendency I followed several times with the Yankees later. One night that winter I told my father, "Dad, I'm thinking about writing to Judge Landis."

He asked why.

"Well, I read in the paper where Cleveland is going to trade me and Milwaukee is going to sell me. I wonder which team I belong to, and there's only one guy I trust on this—Judge Landis."

"That makes sense. You think Landis is the right one to write to?"

"Dad, if there's anyone at all on the side of the players, it's Landis. It's certainly not the owners."

That would suit Dad just fine. He was a big Landis admirer, especially after Landis, as a federal judge, ruled in favor of his labor union, the plasterers, in a dispute with management. Landis said he liked plasterers because "at the end of the day you can always see what they've done."

I wrote the letter a few nights later, and I put it on the breakfast table for Dad to read before he left for his job. He read it and even initialed it, adding a note of his own: "I wouldn't change a word." I sent it.

It was a time when workers all over America were beginning to assert themselves, and maybe that mood prompted me unconsciously to start thinking about sticking up for myself. At the Ford, Chrysler, and General Motors plants, workers were on "sit-down" strikes; they would occupy their plant and wait it out until management agreed to talk to them about higher salaries, better working conditions, a forty-hour work week, or allowing a vote on forming a union at their factory.

Henry Ford and others didn't like this business one bit. Ford said, "Labor unions are backed by war-seeking financiers and take away a man's independence. They are the worst thing that ever struck this earth. . . . The financiers want to kill competition so as to reduce the income of workers and eventually bring on war.''

The automobile business wasn't the only industry affected. Workers at the Holde & Horst Company in Reading, Pennsylvania, the largest manufacturer of hosiery in that region, were staging a sit-down strike of their own. In another Pennsylvania town, Hershey, the 2,600 employees at the chocolate plant were arguing for the right to vote on whether to be represented by the CIO— the Committee for Industrial Organization.

That was the mood among America's workers when I sent my letter to Commissioner Landis. A response was not long in coming, but it wasn't what I had hoped for. It didn't say what I wanted, and it wasn't even from Landis. It was from his assistant, Les O'Connor. He told me Landis was on vacation in Florida, then added as his answer to my question, ''Our records show you are the property of the Milwaukee Brewers.''

In my independent attitude I decided immediately that neither of those statements from O'Connor was acceptable. I wrote another letter, appealing to O'Connor to send my original one to Landis in Florida. Spring training was close. I needed some answers soon—and from Landis.

To his credit, O'Connor took no offense at this request from a young minor-league player. He forwarded my letter to Landis quickly, and the response was a telegram from Landis. As an experienced jurist, he wanted proof, not just hearsay. So I obtained statements from Cleveland's general manager, Cy Slapnicka, and other parties and sent them to Landis to help him answer my basic question: Whose property am I?

Landis again answered quickly. It became clear to me later that one reason Landis was being so prompt in responding to me each step of the way was that he knew, even if I didn't, that I was raising a question of profound implications for many other players and teams. He told me to report for spring training with the Brewers in Biloxi, Mississippi, and promised he would contact me later.

Sure enough, several weeks into spring training I received another telegram from Landis ordering me to report to his suite at the Roosevelt Hotel in New Orleans for a hearing on the subject. I went eagerly and optimistically, part of my enthusiasm coming from my mistaken impression that Landis would act as my representative during this hearing.

That was a mistake caused by my youth. Landis wasn't there to help either side. He was there to help the game, by resolving my specific situation and the thorny issues it raised for the rest of baseball.

There I was, twenty-four years old the month before, in a room with the commissioner of baseball and the executives of the Cleveland Indians, New Orleans Pelicans and Milwaukee Brewers and their attorneys. Me? I didn't have anyone—just the truth and a lot of guts.

I gave Landis my story, and the teams gave theirs. They stated their cases convincingly and professionally. I was clearly outclassed as far as the presentations were concerned. It was David against three Goliaths.

We broke for lunch, and I was walking alone in the lobby when a New Orleans sportswriter, Pie DuFour, came over to me and asked how things were going behind the closed doors.

"Not well," I said. "I think those guys are going to blackball me."

Listening to those strong presentations had given me a new scare: I might get frozen out of baseball as a result of this. Instead of getting an answer to my simple question of who owned me, the word might get around: "Don't get Henrich on your team. The kid is trouble." I was becoming afraid that I might never get a chance to play baseball in the major leagues and might not even get much of a chance in the minors, either.

In the afternoon session, Landis asked me a key question: "Why did you sign with Milwaukee when you were writing to me at the same time?"

I was on the spot. If I didn't explain it well, Landis might think I was playing games with him. I didn't have any smooth lawyers on my side, but I did have the truth, so I told it.

"The way I figured it," I said to Landis, "was that if you find there's something wrong with the transactions involving Cleveland, Milwaukee, and New Orleans, I wouldn't belong to any of them anyhow, so the contract with Milwaukee wouldn't be binding."

Landis agreed with me, to my immediate relief.

Then we got down to a my-word-against-his confrontation between the Indians' Slapnicka and me. I had written to Landis that a Cleveland official admitted to me he could have sold me to several other major-league teams. Landis read that portion of my letter aloud, and Slapnicka immediately said, "I deny that,"

Landis, concerned that the Indians might be blocking my career path, looked at me with his piercing eyes and said, "You state here that an official from the Cleveland club made that statement. Who was that official?"

I said, "Mr. Slapnicka."

Slapnicka was sitting next to me on my left. Again he said, "I deny that."

Landis asked each of the others if he had a final statement. Then he turned toward me and said, "Mr. Henrich?"

I said, "Yes, sir—just one thing. When I say that an official of the Cleveland club told me he could have sold me to several other major-league teams, *that happened.*"

For the third time, Slapnicka said, "I deny that."

Landis said we would hear from him in two weeks.

Two weeks later, as the Brewers, with me as one of their outfielders, were traveling through Nashville on their way from Biloxi to Milwaukee for the start of the season, Lou Nahin, the general manager, said he had heard from Landis. We were due in his office in Chicago at nine o'clock the next morning.

At the appointed hour, the Milwaukee delegation was in the commissioner's office: Nahin, our manager, Al Sothoron, and me. Landis came out of his private office into the reception area and said, "Mr. Henrich, you come in. Mr. Sothoron, you come in. Mr. Nahin, you wait outside."

Inside, Landis said, "Mr. Sothoron, raise your right hand and repeat after me." I'm sure Al was as surprised as I was. This wasn't a court of law. This wasn't a trial. And Landis wasn't a federal judge, not anymore. But I wasn't going to tell him that, and Sothoron obviously wasn't either.

After a few questions to clear up some final points about Al's "testimony," Landis said, "Mr. Sothoron, send in Mr. Nahin."

Apparently Landis did not want both Milwaukee officials in the room at the same time. My guess was that he didn't want them to be able to back up each other's story. He wanted each representative from management to answer his questions without any help from the other. I was delighted to see that. From the beginning, I was out there on the point all alone. Now each of them was too.

The wisdom of the Landis procedure showed itself immediately after Nahin began to answer the commissioner's final questions. Landis asked him a question of clarification, and after Nahin gave his answer, the commissioner snapped, "That's not what Mr. Slapnicka said in here last week."

A few minutes later, Landis said with his usual firmness, "All right, this meeting is over. Call me in an hour and I'll render my decision." As we filed out, Sothoron said to me, "You're in." I told him I was going to find a phone and call Dad, but I didn't know how this business was going to turn out.

Al said flatly, "Tell him you're a free agent."

I wasn't that sure, but Al was. He bet me ten dollars. For a manager who was convinced he was about to lose a starting outfielder, he didn't seem upset. He was happy in his confidence that Landis was going to give a player a fair shake and hand me my release from everybody so I could sign with any team I liked.

Sothoron was so sure, in fact, that he wanted to double the bet. Twenty dollars was an enormous sum for anything in 1937, especially a bet by a young man who might be facing an extended period of unemployment. But I took the plunge and bet the twenty, hoping I would lose the bet.

An hour later, Nahin called Landis from the train station, where we were waiting to leave for Milwaukee. He returned after only a minute or two and said simply, "Well, Tom, you're a free agent." I headed home to Massillon happy—but twenty dollars poorer.

I received calls and telegrams from eight major-league teams. This was back in the days when folks went years or even entire lifetimes without getting a long distance telephone call. In our small town, the normally quiet Henrich household was alive with excitement.

I got a telegram from Bill Terry representing the New York Giants. Pants Rowland of the Chicago Cubs called. So did Connie Mack of the Philadelphia A's, who could offer me as much money as he wanted because he was his team's owner as well as its manager on the field.

I told Mr. Mack I wanted a bonus of $30,000 to sign, plus whatever salary we agreed on for the 1937 season. He was a real gentleman about it. I knew the A's didn't have that kind of money, but I had to ask for what I thought I was worth.

"I'm sorry, son, that's too much money for me. But good luck." I appreciated that, coming from such a living legend as Mr. Mack, because I knew he meant it.

Chuck Dressen of the Cincinnati Reds called, and so did scouts from the Detroit Tigers and Boston Braves. Jack Fournier of the St. Louis Browns even met my demand for the signing bonus. But there was one team I was especially anxious to hear from—the New York Yankees. With the image of Babe Ruth hitting a home run still vivid in my imagination, I wanted to be a Yankee.

Unknown to me, one of their scouts, Johnny Nee, followed me from the final two weeks of Milwaukee's spring training season. Then he went one better. After Landis declared me a free agent, Nee came to Massillon and talked to Dad and me. We listened and asked a few questions, but we weren't going to make a decision in his presence, and he knew it. We promised to talk to him again before I signed with anyone.

That was on a Saturday in early April. Later that day I went down to the Brunswick, our local pool hall with four bowling alleys as an added attraction, to hang around for some relaxation. By the time I got there, I knew what I was going to do. I was going to sign with the Yankees. I wasn't going to fool around, either. I was going to do it the next day.

While I was there, the local boys started asking me my decision. I told them I hadn't made it yet, even though I had. One of the patrons, a stranger to me, said with emphasis that I should join the Braves because, since they were not a strong team, I'd have a good chance of breaking into the starting lineup. That wouldn't have been news to anyone in my situation, but I thanked him for his advice. I've often wondered what that guy thought when he heard the news the next day.

Dad wanted to be sure I considered all the possibilities and pitfalls, so we talked about it again later on Saturday. He asked if I thought I could make the Yankees.

I told him my logic: "Suppose I sign with the Browns—they've already agreed to pay me the bonus—and find I'm good enough to play major-league ball. Then I'm stuck with the Browns, one of the worst teams in baseball. But if I sign with the Yanks and find I can make it as a big leaguer, I'm sitting pretty with the *best* team in baseball."

I assured Dad, "I'm willing to take that chance."

I signed my contract the next day, for a bonus of $20,000 and a first-year salary of $5,000. It was less than what the Browns offered me, but there was this big plus: I belonged to the New York Yankees.

My case sent shock waves throughout major-league baseball. Judge Landis didn't stop with me. He looked into things more deeply and found that several major-league teams were hoarding hundreds of players on their minor-league teams. Many of them were talented enough to make it in the majors, but they were being denied that opportunity because of the greed of the parent team. The Detroit Tigers and the St. Louis Cardinals were the chief culprits.

Branch Rickey, the Cardinals' general manager, was known throughout baseball for signing every player he could get his hands on, a practice he continued when he moved to the Brooklyn Dodgers. There's nothing wrong with that on the surface, but two things that everyone in baseball knew about were definitely wrong. The Cardinals paid starvation wages to the hundreds of players in their minor-league farm system, and Rickey and Sam Breadon, the owner, knew that many of their players deserved the chance to play big-league ball.

Around the National League, and even in the American League, the Cardinals' organization was known as "the St. Louis chain gang." Their players, even those in the high minors only a step or two below the major-league level, were paid only $100 or $175 a month. To this day, Johnny Mize resents the way he was treated by the Cardinals, and his teammate, Enos "Country" Slaughter, verifies it.

Mize was stuck in the Cardinals' farm system for five years and had a great season everywhere he went, yet he could never make as much as $200 a month in the minors.

Slaughter remembers playing professionally in Martinsville, Virginia, for $75 a month in 1935. He also remembers hitting .382 in Double A ball, only two notches below the Cardinals, and then asking Rickey for a bonus to add to his salary of $150 a month. Rickey said Slaughter had been talking to the older players. Country never got his bonus.

This kind of treatment turned some players, including me, against Rickey. He used to quote the Bible, but the complaint against him was that what he was doing conflicted with what it taught. Rickey never attended a game on a Sunday, and the story was that he stayed away because of a promise to his mother on her deathbed. When I heard that, I had one question: Did he promise her he wouldn't take the gate receipts?

In later years a writer told me that Rickey was watching me and making notes on my performance with an eye toward the possibility of getting me in a trade with the Yankees. I told the writer, "I hope he doesn't waste any more of his time, because I'm not going to play for him."

The feeling among the players was that what Rickey was doing was at least morally wrong, if not a violation of baseball rules and maybe even the law itself. Landis agreed. He declared seventy-four minor league players in the Cardinals' farm system to be free agents in 1938, and in 1940 he released ninety-one players from Detroit's system. Many of them made it to the big leagues with their new teams, and some became stars, including Pete Reiser, Mike McCormick, Danny Litwhiler, Benny McCoy, Roy Cullenbine, and Johnny Sain.

It wasn't the first time that Kenesaw Mountain Landis came down hard against the big boys on the ownership side. He was the judge in the famous case brought by the government against Standard Oil Company of Indiana, in which the company was charged with operating a monopoly in collaboration with the Chicago & Alton Railroad. Standard Oil allegedly gave the railroad a kickback on each carload of oil shipped between Whiting, Indiana, and East St. Louis, Illinois.

Landis forced John D. Rockefeller, Standard Oil's president, to testify, and every newspaper in the country sent its best reporter to Chicago to cover the trial. After six weeks of testimony, the jury voted to convict Standard Oil. Landis deliberated for several days before imposing his sentence, and it was a shocker: $20,000 on each of the 1,462 counts, a total of $29,240,000, the largest fine in the history of the United States to that time.

The sentence was later overturned by a court of appeals, but the trial and the sentence made Landis a national celebrity. There was even talk that he should run for president. In the kind of response that people came to expect of him, Landis said, "To think that I would accept political preferment as a reward for what I have done on the bench is to impeach my integrity as a judge and my honor as a man."

He didn't take excuses, either, something the owners learned during my case and its aftermath. While he was a judge he sentenced a man to two years in the state penitentiary. The convicted prisoner told Landis, "I can't do it, Judge. I just can't."

Landis replied, "That's all right. You just run along and do the best you can."

Landis never had trouble making decisions, even where they involved himself. As he was dying, in 1944, he was in control of the medical bulletins about his condition. He told officials at St. Luke's Hospital in Chicago, "Make them more optimistic." When he breathed his last on November 25, his body was cremated that same day, and there was no funeral, all in accordance with his own firm orders.

This was the man the baseball owners picked to be the first commissioner in the history of their sport. He was such a baseball fan and such a frequent visitor to games in Chicago that Will Rogers said the owners should choose "that old guy who sits behind first base all the time. He's out there every day anyhow."

Landis said the players stuck in these enormous farm systems were being denied a fair opportunity to advance in their profession. Rickey was always free to leave the Cardinals, which he did a few years later when he joined the Dodgers. His minor-league players were merely being given the same kind of opportunity.

But they never got it from Rickey. In 1947, Rickey gave black players a chance to play baseball in the big leagues. In 1937, Rickey's players had to get their chance from Judge Landis.

That's how the Dodgers got Pete Reiser. He chose to leave the Cardinals and sign with Brooklyn for a bonus of $100. Four years later, having escaped from the St. Louis chain gang, Reiser was the National League's batting champion and led his team to the 1941 pennant. Without Landis, he might never have been given the chance.

Roy Weatherly was mired in the Indians organization. Landis set him free, too. The Yankees were after him, but he decided to play for Cleveland. "Stormy" went on to ten successful seasons in the big leagues and became known as an excellent hitter. Like so many of us, he missed prime years because of military service during World War II.

Looking back now, it seems almost inevitable that Landis would rule in my favor and act in support of all those others as well. The common complaint about baseball commissioners, and those of other sports too, is that they are employed by the owners and therefore will always come down on the side of management. Not Landis.

He never felt he "worked for" the owners, and maybe that sense of independence came from his years on the bench. He believed he was in charge of a public trust, another sentiment that may have stemmed from his judicial years, and represented all of those who loved baseball—the players and the fans—and not just the owners who hired him.

Two weeks after I joined the Yankees on Opening Day in 1937, my logic in choosing them was beginning to look questionable. I was farmed out to Newark.

Maybe that bellhop at the New Yorker knew what he was talking about.

_____

Three

In the Beginning

I wore the Yankee pinstripes for the first time in the team's last exhibition game before the 1937 season. We played the army at West Point and slaughtered them, 19–4. I replaced Selkirk in the middle of the game, went 0-for-2, and didn't get a chance in the field. I did manage to score a run. It wasn't the most productive day you could have in your first game, but I was a Yankee. Success would come—I hoped.

The American League season opened the next day when President Franklin D. Roosevelt threw out the first ball in Washington, where 32,000 fans turned out at Griffith Stadium and saw the Senators lose to the Philadelphia A's, 4–3, in ten innings. It was the first loss for them under FDR, who brought them so much good luck that their owner, Clark Griffith, used to call Roosevelt the team's mascot.

It was traditional for Washington to open its season at home and to do it one day ahead of the rest of the games so the Presidential Opener could get a big play in the papers and on the radio around the country and in the movie newsreels the next week.

That's one of the things I miss now that baseball is not represented in Washington. That's too bad. I think we hit the very bottom of that situation at the beginning of the 1990 season, when the president of the United States not only didn't throw out the first ball of the baseball season in Washington, he didn't even do it in the United States. President George Bush went to Canada and performed the tradition at the home opener of the Toronto Blue Jays. Who would have thought it?

Joe McCarthy called me into his office at Yankee Stadium after batting practice before a game in the 1937 season and gave me the dreaded word that he was farming me out to the Newark Bears. The Bears were one of the greatest teams in the history of minor-league baseball that year and through the rest of the 1930s, but that was small consolation. I wanted to play in the big leagues. What made it even harder for me to take was that I hadn't been given a chance in my brief stay with the Yankees.

I told McCarthy, "You don't know if I can play. You haven't even seen me in a game."

McCarthy, always the boss, said, "I know what you can do."

"Yes, but—"

"Son, I can *ask* you to go to Newark. Or I can *make* you go."

That was the end of the conversation and the end of my first taste of life as a big leaguer.

I set some kind of a record that day. As I walked out of Yankee Stadium, not knowing when—if ever—I might make it back to the top, George Weiss, the farm director who later became the Yankees' general manager, was waiting for me in a Cadillac to drive me to Newark.

When we got there, the Bears were still playing that day's game. I signed a contract and put on my uniform, and the manager, Oscar Vitt, put me into the game in extra innings to pinch-hit. I struck out. But I had taken batting practice as a major leaguer and played as a minor-leaguer both in the same day, under contract to each team. I seemed to have a certain ability to find myself in unusual situations where contracts were concerned.

My stay at Newark wasn't any longer than my first stay in New York, thanks to Roy Johnson's remark in Detroit and McCarthy's good hearing. I was with the Bears for only ten days, and three games were rained out, so that phase of my career lasted only seven games.

The Yankees couldn't get anybody for Johnson, but Barrow had McCarthy's word: Get rid of him. So they sold him on waivers to the Boston Braves on May 11 after 12 games. Roy was on the Yankees' World Series championship team in 1936. We won the Series again in '37 and '38, but he wasn't with us. He was with the Braves, who didn't win anything. Seldom has an overheard remark cost a player so dearly.

The first man to greet me when I walked into the Yankees' dressing room on my return from Newark was Lou Gehrig. One of the biggest heroes of my teen years was now my teammate, or I was his, greeting me warmly and welcoming me back to his team—*our* team.

Joe McCarthy was in firm command of the Yankee team. His control and influence even extended to such supposedly little things as smoking a pipe, which to McCarthy was no little thing at all. He didn't like pipe smokers. He considered the pipe to be a sign of contentment, and McCarthy didn't want any contented athletes.

He smoked, like most men in those years, but his choice was cigars. Fortunately, they were what I smoked too—and I smoked them before I made it to the Yankees. Today? I smoke a pipe.

The McCarthy agenda included a subject called "beer legs," something I've never heard about from anyone else. He told us he knew most players were going to drink, and he discouraged beer as the drink of choice. He said beer could "go to the legs of some players" and slow them down. So if we were going to drink at all, "drink whiskey."

McCarthy was a man who practiced what he preached. He drank White Horse Scotch, on the rocks.

The atmosphere in the Yankee dressing room was always the same under Joe McCarthy. It was an environment of professionalism. Like any clubhouse, ours had its cutups and its good times, but it was all business before a game, and there wasn't a whole lot of hell-raising after one either. McCarthy simply wouldn't allow it.

Even in star-filled New York, celebrities were not welcome in our clubhouse. The Dodgers always had show people in there with them after a game—Milton Berle, Phil Silvers, Zero Mostel, Buddy Hackett, and others. In our clubhouse, not even our own general manager was allowed.

Ed Barrow flagged me down one day as I was approaching the clubhouse from the parking lot. He called out, "Hey, Tom! Tell McCarthy I want to see him." Here was McCarthy's boss telling me he wanted to see Joe—but he didn't dare go into that clubhouse. Why? McCarthy's orders.

The clubhouse atmosphere is an important part of a team's feeling about itself, something that few fans realize. The dressing room environment reflects the team's personality and attitude. A clubhouse that's as professional as ours was reflects the professionalism of the team and adds to it. A team that's relaxed and confident will have a clubhouse that's the same way. And a clubhouse that has an I-don't-care attitude is occupied by that kind of a team.

I visited the Yankees' clubhouse in New York a few years ago, and it told me something. I thought to myself, "There's no more feeling in this room that they're going to play a game today—much less play it as a team—than in any other room in New York. There's nothing here." And there wasn't. That team did nothing.

I looked around that clubhouse on my first day back in '37 and saw the men who would be my teammates as long as they stayed with the Yankees—because I was destined never to play for another team. Only one would be a Yankee with me throughout my career, "the great DiMaggio."

I didn't get to play with Joe in that two-week stretch before Newark. When I joined the team on Opening Day, Joe was being released from Lenox Hill Hospital, where he had just had his tonsils removed. He missed the first two weeks of the season. By the time he got back into the lineup, I was gone.

After my brief exile, though, we played next to each other in the field. Charlie Keller joined us in 1939 to make up what many people say is the greatest offensive outfield in baseball history. And as if that didn't put me close enough to Joe, we hit back-to-back in the Yankee batting order, with me third and Joe fourth.

I was his teammate longer than anyone else, so maybe I'm in the best position to appreciate him. Joe was unquestionably the greatest baseball player I ever saw. In fact, he was the greatest player of all time except maybe for Ruth, who might be rated ahead of Joe simply because Babe was also an outstanding pitcher for six seasons before becoming a full-time outfielder.

Joe might even have broken Babe's home-run records if he had played in another home park. Yankee Stadium was not built for Joe. He hit a ton of long fly balls that died in left center, the stadium's "Death Valley." In another ballpark, many of them would have been home runs.

Without question, his approach to a game was predicated 100 percent on winning, and that was the driving force in his makeup. He was the most valuable player I ever saw on a ball field. He had the strongest drive for winning of any player I ever played with or against. His attitude was that the best way for his team to excel was for him to excel, and that inner toughness put him above all the other greats.

If you had to pick one player in history to start a team with, you'd take him.

He took such tremendous pride in his performance that he never wanted to look bad. Tex Hughson of the Red Sox stuck a fast ball into Joe's ribs once, and he had to be in dire pain. But he just flipped his bat aside in disgust and started walking to first base. He couldn't run or even trot because of the pain. McCarthy was managing the Red Sox by that time, and in the dugout he told his players, "Look at him. He won't rub it." And he didn't.

McCarthy complimented Joe more than once. On another occasion, when several writers were talking about DiMag's greatness as a hitter, one of them asked, "Can he bunt?"

McCarthy said, "I'll never know."

My teammates in '37 told me that Babe Ruth accorded Joe the greatest compliment Ruth could ever give anybody, and Lefty Gomez made sure Joe realized its significance. It happened the day Joe hit the first home run of his major-league career, one that landed in Yankee Stadium's right-center-field bleachers.

Ruth, who called almost everyone "kid" because he was the world's worst at remembering names, came into the Yankee dressing room after the game, one of the few times he did. He walked up to DiMag, stuck out his hand and said, "Hello, Joe." DiMag returned the greeting.

Gomez, Joe's close friend, described just what that meant. "With the Babe," he told Joe, "veterans are 'Doc' and rookies are 'kid.' You're the first guy I ever heard him call by name."

When we played against Bob Feller, the best pitcher of our time, you could see the veins sticking out of Joe's neck. Charlie Keller used to talk about it, too. Joe was determined that he was not going to look bad against the best.

People remember how graceful he was, gliding around the bases, roaming the outfield with ease as our center fielder while making difficult catches look easy. But he was also a fierce competitor. He always had strawberries on his legs from sliding into the bases so hard. And they stayed with him, because he aggravated them every day. He'd just go into the clubhouse after the game and say to the trainer, "Fix them up, Doc." And the next day he'd be right back out there, playing with strawberries on both legs and sliding hard again, knowing he was sliding into more pain.

Joe quickly became the team's leader, and he led the way all great leaders do—by example. He was at his best under pressure, getting the hit to win the game or making the catch to save it, taking an extra base as a runner or cutting down the opposing runners with his strong, accurate throwing arm. And I never saw him throw to the wrong base.

We never collided in the outfield, never even came close. If I called for a fly ball, Joe would let me take it. If I didn't call for it, my responsibility was simply to get out of the way because that ball was not going to drop to the ground. Joe was going to get there. He had the same beautiful playing arrangement with Charlie Keller, our left fielder.

I saw him hit three triples in one game off Johnny Allen in Yankee Stadium. That's unheard of. The triple is supposed to be baseball's most exciting hit because it requires a combination of power and speed. To get three of them in one game, and off a good pitcher, would pop anybody's eyes.

In Yankee Stadium I saw him get a hit to left that looked like a double, but the left fielder got to the ball quickly, released it in a hurry, and made an exceptionally strong throw to second base. Joe was running hard from the start, but when he saw what a good play the left fielder had made, he somehow found even more speed and made it to second safely. I was sitting next to Bill Dickey in the Yankee dugout when it happened. Bill said to the rest of us, "You know something? That guy can run as fast as he has to."

Joe never knew how much I admired him. He was a loner to us on his team as much as he was a loner to the general public. Lefty Gomez was the one he enjoyed. They shared an apartment in Manhattan and eventually roomed together on the road, too. Before that, I was Lefty's roommate on trips for three years, yet even then I hardly ever saw Joe. Lefty saw him socially, almost every day and night, but the rest of us didn't. He was just never in our social circles, even when Gomez was.

Joe and I were Yankees together from 1937 through 1950, with the same three years—'43, '44, and '45—out for military duty in World War II. In our eleven seasons together, the Yankees were in the world Series eight times, and we won seven. Our only loss came to the Cardinals in '42, two months after I was called to active duty with the Coast Guard.

Eventually they started calling me "Old Reliable," and Joe was "the Yankee Clipper"—and more. He *was* the Yankees, period.

Tony Lazzeri was on that '37 team, playing the last season of his twelve years as a Yankee before finishing up with the Cubs, Dodgers, and Giants. Lazzeri typified the Yankee emphasis on toughness and a professional attitude. He was an epileptic, but you'd never know it. On the field he was as tough as any of the rest of us, or tougher. He's finally been enshrined in the Hall of Fame, voted there in 1991—forty-five years too late to enjoy it. He died in 1946.

In my rookie year he was talking about the American League pennant race of the year before, when New York won it by the enormous margin of nineteen and a half games. He told me the team pulled into Cleveland for what the local papers there were calling "a crucial series." He griped, "Yeah, we went out there and played them. But they *quit* on us." He was still steaming about it a year later.

He said he had been looking forward to the challenge of playing the Indians in what was still an important series at that stage of the season. He felt the Indians had approached the games with a defeatist attitude, and Lazzeri, always the competitor, was disappointed that Cleveland didn't give the Yankees more of a fight. The Indians finished in fifth place.

The 1937 season was almost as much of a runaway as '36. We won the pennant again, this time by thirteen games over the Tigers. After we clinched it, Lazzeri decided to have some fun. We were playing the Philadelphia A's in Yankee Stadium. I was out of the lineup with an injured knee. Bob Johnson, the A's consistent home-run hitter—he hit at least twenty-one in each of his first nine seasons—came to the plate to lead off the eighth inning.

Johnson swung at the first pitch and fouled it back to the screen behind home plate. Our bat boy, Timmy Sullivan, retrieved the ball immediately and brought it back to our dugout without giving the home-plate umpire, Bill Summers, the chance to decide whether to keep the ball in the game.

Billy Werber, the A's third baseman, comes charging out of the dugout and starts an argument about the ball. Johnson, in the meantime, turns to Summers and asks in disbelief, "What was that?" The ball just didn't look right to Johnson, and Werber smelled something fishy.

Summers quickly puts two and two together and calls to Lazzeri at second base, "Give me the ball."

Lazzeri gets the look of innocence on his face and says, "What ball?" Tony didn't have it. The bat boy had it in the dugout.

Then we found out what Summers suspected: Lazzeri was guilty of conspiracy. Before the game he had taken a ball and rubbed it with soot from the ground below Yankee Stadium so that it was black. By the eighth inning, with darkness creeping in, no hitter was going to be able to see a black baseball until the pitch was past him, and that's exactly what happened.

Lazzeri knew the game was meaningless to both teams by that point in September, so he was having some fun at the expense of

Johnson, the man we called "Indian Bob" because he was part Cherokee. He was the gentlest of men and one of the great players of our era, the perfect target for Lazzeri's gag.

Summers didn't count the pitch. To make matters worse for him, he had to write a report to the league office.

We had three San Francisco Italians on that team—DiMaggio, Lazzeri, and Frankie Crosetti, our shortstop. We called Crosetti "The Crow," and he was a Yankee player for seventeen years, from 1932 through 1948, and a coach with them for twenty years after that.

Frankie was an outstanding shortstop, one who knew every trick in the book. He was a conniver on the field, gaining every edge he could against the opposition. His specialty was the hidden ball trick. He was famous for it.

I was curious about how he performed his act, so I watched him carefully during a game in Fenway Park. Red Ruffing was pitching for us. The Crow had the ball in his right hand after taking a throw from the outfield on a double.

Crosetti walks to the mound and goes through the motions of tossing the ball to Red—only he doesn't toss it. He quickly brings his left hand over the top of his right hand, catches his own toss, and then slips the ball inside his glove. Ruffing then goes to the resin bag near the mound and pretends to be dabbing resin on his pitching hand. What he's really doing, though, is stalling while the Crow tries to catch the runner napping off second so he can slap the tag on him. He was a magician, with a hand quicker than the runner's eye.

Frank was skilled in another specialty, too: getting hit by the pitch. Well, *he* didn't get hit by the pitch. His shirt did. Before he came to bat, he used to fluff up that flannel shirt we wore so that it bulged around his waist. If the pitch was close to him, he'd lean ever so slightly into it, and with that the ball would flick his shirt and the umpire would wave him to first.

The Crow was an artist at it—another example of a player helping his team any way he can. He was getting on base so one of us behind him could drive him in. In doing so, he was foregoing the chance to get a hit and add to his batting average, but he knew he was helping his team. That meant more to him.

McCarthy loved Crosetti because he was another tough competitor, like so many of the Yankees. It was no accident we had a lot of players with that attitude. That's the only kind McCarthy wanted.

One of our outfielders, Myril Hoag, was aggressive like Frankie, and they both had a fondness for trying to steal third base. Hoag, however, was getting thrown out almost every time he tried it (maybe because he wore only a size six shoe), so McCarthy told him to stop trying. Hoag said, "Why? Crosetti does it."

McCarthy said, "There's one difference—Crosetti makes it."

The three San Francisco Italians enjoyed each other's company, but you'd never know it from the conversation—or the lack of it. Those three seemed to go days without talking to each other even though they were spending hours on end together. In fact, Joe remembers the time their silence really did extend over a period of days.

In Joe's rookie year, the three decided to drive to spring training together, covering more than three thousand miles from San Francisco to St. Petersburg on the Florida Gulf Coast. At the start of the trip, Lazzeri and Crosetti took turns behind the wheel. Joe tells the story:

"We drove all the way from San Francisco to Amarillo, Texas, and not a word passed among us . . . I sat in the back seat looking at cactus. At Amarillo, Lazzeri broke the silence, saying, 'Gotta get some gas.' Then he added to Crosetti, 'Let's let the kid drive.'

"They knew beforehand that I had never driven a car in my life. When I told them, Lazzeri, who was a great kidder, said with a perfectly straight face, 'What say, Frankie, should we let the bum walk?'

"Crosetti says, 'Yeah, that's a good idea.'

"I was as green as a pea and thought they were serious. But Lazzeri's face broke into a smile just as I was opening the door. We continued on to Florida—but I'll swear that's as many words as we said on the trip."

One of the New York writers said he saw DiMaggio, Crosetti, and Lazzeri sitting in the lobby of the Chase Hotel in St. Louis, across the street from beautiful Forest Park, without a word spoken by any of them for an hour.

Finally Joe clears his throat.

Crosetti says, "What did you say?"

And Lazzeri says, "He didn't say a damn thing. Shut up."

Lefty Gomez was a key player on that '37 team. His first name was Vernon, but nobody called him anything but "Lefty," because of the way he threw, and "Goofy" because of the things he said and did.

But Lefty was no clown. He was a talented pitcher who is now a member of the Hall of Fame. He was a 20-game winner four times and led the American League in wins twice, complete games once, strikeouts three times, and shutouts three times. In my rookie year he led the league with 21 wins and won both of his starts — the opener and the final game — in the World Series against the Giants, pitching a complete game both times.

Aside from his skills as a pitcher, his contributions to our team included his humor and his close friendship with DiMaggio. They were the best of friends from Joe's rookie year in 1936 until Lefty died in 1989.

Lefty was the funniest man I ever met. He was good for Joe. He saw humor in everything, even defeat. I was in my second month of service in the Coast Guard, when the Yankees lost the 1942 World Series to the Cardinals, so I wasn't there, but the guys told me that in the dressing room following the last game, Gomez announced: "Fellas, the victory celebration this year will be held at Horn and Hardart's, the Automat."

He once picked up a ground ball and threw to Lazzeri at second base when he didn't have a play there. When Lazzeri asked why Lefty threw it to him instead of one of the other bases where he did have a chance for an out, Gomez said, "You have the reputation of being the smartest man on this ball club, and I didn't know what to do with the ball, so I figured you would."

He had that Yankee team attitude that McCarthy loved, but once it brought a scolding from Joe. Ted Williams hit a home run off Lefty, and I hurt my back banging into the fence trying to catch it. I had to be taken to the hospital, and when McCarthy asked for a volunteer to ride with me in the ambulance,

Lefty, who had been lifted from the game, got up and said he'd go.

McCarthy said, "You sit down. You almost got him killed already."

In another game, Lefty fielded a ground ball and threw to Lazzeri at second when he should have thrown to Crosetti at third. After the inning, McCarthy got hold of him in the dugout and demanded to know why he threw to Lazzeri. Lefty told him, "I heard everybody yelling, 'The Dago! The Dago!' I just threw it to the wrong one."

McCarthy said, "Why didn't you throw it to center field? We have one out there, too."

Those veterans were a great influence on a rookie. Our catcher, Bill Dickey, would correct you with a kind and gentle touch; he'd call you aside to tell you that you made a mistake out there today and then tell you what the proper play would be in that situation. Gehrig and DiMaggio would simply look at you. Crosetti would tell you out loud, in front of the rest of the team.

Robert "Red" Rolfe, our third baseman, was another bear-down guy who would let you know when you made a mistake that hurt the team. Our ace relief pitcher, Johnny Murphy, was that way, too, and so was our right fielder, George Selkirk. They called him "Twinkletoes," and he was good enough under fire to make it as a starter on the Yankees, the man who replaced Babe Ruth. He even had the burden of wearing Ruth's old number 3. Any player who can perform under that kind of pressure is going to demand the same thing from his teammates, including us rookies.

Even our third-string catcher, Arndt Jorgens, stayed on top of the guys when they made a mistake or he thought they weren't giving 100 percent. Arndt was born in Norway, and he never played more than fifty-eight games in any season, but he was in the big leagues for eleven years and was a Yankee that entire time. Why? Because McCarthy loved his attitude.

He was a little guy for a catcher, only five-feet-nine and 165 pounds, but that didn't stop him from his self-appointed role of staying on top of the rest of us. His position as a third-stringer didn't make any difference, either. He'd yell at us first-stringers anyhow. He saw me clowning in the dugout before a game in my rookie year and let me have it: "C'mon, Tom! Bear down!" And I did.

I always included the mental part of baseball in the way I played the sport, and I popped a few eyes with a play in my rookie year that led to a change in the rule book.

The Red Sox had runners on first and second with one out when the batter hit a fly ball to me in short right field. I got to it in plenty of time, then dropped it on purpose and fired to Frank Crosetti at second base. He tagged the runner, who couldn't get back to the bag in time, then tagged the bag for a forceout on the runner on first. Double play.

Joe Cronin was the Red Sox player-manager, and he had a fit. He swore he'd get something put into the rule book making that play illegal. He did, too. Now an umpire can call the batter out on a judgment play if he thinks the outfielder dropped the ball on purpose. It's similar to the infield fly rule except the batter is not automatically out when the ball is hit into the air—only if the outfielder drops it.

Unfortunately for Phil Rizzuto, he broke in with us before the rule was changed. Every time I pulled that trick, he'd tell me in the dugout later, "I hate that play. I never know which runner to tag."

Gehrig gave me some good advice, but with the wisdom that all rookies possess, I decided I knew more than he did. We were playing the White Sox on a Sunday and facing Ted Lyons, their star pitcher, who is now in the Hall of Fame. I knew how good he was. This was his fifteenth season with the White Sox, the only team he ever played for, and he would pitch another six years and win 260 games in his brilliant career.

I asked Gehrig what I should look for from Lyons. His advice: "Hit the first good fastball he throws."

With my usual curiosity, I asked why.

"Because," Lou said, "he gets tough after that."

The first pitch from Lyons to me was a fastball on the outside corner. I thought to myself, "I can't make a living trying to hit one that's out there. I'll wait for one a little closer."

Strike one, called.

Then it dawned on me: "That was the first good fastball that Lou was talking about. I was supposed to swing at that. No worry. I'll get something better."

The second pitch came in shoulder high—until it dropped straight down just in front of the plate, right into the middle of the strike zone. This time I thought to myself: "That had to be a fluke. He surely can't do that again."

Strike two, called.

The third pitch from Lyons came to me on the outside, but then it broke in toward the plate. In my anxiety I took the weakest swing you ever saw.

Strike three, swinging.

I took that long walk back to the dugout, the one that's always longer when you strike out, knowing that Gehrig gave me excellent advice, and I ignored it. When I returned to the dugout, Lou was too nice to say anything.

The story has a happy postscript to it. In my second season, I got another chance against Lyons. This time I knew better than to ignore Lou's advice. I committed myself to hitting the first good thing he threw me.

It came on the first pitch. All I was able to do was foul it back, but I knew I had taken a good cut. Obviously Lyons did too, because he walked halfway to the plate and said, "How do you hit the knuckleball?"

I told him, "The last time a guy threw me one, I hit it to that scoreboard out there."

Lyons said, "Well, get ready, because that's all you're going to get."

He was telling the truth. He threw me nothing but knuckleballs on that at-bat. I doubled down the right-field line. Two years later I hit a home run off him in Chicago on one of his fastballs.

I can't brag about anything else in my performances against Lyons. We played against each other for six more years before he retired after the 1946 season. I never got another hit against him, but I wouldn't have gotten anything at all if it hadn't been for that advice from Gehrig.

I started hitting well early in my rookie year, but only after McCarthy got through to me when he felt I wasn't doing what he wanted. That was one of his great talents as a manager of men.

I was having trouble hitting the low, inside curveball from a right-handed pitcher, which isn't unusual for a left-handed hitter, and McCarthy told me I would have to stop swinging at it if I was going to make it as a hitter in the big leagues. "I want you to lay off that pitch," he told me. "The pitchers are making a sucker out of you."

When I continued that habit, McCarthy invoked the Yankee threat: Newark. All of us on the Yankees were all too aware that New York's top minor-league team was loaded with talent. We played every season knowing that if we didn't perform, we could be replaced with one phone call to the other side of the Hudson, the same way many of us got to New York ourselves.

This time, a week later, McCarthy said, "Tommy, I told you to lay off that low, inside curve. Now either lay off or you'll learn to hit in Newark." I knew that Charlie Keller was over there hitting a ton, so when McCarthy mentioned the dreaded word *Newark*, I listened—and became a better hitter.

That order from McCarthy (and that's what it was) provided an insight into one of his characteristics as a manager. He was never good enough to play in the major leagues, so he did not presume to tell major leaguers how to do the technical parts of their jobs. But he did tell us *what* to do. In this case, he was telling me to lay off the low, inside curveball. He didn't tell me how. That would be up to me. What he was telling me was to exercise the discipline required to figure out how to carry out his orders.

Emphasis on discipline—not just in the sense that you did what you were told, but in the larger definition of controlling yourself and your performance—was one of the hallmarks of the McCarthy management. He didn't just *want* discipline in the way you played, or *ask* you for it, he *demanded* it. And if he didn't see it in you, you could shake his hand, because you'd be leaving soon.

The pursuit of it created the air of professionalism we brought to our clubhouse, our train rides, our hotel stays, and everything else we did as New York Yankees. And it's why we won.

It was also one reason McCarthy did not like managing Babe Ruth and was crazy about managing Lou Gehrig. Gehrig was his favorite. Mccarthy simply loved the man, just as the rest of us did, but for some additional reasons.

Lou was the perfect team man. He did what he was told, and in so doing, he set the example for the rest of us. If this towering star was willing to obey his manager and approach the sport with the same deadly seriousness that McCarthy did, then who were we to do any less?

Ruth, however, obviously clashed with the McCarthy personality and attitude. The Babe left the Yankees two years before I joined them, but it was clear from being around McCarthy, listening to his comments and watching his reactions to the comments of others, that he was no fan of Ruth, at least not as a manager.

Joe felt that Ruth considered it beneath him to take orders from a manager—any manager. I once heard him say he didn't want to hear anyone praising Ruth. On another occasion, our trainer, Doc Painter, was saying some flattering things about the Babe when Joe overheard him.

"Knock it off," he said, "and get back to work."

The low point of my first season came when I hurt my knee on July 25. I was off to an exciting start and was hitting .320 when we went into Chicago. In the fourth inning, White Sox second baseman Tony Piet got a hit to right center with a man on first. The runner was able to take third, but I thought I could hold Tony to a single, so I stopped sharply on my right leg and twisted to throw to my left, trying to snap the ball into second.

As soon as I did that, I felt something wrong around my left knee, the same knee I had heard go "click" when I slid into Charley "Greek" George in an exhibition game that spring in Biloxi while I was still playing for New Orleans. As I buckled, off balance and in pain, the White Sox players, always the hardest bench jockeys in the league under manager Jimmy Dykes, started hollering out to me, "Stumblebum! Hey, Stumblebum!" The nickname stuck with me for the rest of my career as far as any White Sox player was concerned. They always called me Stumblebum, and I always answered. I never resented it, because on that play I *was* a stumblebum.

I stayed in the game. I didn't want to tell McCarthy about my injury. When you're a rookie hitting .320 with the great New York Yankees, you don't want to come out of that lineup for any reason in the world.

In the sixth inning, I hit a home run with a man on to tie the game. In the eighth, with Gehrig on second, the Sox walked Bill Dickey intentionally to pitch to me, apparently not remembering my batting average or that home run on my previous trip to the plate. I hit another home run. The Sox scored three in the bottom of the eighth and another in the ninth to win it, but I had gotten their attention.

The knee stiffened up overnight, and by the time we got back to New York I couldn't play on it at all. I had torn some of the cartilage. I was able to get back into the lineup only for a few appearances in August and September.

With my injury, I wasn't able to enjoy playing every day, but I was able to enjoy New York. The big city didn't intimidate me or make me homesick, as it did some rookies, despite my small-town background. By this time I was in my fourth year away from home, doing the only thing I really wanted to do, and playing in New Orleans and on the road had conditioned me to life in big cities, so New York was never anything but a pleasure for me.

I discovered Radio City Music Hall in that first year and was a frequent visitor there throughout my Yankee career. To be able to watch a good movie and see a first-rate stage show all at the same place was my idea of a great time. The combination attracted me to the Paramount, Loew's and the Palace, too.

You could see Paul Muni and Miriam Hopkins in *The Woman I Love* at Radio City, plus those Rockettes. At the Paramount on Times Square there was *Swing High, Swing Low*, starring Carole Lombard and Fred MacMurray. Onstage, in person: Louis Armstrong and His Band "with a gala array of stars."

At one of the other Times Square theaters, the Rialto, Lionel Barrymore and Mickey Rooney were in *Family Affair*. The big ad in the paper said, "The grand stars of 'Ah Wilderness' in MGM's timely drama of one old man who didn't fear to call a law unconstitutional!"

The Ringling Brothers & Barnum & Bailey combined circus was playing at Madison Square Garden when I broke in with the Yankees. You could thrill to "10,000 marvels" for the price of admission: one dollar, half-price for children under twelve.

After a show, you could dine among the stars at Jack Dempsey's restaurant, where you could "meet the celebrities for dinner" in "the meeting place of the world." Entrees for dinner began at eighty-five cents. If you really wanted to go first class, you could enjoy a turkey dinner on Sunday at the Brass Rail on Seventh Avenue at 49th Street for $1.50.

Players' wives could buy saddle-stitched pumps at Bergdorf Goodman on Fifth Avenue for $14.75. If they wanted to add some attractive lawn furniture to the family surroundings, a rattan chaise "with rain resistant fabric" was on sale for $24.99 at Macy's. To help with our letters home, there was Macy's own brand of new portable typewriters for $36.95, featuring automatic ribbon reverse and a "stencil-cutting device." You could buy carbon paper there, too, "inked to give sharp impressions and long wear," twenty-five sheets for thirty-nine cents.

If you wanted to enjoy a night in Brooklyn, you could catch the new Jack Benny movie, *Transatlantic Merry-Go-Round*, at the Strand.

I didn't have any real close friends on the ball club in my rookie year. Most of my teammates were married and their wives were with them during the season. So I was alone most of the time and perfectly happy about it. I lived by myself in a room at the Greystone Hotel at 91st and Broadway, several steps up in class from the Grand Hotel in Monessen, and was the subway system's best patron, hopping on it at every chance to run to midtown Manhattan and enjoy those shows.

Radio was approaching its heyday, and I was one of its biggest boosters. As a lover of music of every kind from Dixieland to classical, I used to lug my "table model" with me on our road trips in the minor leagues, enjoying everything from Milton Cross and the opera on Saturday afternoon broadcasts from Carnegie Hall to the barbershop songs by my fellow members of the Society for the Preservation and Encouragement of Barber Shop Quartet Singing in America, Inc.

Lou Gehrig introduced me to the marvels of the 1930s when I was a rookie. As we were getting comfortable on the team bus for the drive to Penn Station to start one of our road trips, Lou called down the aisle to me, "Hey, Tommy! Look what I have."

What he had was something new called a "portable radio." Lou was a fellow music lover, especially of serious music, classical and opera. Just like today's players, we enjoyed taking our music with us.

I was perfectly content to haul my table model around the American League with me so I could enjoy music in my hotel room. A radio in your room was about the last word in hotel luxury. But

Lou had this portable model, and I was fascinated by it. It didn't have a wire or a plug at all. It ran on batteries, which I found hard to believe. But it worked as well as my table model even without a cord, so I went out and bought one with some of my first-year money and carried it with me on every trip.

I got to go on the radio myself in my rookie year, and with Babe Ruth, no less. The Babe had a baseball show on a New York station, and he interviewed me after I made it back from Newark. He kept calling me "kid" and talking to me about the Yankees' management, including Colonel Jacob Ruppert, the owner and beer baron (Ruppert's Beer, of course).

The Babe asked me if I had cashed my bonus check of $25,000 yet. When I told him no, he gave me an encouraging word about the financial stability of the organization: "Don't be afraid to cash it. If it was signed by Colonel Ruppert, it's good."

It was no surprise that we won the American League pennant in a romp. To use some of the present statistical categories for illustration, we led the league in runs scored, home runs, and slugging average, and our pitchers had the most complete games, saves, and shutouts plus the lowest earned run average.

Joe led both leagues in home runs with 46, and that's why I say that with a different home field he could have broken Ruth's records. Maybe the war would have kept him from breaking the career record, but he certainly could have set the single-season record—and his total might have been well into the sixties. Any right-hander who can hit 46 home runs with a canyon like the one in Yankee Stadium's left-center field would be a strong bet to hit 60 or more in a right-handed hitter's park like Briggs Stadium in Detroit or Fenway Park in Boston.

The year after he retired, Joe told one of the New York writers, Tom Meany, that he could have hit more homers in another stadium in 1937. "I could have hit 70 in a field which favored right-handers," he said. "In addition to the 46 homers I got, I hit 15 triples that could have been homers. It seemed that every long ball I got hold of that season was a 400-footer, even the outs."

One of the most qualified judges in baseball also thought Joe was a threat to become the all-time home-run champion. In August of 1937, before we realized that there was a war in our future, Connie Mack told a magazine writer: "He has an excellent chance not only to draw as well as Ruth but even to beat the Babe's home run record. He is one of the most amazing players in the history of the game . . . I know it's asking a lot of a right-handed hitter to beat Ruth's record, but I do think it lies within the ability of DiMaggio to do so."

Joe hadn't finished his second year in the majors, yet Mr. Mack, one of the senior members of the baseball world, was giving this enthusiastic evaluation of his almost unlimited potential. His greatness shone brightly on defense, too. He led all outfielders in both leagues with 413 putouts.

Joe's contributions to the success of the organization didn't end there. One published report said, "The Yankee front office admits that he is drawing even greater crowds than the mighty Babe did."

Gehrig was still going strong, not showing even a hint of the illness that was to strike him down little more than one season later. In 1937 he was the second leading hitter in the league with a .351 average, five points ahead of DiMag, and third in home runs with 37 behind Joe and Hank Greenberg.

Joe finished second in runs batted in, ahead of Lou and Bill Dickey, and Joe and Lou finished one-three in total bases. We had the top three leaders in runs scored: Joe, Red Rolfe, and Lou, in that order.

I was able to contribute until my injury. My .320 batting average held up, covering 67 games and 206 at-bats. I could have pinch-hit against the Giants in the World Series, but the Yankees didn't really need me. We won it in five games, and our closest win was the final game, 4–2. Our other wins were by comfortable scores, 5–1 and two 8–1 games.

Before the first game of the Series, Judge Landis sent an usher over to the Yankee dugout with instructions to bring me to the commissioner's box. When I got there, Landis said, "Hello, Tom. How are they treating you?"

I said, "Fine, Commissioner. Just fine."

Landis said simply, "Well, they'd better."

It was a neat bit of judicial follow-up. He wanted to make sure that the kid from Ohio whose case had caused all that fuss before the season started was not being given any kind of cold shoulder by his team or anyone else in baseball.

Even though my teammates didn't need me on the field, I was able to make a contribution to our victory—sort of. McCarthy never overlooked a thing, and before that last game he told those of us who were not in the starting lineup, "You guys who aren't playing—get on those Giants."

We started to ride them early in the game, all except Frank Makosky, a twenty-five-year-old right-hander from Boonton, New Jersey, who won five games that year, his only year in the big leagues. He was the quietest teammate anyone ever had. McCarthy told him, "Makosky, you go down to the bullpen. You're no good to us around here." He knew Makosky wasn't going to say boo to the Giants.

Jake Powell, who was the hitting star of the previous World Series, was on the bench with me. Both of us were carrying out our orders from McCarthy with great delight, sticking a sharp verbal needle into the Giants at every opportunity, especially after their shortstop, Dick Bartell, had trouble with a ground ball. Bartell was known for his short fuse, and if Jake and I could get him upset or thrown out of the game, that would be playing right into McCarthy's hands. As soon as he juggled that grounder, Powell and I got on him. I yelled at him, "Great shortstop, my foot!"

What does Bartell do? What every great athlete does in that situation: He makes an outstanding play on his next chance. It was the third out of the inning, and as he began to trot toward the Giants' dugout, he took the time to look at ours—and glare right at me. He knew who the loudmouth was. What he didn't know was that I was doing it under orders from McCarthy.

I was so determined to help my team in the role that McCarthy assigned to me that I kept yelling at the Giants throughout the game. In the late innings, when DiMaggio came to bat for the last time in the World Series, the Giants' catcher, Harry Danning, said through his mask, "Joe, do me a favor, will you?"

Joe said, "What's that, Harry?"

"Tell McCarthy to send Henrich up here just once."

Hits, Runs and Stolen Signals

From the very beginning of our 1938 season, we knew we had a chance to do something great: win three World Series in a row, something that no team had ever done.

But there was a cloud on the horizon, a huge one, and it extended all the way from our spring training site in St. Petersburg to San Francisco. Joe D. was holding out for more money.

No wonder. In only two seasons, he had become our real leader, even though Gehrig had been our team captain since Babe Ruth had gone to the Boston Braves following the 1934 season, for what would be his last year.

Joe was a star from the very beginning in 1936, making an immediate contribution to the Yankees' success both on the field and at the gate. As a rookie he hit .323 with 29 home runs and 125 runs batted in. In '37 he did even better, with a .346 average, those 46 home runs that topped both leagues, 151 runs scored that did the same, and 167 RBIs.

Joe had forty more runs scored than the National League leader,

Ducky Medwick, and thirteen more RBIs than Medwick, who led the National League in that department, too. The only reason Joe didn't lead both leagues in RBIs was that in the American League Hank Greenberg drove in 183 runs for the Tigers.

As for his performances in the World Series, he hit .346 against the Giants in his rookie season. In '37, when we beat the Giants again, he drove in two runs with a bases-loaded single to help us win the first game and hit a home run to help us win the final game.

But the Yankee management, in the attitude of management on almost every team in those years, with the notable exception of Tom Yawkey of the Red Sox, decided Joe wasn't worth as much to the organization as the rest of the world thought he was. Joe has written that he was paid $8,500 as a rookie in 1936 and $15,000 in '37. After what he had accomplished for the team in his first two seasons, and the money he was making for management, he wanted more than the $25,000 they were offering him for 1938.

This was in the days when multiyear contracts were so rare as to be almost unheard of. You played from one year to the next. Thus, you were paid not on what you were doing this season, but on what you did last year. And when spring came, if you didn't like what management was offering, you became a "holdout." You held out for more money, and you stayed home while your teammates began spring training in sunny Florida in late February or early March.

If things reached the ultimate stage, you had no choice but to sign or sit out the season. You couldn't do like an employee in any other field and decide to quit your job and go to work for someone else. Baseball contracts had a "reserve clause," which bound you to your team for the year after your one-year contract expired, whether you liked it or not. But as the owners interpreted it, it also applied to the next year, and the next, and so on until they were through with you. The players went along with that assumption until 1975, when Andy Messersmith and Dave McNally questioned it in arbitration. Arbitrator Peter Seitz ruled in their favor, saying "one year" meant just that, and the courts upheld his decision. The result was the virtual creation of free agency in baseball.

Unable to invoke free agency in 1938, Joe was in a showdown

with management. He had settled for less than what he wanted after his rookie season. He didn't want to do the same thing after his second season. He asked for a large raise. The figure we heard was $45,000.

Ed Barrow summoned all of his business manager's firmness and said to Joe, "Young man, do you know how long Lou Gehrig has been with this club? Well, I'll tell you—thirteen years. And do you know how much he gets? $41,000. What do you have to say to that?"

Joe didn't hesitate: "Mr. Barrow, Gehrig is badly underpaid."

Barrow exploded at DiMag, who promptly left the general manager's office and went home to San Francisco, where he stayed until April 20, two weeks into the season. Then he gave up and signed for the $25,000, only to be informed that he would be fined for every day it took him to get into shape. Joe had been working out in San Francisco, so it didn't take him as long as spring training normally does, but it still cost him $1,944 in fines.

Joe remembers that Charley Ruffing was fined for holding out for two weeks the year before, but it was refunded to him when he began pitching and winning. But not Joe. He says Barrow never did give him his money back, even though he was blistering the ball right from the start.

When he returned to our lineup, Joe was booed in every American League park. The country was still in the Great Depression, and the fans had trouble—understandably—relating to a baseball star's holdout when they couldn't find a job.

He says he was shocked when he trotted onto the field for his first game of the season. "The fans at Griffith Stadium in Washington burned my ears with the loudest booing I'd ever heard," Joe wrote in a magazine article. "I couldn't understand it. I'd never been booed quite as lustily before. They repeated it every time I came to bat. It happened in every city thereafter, and it was loudest in Yankee Stadium . . . I was pretty upset . . . I don't know of any other disappointment that affected me as deeply."

Yet he never said anything to his teammates, at least not to me. On the field, Joe handled it well, as he always did when the public put pressure on him. He hit .324, with 32 home runs, the fifth best in the league, and 140 runs batted in, the third highest total in that category.

After his first three seasons, "the great DiMaggio" had 107 home runs and 432 runs batted in. He was twenty-three years old.

I received my own quick indoctrination in the facts of big-league life during that same winter. Ed Barrow, who was the Yankees' secretary and business manager, sent me a letter dated January 25, 1938, that was something less than a model in employer-employee relations. The issue was a difference of a couple of thousand dollars between the salary I wanted and Barrow's offer.

He didn't address me by my first name, or call me mister. He began bluntly and coldly:

My dear Henrich:
    We were quite surprised to receive your letter of January 24th, returning copies of your unsigned contract.

Barrow went on, "You are still on trial as far as the New York Club is concerned." He let met know management still had reservations about my knee. Then he said that, out of the goodness of their hearts, he and Colonel Ruppert had agreed to pay me a bonus of $1,500, giving me a total of $7,500 for the 1938 season. He closed with a stern warning:

    . . . if you are as smart and as fair and sensible as you always seem to be, you will sign and return both copies of your contract to this office without further argument.

I did.

We were a powerhouse team again that year. We beat out the Red Sox by nine and a half games to win the pennant, and we did it with power. We led both leagues with 174 home runs and 966 runs scored, and no other team anywhere was even close. To make us even tougher to beat, our pitching staff of Red Ruffing, Monte Pearson, Spud Chandler, and Lefty Gomez had the best earned run average in the American League, and Ruffing led the league with 21 wins.

McCarthy was getting the most out of all of us, which was a key part of his genius. He knew how to motivate a player, and he knew how to motivate an entire team. Sometimes he fired up the team by firing up one player. And it was always the same player: Jake Powell. Jake was a hard-hitting, hard-playing outfielder from Silver Spring, Maryland. He was the hitting star of the 1936 World Series for the Yankees with a .455 average against the Giants in his second full season as a big leaguer.

Jake was a talented athlete, but he was also his own worst enemy. He had a way of getting himself into controversies that never would happen to any one of the rest of us. A winter radio interview was one example.

He was a guest on a radio show in Chicago, and when the interviewer asked Jake what he was doing during the offseason, Powell told him he was a police officer in Dayton, Ohio. The interviewer asked if he liked police work, and Jake told him, "Oh, yeah. What I like to do is go around beating those niggers on the head."

The uproar that followed was predictable. The station spent the rest of the day disassociating itself from Powell's remark.

On Memorial Day of our 1938 season, when we were playing the Red Sox before 78,000 fans in Yankee Stadium, McCarthy singled out Powell again for the task he handled so well: getting the other team mad. We were facing the great Lefty Grove, and McCarthy saw that Lefty was getting tired in the later innings. He was wild, and his pitches were inside. That gave Joe the opportunity he wanted.

He turned to Jake in our dugout and said, "Jake, do you see what Grove is doing out there? He's throwing at us." McCarthy knew full well Lefty was just losing his sharpness as his fatigue increased, but Jake either didn't realize it or didn't care. By the time he came up to bat, he was itching to do battle.

But something changed. Joe Cronin lifted Grove and brought in a new pitcher, Archie McKain. Archie had no reason at all to throw at the hitters, and if he did, it wouldn't make any difference anyhow because his pitches, as the players say, "couldn't break a pane of glass."

As luck would have it, McKain's first pitch was low and inside. Jake got upset all over again. He wanted to bunt the second pitch and drag McKain or one of the Boston infielders into his path, which is always a convenient and subtle way to start a fight.

But the pitch was inside and, of all things, it hit Powell. That fit into McCarthy's scheme perfectly. Jake, naturally, charged the mound to do battle with McKain. The umpire threw him out of the game and Cronin, Boston's player-manager, got kicked out, too.

The whole flare-up ignited our team. We came back to win the game because of McCarthy's subtle little tactic. It was ironic, because McCarthy would never in a million years condone that kind of conduct by a player acting on his own. Joe always picked Jake for that assignment, and Jake never knew he was being used. It worked every time.

With my left knee healthy again, I was able to play my first full season in the major leagues. I finished with a .270 batting average, 24 doubles, 7 triples, 22 home runs, and 91 runs batted in. I was also showing discipline with my power. I struck out only 32 times in 471 times at bat, and I drew 92 walks.

I had by far my best game against an established pitching star, Buck Newsom. It was the kind of game you can go a whole career without experiencing. Newsom, who took the nickname "Bobo" later when he made himself into a personality to help prolong his career, pitched for the Red Sox in Yankee Stadium and held us to four hits. His opponent was Charley Ruffing, one of our best pitchers.

I hit two home runs and a double in our 4–2 win, driving in three runs and scoring the fourth.

That evening, Charley took his wife, Pauline, to dinner at the Pennsylvania Hotel. He was a great fan of the Big Band sound and went to the Pennsylvania and other spots in New York every chance he had to enjoy the hit songs played by Glenn Miller, Jimmy and Tommy Dorsey, Benny Goodman, and all the rest. The Ruffings ran into Newsom, that night, and Buck was gracious in defeat. He congratulated Charley on his outstanding performance, but Ruffing was honest and said, "Thanks, Buck—but you outpitched me. It's too bad you had to lose a game like that."

Newsom said, "That busher beat me."

The next day at the ballpark, Ruffing told me the story, including the fact that Newsom called me a "busher," the ballplayers' term for someone they resent. It's a reference to someone who belongs in the lowest levels of the minor leagues, the bush leagues.

"That's okay," I told Ruffing. "As long as he keeps giving me that fastball of his, he can call me anything he wants to."

McCarthy had me hitting third in the batting order again, just ahead of Joe, who remained our cleanup hitter, the one who is responsible for "cleaning" the bases after one or more of the first three hitters get on base. I told myself that my numbers weren't bad at all for a guy playing his first full season in the majors. Still, I wasn't entirely sure I was going to stick. There were so many other good players on the Yankees, and on every other team, too. And so many pitchers throwing so many curveballs.

We picked up a valuable addition to McCarthy's preferred combination of power and team play when Joe Gordon came up from Newark to begin his big-league career. He was an immediate help with 25 home runs and 97 RBIs, and he was such a sensational performer around second base that we quickly nicknamed him "Flash" Gordon after the popular comic strip character.

If Joe had been more selfish, he might be in the Hall of Fame today. He did all the unselfish things that team players do: hitting the ball to the right side with a man on second and nobody out, hitting the outside pitch to the opposite field to start a rally in the late innings, taking that extra base every chance he got instead of running the bases only ninety feet at a time, and taking charge of anything hit near him in the field.

McCarthy himself was a great one for doing everything he could dream up to help us win a game and exercising his leadership in every way imaginable. Once during the '38 season, Gerry Walker of the White Sox was taking batting practice when some of us decided to start riding him from the bench.

We called him "Gee-Gee," and McCarthy knew all about him. Walker was in his eighth season in the league, and he could beat you with his bat. He already had five .300-plus seasons, including two years when he hit .335 and .353, and he was hitting over .300 at this point, too.

But he was a nice, easy-going guy, the kind you can have some fun with, so we started hollering at him. McCarthy shut us up right away. He yelled at us, "Knock it of!"

When one of us asked what was wrong with a little good-natured ribbing, Joe said, "Gerry is sleeping today. Let's not wake him up."

Gerry helped us out once the year before, when Walker was with the Tigers, and Joe didn't want him getting any angrier at us than he was already. That came about during a game when Charlie Gehringer was on third and Gee-Gee was on second. All of a sudden, Walker takes off lickety-split for third and slides in with great flourish, obviously forgetting that one of his teammates was already there. Our third baseman, Red Rolfe, calmly tagged him out.

Gehringer, a man of few words, looked down at Walker on the ground and said, "Where the hell are you going?"

Gee-Gee said, "Back to second, if I can make it."

I was learning more about Lou Gehrig, and my admiration for him as a person and as a championship athlete continued to grow. He was a marvelous human being, with that beautiful blend of kindness and consideration for others mixed with the pride and determination that makes a talented athlete a champion.

As I was walking down the aisle of our Pullman car on a trip west in 1938, I spotted a card game in progress at the back of the car. Gehrig and Powell were playing hearts with a few teammates. Lou was sitting next to the window, and Jake was in the aisle seat.

Powell kept topping Gehrig's every play, until one of the other players in the game led spades. That was just the moment that Gehrig was waiting for. He had been sitting there all that time holding the queen of spades, waiting for someone to lead spades so he could play his queen and catch Powell for fifty points.

Lou suddenly jumped up, stood on the seat, and hammered the queen down onto the table with a *splat!* Then he turned to Jake and said, "I finally nailed you!"

I began to notice two other Gehrig characteristics—confidence, and respect from his teammates—in our card games. Both came to the surface in a game involving Lou and Bill Dickey, a superb bridge player.

To Gehrig, Dickey was more than just an excellent bridge player, one who usually was able to beat Lou at the game. The two were also the best of friends, respecting each other as athletes, teammates, and men.

Lou always wanted to improve himself. He valued culture in a person, and his wife, Eleanor, helped him increase his knowledge and appreciation of good music and other forms of culture. He made himself one of the best-informed members of the Yankees on current events, and in the late 1930s, as Hitler made noises in Europe and we were fighting our way out of a Depression at home, there were plenty of current events to read about. The rest of us often came to him for discussion of the day's news and what it might mean.

Lou's education at Columbia University was one of his early steps in acquiring the education and culture he desired for himself. Playing bridge was another part of that, especially playing with Dickey.

I was watching them in a game on the train one evening after dinner, when they were on the same team. They were playing against Red Rolfe and Charlie Keller. After losing a hand, Bill started to tell Lou how he could have played his cards differently and maybe won the hand.

"Lou," he said, "you could have made that hand . . ."

Gehrig cut him off. "Bill, the hand couldn't be made."

Dickey tried again. "But back there when . . ."

"Bill, the hand couldn't be made."

Dickey tried a third time. "Here, Lou, let me show you . . ."

Gehrig was firm and final: "Bill, I said the hand couldn't be made."

Dickey said only, "Okay." He was acknowledging Gehrig's superior status among us.

Gehrig wasn't the fiery type like Jake Powell, or the flamboyant type like his teammate of earlier years, Babe Ruth, but the fire of competition burned just as hot inside him as in any other athlete of his time or any era.

I remember one afternoon when we were facing Johnny Allen of Cleveland. Johnny was a good right-handed pitcher who won 142 games in his career. He broke in with the Yankees under McCarthy in 1932 and pitched for them through 1935, but McCarthy felt he was too difficult to manage, so he traded him to the Indians for two other pitchers, Monte Pearson and Steve Sundra.

Difficult to manage or not, Allen was a good pitcher. I struck out against him in this game, and after I went back to our bench—sitting on the far end, at the opposite end from McCarthy—I muttered to the guys right next to me, "Man, that guy's got good stuff."

McCarthy, all the way at the other end, heard my remark, leaned forward across the row of Yankees between us, and said sternly, "The guy's got nothing."

In the ninth inning, I got a hit off Allen and helped us to stage a four-run rally to beat him. In the clubhouse after the game, I was sure I was the happiest Yankee of them all. I had gotten a key hit off a good pitcher and Yankee rival, and we had won the game with a dramatic rally.

Across the clubhouse, sitting on the stool in front of his locker with his legs crossed and a cigarette in his hands, was Gehrig. He caught my eye and motioned me over.

When I got to his locker, he said, "Tom, I know you're a happy man. But you're not the happiest guy in this clubhouse. I am, because we creamed Johnny Allen."

It was the Gehrig pride rising to the surface again. That pride—no wonder they called his movie *Pride of the Yankees*—was one of the many ingredients that prompted McCarthy to love Gehrig. Lou was the apple of Joe's eye, and it was plain for all to see.

I was learning about the personnel on the other teams in the American League, too: the hitters and their tendencies, what certain players did when they were running the bases, where a particular team positioned its fielders when I was at bat—everything I could.

Chicago's shortstop, Luke Appling, was destined for a plaque in the Hall of Fame. He was a likeable guy, and one of the greatest all-around players I ever saw. He could beat you any way it was necessary—with one of his 2,749 hits, great plays at short, stolen bases—and he was the greatest hit-and-run man I ever saw.

He was a magician with the bat, waving it like a magic wand to foul off any pitch he didn't like. In twenty years as a big leaguer, all with the White Sox, he never struck out more than 41 times, and that's with five or six hundred at-bats every season. He led the league in hitting twice, including a .388 average in 1936.

One thing I learned quickly about Appling was his exceptional ability to hit behind the runner on a hit-and-run play, enabling the runner to advance from first to third. The runner would break for second like on a steal attempt, the second baseman would break for the bag because it's usually his to cover with a right-handed hitter, and Luke would punch the ball right through the spot just vacated by the second baseman.

That's bat control. And as if he didn't impress the rest of the league enough on those hit-and-run plays, he showed his bat control in even more convincing terms one day when he was mad at management for turning down his request for a raise. He fouled off eighteen straight pitches, costing the front office the price of eighteen baseballs.

Luke went hunting one fall down home in Georgia with one of our star pitchers, Spud Chandler. The longer they waited for the birds to show up, the more white lightning they consumed. Late in the afternoon, Chandler felt fortified enough to ask Luke how he put on the hit-and-run sign.

Luke, feeling the same warm glow of fellowship, told him: one hand on the bat followed by one tap of the bat on home plate, or two hands and two taps.

The next season, Luke is the hitter with a man on first, and he pounds the plate once while holding the bat with one hand, so our catcher, Bill Dickey, calls for a pitchout so he can nail the runner trying to reach second.

Only the runner doesn't go. Next pitch, same thing. We went to a 3–0 count from three straight pitchouts. Finally Luke walks.

After the inning, Dickey comes back to our dugout and says to Chandler, "Which one of you guys did you say was drunk last fall?"

When it came to signals, the Yankees led the league there, too, and no one ever knew it. We got away with stealing the signals of every other team in the league for years.

The baseball world has no idea to this day how many pitches two of our coaches, Art Fletcher at third base and Earle Combs at first, stole for our hitters. They put all of us at a clear advantage by stealing signs or picking up some characteristic in the pitcher's motion. And it never reached the newspapers.

Chuck Dressen was almost as good—but you'd never get

DiMaggio to agree with that. Joe was hitting one day when Dressen, one of our coaches in the 1940s, tipped him off that a curveball was coming. It was a fastball high and inside. Only Joe's exceptional reflexes kept him from getting hit in the head.

That's the risk when you're stealing signals or picking up a habit that the pitcher has on a certain pitch. If you're wrong, the hitter can get killed, thinking it's a curveball headed toward him that just hasn't started to break yet when in reality it's a fastball coming at him that's much harder than a curve and isn't going to break.

That's also the way you can stop the other team from stealing your signals. Your catcher flashes the sign for a curveball, the coach at first or third relays that information to the hitter after spotting the signal, but you've already arranged with the pitcher to throw a fastball instead. The hitter gets knocked down, and he'll never believe that coach again.

When it happened in Dressen's case, whether it was intentional on the part of the other team or not, that was all DiMag needed. He came back to the dugout after finishing his turn at bat and told our manager that year, Bucky Harris, "Either you tell Dressen not to call any pitches for me, or I will." Bucky told him.

But Fletch and Combs were the best, even better than Del Baker, who had the reputation of being the best in the business. That just made Fletch and Combs even more effective, because the rest of the league didn't know they were doing it and giving the Yankee hitters valuable secret information.

McCarthy was so secretive about signals of any kind that he bordered on the paranoid. Even his own players didn't know what his signs from the dugout to Fletcher and Combs were in a bunt situation, or hit-and-run, steal, sacrifice, whatever the occasion might suggest. All we knew were the signs we got from Fletch in his third-base coach's box.

Many years after all of us retired, I was talking to Joe at an Old Timers Game at Yankee Stadium. I asked him, "Joe, have you ever told anybody what your signs with Fletcher were?"

He said, "No. Why should I?"

We were playing the Tigers once when Rudy York came to bat in the ninth inning with a man on. McCarthy motioned one of our relief pitchers, Bill Zuber, into the game from the bullpen. As McCarthy and our catcher, Rollie Hemsley, were waiting on the mound for Zuber, McCarthy said he wanted Zuber to give York nothing but fast balls.

Hemsley, always alert, said, "In that case, Joe, should we tell him to pay no attention to my signs?"

McCarthy exploded, "Judas priest! Don't tell me he knows them, too!"

McCarthy kept close tabs on everything we did on the field. Some managers who were not pitchers prefer to delegate that part of the game to a coach because it is such a specialty, but not McCarthy. He knew what he wanted from his players at every position, including his pitchers.

If he didn't approve of a pitcher's performance, he was perfectly willing to let him know it for the good of the team. Like the time Kemp Wicker, a left-hander from Kernersville, North Carolina, gave up a home run to Hal Trosky, the big, slugging first baseman of the Cleveland Indians.

Wicker, who won a total of nine games for us over three seasons before the war after making it to the big leagues as a thirty-year-old rookie, came storming into the dugout after the inning. McCarthy said to him, "Don't worry about it, son. He's hit homers off pitchers who are a lot better than you are."

In another game against the Indians, Bill Zuber came in from the bullpen for us in the late innings with one man on base and one out and promptly gave up a home run to Ken Keltner. Then he struck out the next two hitters on six pitches.

When Zuber came into the dugout, McCarthy asked him, "What did you strike them out with?"

Zuber told him, "My sinker."

"What did Keltner hit?"

"My curveball."

"What's your best pitch?"

"My sinker."

"That's right, Bill. Save it until the game is gone."

As we closed in on the pennant with a comfortable lead over the Red Sox, McCarthy became anxious to win a hundred games for the third year in a row. But it didn't turn out that way, and to say that we backed in would be an understatement. We won the pennant on a day when we lost a doubleheader—to the lowly Browns, yet. The Red Sox were rained out, and that eliminated them mathematically from any chance of winning the pennant. We won 99 games.

One group who didn't care how we won was our wives. An extra paycheck for playing in the World Series always came in handy in managing the family budget or buying a new coat for the coming winter.

We were lucky in that respect. The Yankee wives were our biggest fans. Maybe the most faithful of all was Red Rolfe's wife, Isabella. She was one classy lady. She came out to Yankee Stadium often and enjoyed the games like any other enthusiastic fan. She never berated an umpire for making a call against Red and never second-guessed McCarthy or any of us. Wives like that help make you a better player and a better team.

Charley Ruffing's wife, Pauline, was another faithful fan. She was as much of a needler as he was. She sat away from the rest of our wives, making more noise than any of them. Crosetti's wife, Norma, sometimes would sit with her to keep her company, but she left the screaming to Pauline.

Those of us who were still single didn't realize it, but the member of the front office with the most delicate job was the ticket manager, Mike Rendine. He told me he felt he had to give careful consideration every day as to which tickets to give to which wives. For instance, he tried not to put the wife of a so-so defensive player next to that day's starting pitcher. The player might cost the pitcher the game, and the two wives might take it out on each other. Seating the wives was more than just a social question. With Mike it was a protocol problem as well.

In the '38 World Series, as we made a bid for three in a row, our opponents were the Chicago Cubs. They had a much closer race of it in the National League than we did in the American. They won the pennant by two games, overtaking the Pittsburgh Pirates in September, and pitching is what won it for them.

Stan Hack, their third baseman, was the only Cub among the leaders in any offensive category, and he didn't finish first in anything except stolen bases; even there he had only 16. He was second in hits and runs scored. The rest of the team's strength was in its pitching.

Their ace was Bill Lee, a six-foot-three right-hander from Plaquemine, Louisiana. He led the league that year in wins (22), won-lost percentage, earned run average, games started, and shutouts. Clay Bryant was another big man on the mound for the Cubs that year. He was a tall right-hander, too, just under six-three, in his best year by far of a big-league career that lasted six seasons. Bryant won 19 games and led the league in strikeouts. Except for that year, the most games he ever won in a season was nine.

Outside of Lee and Bryant, the biggest winners on the Cubs' pitching staff that year were Larry French and Tex Carleton, who won 10 games each. But Carleton was barely a .500 pitcher because he lost 9, and French's record was far worse with 19 defeats.

The other major factor in their pennant victory was the Cubs' defense. They led the National League in team fielding average and allowed their opponents the fewest runs. The proof of how tight their defense was could be found in the number of runs the two Series teams allowed. The Cubs gave up 598 runs, the lowest number in either league. We had the lowest total in our league— 112 more than the Cubs allowed.

Their first baseman, with the great name of Ripper Collins, and their second baseman, Billy Herman, led the league with the highest fielding averages at their positions. The Cubs had some other veterans who also knew what it took to win over the long haul.

Baseball isn't like football, where you play only sixteen games and your season can be made or broken with two or three wins or losses in a row, or basketball, where you play only eighty-two games. Part of baseball's great appeal is in its test of consistency. You have to be the best over a long stretch. If you run off four or five straight wins, that's still not going to be good enough to win the pennant or the division championship for you. You have to be better than that. And if you lose four or five in a row, you can still shake that off, pick yourself up as a team, and have time to get back into the thick of things.

McCarthy managed the Yankees that way, always aware that we had to play 154 games. Winning a few in a row wasn't any reason to start jumping out of your skin or popping any champagne corks. If you won on Opening Day in April, that meant you still had to win almost another hundred times to be sure of playing in the World Series in October. That's a true test of greatness, to win consistently over a sustained period of time, and baseball is the sternest test of that.

The '38 Cubs had veteran players who knew that, too: Hack and Herman, Dizzy Dean and Charlie Root on the pitching staff, Billy Jurges at short, an outfield of Augie Galan, Carl Reynolds, and Frank Demaree, plus Gabby Hartnett, the Hall of Famer, behind the plate, handling the pitchers and hitting one of base-ball's most historic home runs.

For Hartnett, 1938 was a special season. He replaced Charlie Grimm as manager after eighty-one games, when the Cubs were 45–36. Under Hartnett they won 44 games and lost only 27. This World Series was Gabby's only one as a manager, and his last as a player.

Then there was that home run—"the homer in the gloamin'."

Gabby—his real name was Charles, but he had the Irish gift of gab—hit a home run into the gloaming—the dusk—in the last of the ninth to beat the Pirates and propel his team toward the pen-nant. The next day, they defeated Pittsburgh again, 10–1, to clinch it. It was their twenty-first victory in twenty-four games.

Hartnett was known for his ability in every phase of catching, especially his throwing arm. The fans used to delight in coming out to the ballpark in time to watch the Cubs in their pregame practice so they could see—and hear—Gabby's throws to the bases. He'd pop the gloves of his infielders, and everyone in the ballpark loved it.

McCarthy knew all about Hartnett's arm. Joe began his man-aging career with the Cubs in 1926 and guided them to the Na-tional League pennant in 1929. He was Hartnett's manager for five seasons. He told me Hartnett was "the best thrower I ever saw."

Rolfe came to appreciate that throwing arm in the '38 Series. Red, with 44 stolen bases in his career, stole 13 of them in 1938.

He tried to steal second against Hartnett, and Gabby cut him down by a wide margin with his bullet throw to shortstop Billy Jurges, who was covering second. I was the hitter, and I just stood there with my eyes popping and my mouth hanging open at how easy Hartnett made it look. Here was an experienced base stealer, and the play at second wasn't even close.

That was the third out of the inning, and as Hartnett took off his mask and started to trot off the field, he saw me standing there with this look of amazement on my face. He didn't say anything. He just gave me a smile and a wink.

He was telling me, "You ain't playing with kids today, son."

We knew we were catching a hot ball club. But hot teams never scared us. We weren't cocky, but we knew we were tough, we knew we had good players, and we knew McCarthy was going to make sure we played together as a team and not as nine individuals out there for their own glory.

Through all of our years of success from the mid-1930s until Joe and I retired at the beginning of the 1950s, the Yankees never took the field with the attitude that the other team had to roll over and play dead because we were the mighty Yankees. We didn't jam ourselves down anybody's throat.

Our attitude always was: "We're ready to play you. Let's go." If it was a crucial game, we knew we'd have to play even harder, so we did. We had our Yankee pride as our driving force.

That was the way we ran onto the diamond in Wrigley Field for the opening game of the 1938 World Series. We knew we were going to have to be good, to play hard, to beat a team as hot as the Cubs. And that's exactly what we did. We beat them in four straight games.

Charley Ruffing—we didn't call him "Red" as much as the writers and the fans did—and Bill Dickey led us to our first victory. Charley held the Cubs to one run, and Bill helped his battery mate by getting four singles as we beat Bill Lee. The two pals, DiMaggio and Gomez, plus Crosetti were our winning combination in the second game. Joe D. hit a home run with me on base and Gomez got the win, with relief help from Johnny Murphy. The Crow drove in the tying and winning runs with a home run in the eighth inning off Dizzy Dean to put us ahead, 4–3, one of the biggest hits in the series. DiMag's homer came in the ninth after I singled off Dean. The final score was 6–3.

That game was my introduction to Dean, and it shocked me. Diz had been hit in the big toe of his right foot in the All-Star

game in Washington the year before by a line drive off the bat of
Earl Averill. The shot broke his toe. He tried to come back for
the Cardinals too soon after the injury and developed a sore pitching arm by trying to compensate for the discomfort in his toe when
he threw.

Branch Rickey traded him to the Cubs at the start of the '38
season for Curt Davis, Tuck Stainback, Clyde Shoun, and
$185,000, and everyone in baseball except the Cubs knew that
Rickey had scored a major trading victory because Dean simply
was never going to be the pitcher again that he once was.

Dizzy was a pitching marvel until that time. He led the National
League in wins twice with the Cardinals and in strikeouts four
times. He had 121 wins going into the '37 season and managed to
win 13 that year despite the toe injury. With the Cubs in '38, his
performance was remarkable. Pitching with a dead arm and with
only his experience and courage going for him, he won 7 games
and lost only one.

But he was finished. In four seasons after that, he won a total
of nine games. He was elected to the Hall of Fame because the
writers had good memories. They remembered that when Averill's
line drive hit him, Dizzy, with more than 120 wins already, was
still only twenty-six years old.

In my first three times at bat against him, I saw nothing—
absolutely nothing. I knew what the word on him was, that he
couldn't throw any more, but I expected to see at least a trace of
his former greatness, or maybe even something new. An off-speed
pitch, maybe. But there was nothing. Our batting-practice pitchers were throwing better stuff than Dean showed us.

When I came up in the ninth ahead of DiMaggio, I knew all I
needed to know. After seeing Dean for three turns at bat myself,
I reminded myself of one of the cardinal rules of hitting: Wait on
the pitch.

That's one of the hardest things to do, but it's one of the most
important. The longer you can wait, the better chance you have
of hitting the ball for the simple reason that you have longer to
see what kind of a pitch it is, how fast it's coming, and where it's
headed. But it takes discipline, and not all hitters have it, and no
one has it every time.

But in my fourth time against Dean, I had it. I told myself to wait longer than usual. I did, and I pulled a line-drive single to right field.

Yankee power and Yankee pitching won the third game. Joe Gordon didn't let his rookie status bother him in the World Series pressure cooker. He homered in the fifth, our first hit off Bryant, and drove in two runs in the next inning with a single. Dickey added a home run.

We wrapped everything up in the fourth game. We jumped out on top with three runs in the second inning on two singles, an error, and a triple by the Crow. We faced another legendary name in this game, Charlie Root, the man who was the pitcher when Babe Ruth hit his "called shot" home run against the Cubs in the '32 Series.

Root entered the game in the third inning in relief of Bill Lee. Charlie was thirty-nine by that time, but he was still good enough to win 8 games for the Cubs that season in a career that included 201 victories in seventeen seasons. He was a fellow Ohioan, from Middletown, and he was a big name to me from my teen years.

I hit a home run off him in the sixth inning to extend our lead to 4-1, the first World Series homer of my career. Ken O'Dea, the Cubs' backup catcher behind Hartnett, homered in the eighth to cut our lead to 4-3, but between the Cubs' ineffective bullpen and a defense that was less than airtight, we scored four cheap runs and won the game and the Series, 8-3.

I'm sure Root wanted to beat our brains out after what the Yankees and Ruth did to him six years earlier. In 1932, the Babe and the rest of the Yankees were resentful over what they considered the Cubs' unfair treatment of former Yankee infielder Mark Koenig, who was traded to the Cubs during the season and was a key factor in their pennant victory. The Cubs voted him only half of a player's World Series share. That sparked a bitter atmosphere from the beginning of the '32 Series, which the Yankees swept in four games.

Ruth hit his famous home run in the third game after Root got ahead of him in the count, no balls and two strikes. The Babe seemed to point to the center-field stands and tell Root he was going to park one there for a home run.

Then he put his homer where he seemed to have been pointing.

Whether he actually did point is being discussed to this day. Bill Deane, the senior research associate at the Hall of Fame's National Baseball Library, has done the most thorough job of bringing together the conflicting versions of what is still described as "Ruth's called shot."

Deane discovered that Ruth told John P. Carmichael of the *Chicago Daily News*, "I told Hartnett, 'If that bum throws one in here, I'll hit it over the fence again . . . I took two strikes and after each one, I held up my finger and said, 'That's one' and 'That's two' . . . That's when I waved to the fence.

"No, I didn't point to any spot, but as long as I'd called the first two strikes on myself, I had to go through with it. It was damned foolishness, sure, but I just felt like doing it . . . I just laughed to myself going around the bases and thinking, 'You lucky bum.' "

Deane wrote in *Baseball Today* that Root "went to his grave denying the 'called-homer' story." Root's widow, Dorothy, who was at the game, said, "Of course I didn't see him point. Nobody else saw him point because he didn't . . . Charlie would have thrown it right at his head. I knew that and so did all of the players."

Lefty Gomez disagreed with Dorothy. "Ruth pointed with his bat in his right hand, to right field, not center field," Lefty said. "But he definitely called his shot."

Koenig, the man who started it all, said, "Ruth did point, sure. He definitely raised his right arm . . . but as far as pointing to center, no he didn't . . . You know darn well a guy with two strikes isn't going to say he's going to hit a home run on the next pitch."

Deane also discovered in his research that the dispute became the subject of a court case more than fifty years later. Judge George Choppelas of the California Court of Historic Review and Appeals issued a finding in 1986, accompanied by a report that said:

> It is not important if the incidents referred to in . . . legends really did in fact happen. What is important is that a large segment of the people believe that they did occur, and it is for us as individuals to place whatever credence or value on these stories as we might desire . . .

It is the court's opinion that the legend of Babe Ruth pointing to the center field fence in the 1932 World Series shall remain intact for future generations of baseball fans and sports writers to argue about.

As good as the Cub's pitching was in 1938, ours was better in the World Series, and the performance of our pitchers reflects one of the differences in pitching then and now. In four games, with baseball's world championship at stake, McCarthy made a total of one pitching change.

Ruffing went the full nine innings in winning the first game and the last, and Monte Pearson, a right-hander who won 16 games for us that season, went the distance in winning the third game, 5–2, on a five-hitter. Johnny Murphy's two innings in relief of Gomez in the second game was the only appearance by a Yankee relief pitcher in the whole World Series.

For those who weren't around then, that kind of endurance by pitchers may be hard to believe, but that's the way they pitched in those years. Starting pitchers were also finishing pitchers. They had to be stronger and more durable than today's pitchers. The manager didn't hand them a new ball in the clubhouse and say, "Give me six good innings, if you can."

The difference was in pitching philosophy, with relief pitchers called on for an inning or two at the end of some of the games. Today it's unusual for a starting pitcher to pitch a complete game. In those years it was unusual not to.

As a result, there was a difference in the men themselves. You had to be stronger longer in the 1930s and '40s. Today's pitchers might have stronger arms, but only for six or seven innings. In our day, we had ten strong arms we could throw at you, and at least half of them could go the full nine.

I don't mean to sound like someone who says the old days were better, but this much is undeniable: They don't pitch like that any more.

Five _____

Triumph and Tragedy

A Yankee era ended in January 1939, with an impact on all of us. Colonel Jacob Ruppert, our owner, died on January 13, after suffering from phlebitis for years. He passed away at his home on Fifth Avenue shortly after his most famous acquisition, Babe Ruth, came outside with tears in his eyes and said, "Jake is dying."

Ruppert enjoyed great wealth and owned not one of New York's best-known businesses but two. Ruppert's Brewery was the other. He was known and admired as the one who gave New York not only the Babe, the most famous sports star in the world, but also Lou Gehrig, Joe McCarthy and Joe DiMaggio—and Yankee Stadium itself. His funeral was at another New York landmark—St. Patrick's Cathedral—with thousands of mourners who had to be controlled by police lines. I flew from Ohio at my own expense to be there. The flag at City Hall flew at half-staff.

Shortly after Ruppert's death, Ed Barrow was elected president of the Yankees. With his new authority at the top of the Yankee organization, Barrow made it clear immediately that he was going to be firmer than ever in dealing with us players—and just as warm-hearted.

On February 1 he sent me what was becoming his annual ul-

60

timatum, this one blaming the organization's refusal to meet my request on Ruppert, who was unable to give his side of the story:

My dear Henrich:

Replying to your letter of January 31st, beg to advise that Colonel Ruppert fixed the 1939 salary figures for the various Yankee players just one week before he died, and there is no one now living with authority to change those figures.

Am certainly very much surprised at your attitude as Colonel Ruppert, Manager McCarthy and myself all figured that you were being treated exceedingly well when you were voluntarily given an increase of $1500.

You players forget how much it costs the New York Club every year to get together a pennant winner from which the club seldom gets anything but glory.

However, as stated above, there is not a chance in the world of your receiving a further increase for the coming season.

He made his heavy-handed attitude stick. I signed on his terms. In 1939, the only option was to find another line of work.

Barrow was ruthless in negotiating with us. He had no shame. And there was no limit to the number and kinds of excuses he made to deny you a fair salary: You didn't have a good year, you're getting older, you had a knee operation over the winter so we don't know how you'll do. His letters about our contracts were exercises in creative writing.

All of us felt the same way. When Joe Gordon was leaving our victory party at the Commodore Hotel after one of our World Series championships, he said to Barrow, "Mr. Barrow, I have to make a phone call. Can you lend me ten cents on next year's salary?"

Joe didn't have to make any phone call. He was creating an opportunity to stick it to Barrow and embarrass him in front of those of us who heard him.

The same two names that dominated the headlines about the Yankees for three years did it again in 1939, but for tragically different reasons.

DiMaggio was in our lineup on Opening Day for the first time in his career as McCarthy made it our mission to win four championships in a row. DiMag didn't stay there long. A few games later, he tore muscles in his right leg above the ankle while making a sharp turn after another of his outstanding catches. He was out of our lineup for thirty-five games.

When he came back, he hit with a vengeance. He was tearing the cover off the ball, so much that he was hitting .409 with only three weeks left in the season. Then, of all things, a nerve in his eyelid began giving him trouble and made him blink. A hitter who blinks is no hitter at all, and Joe wasn't.

His average began to drop, but McCarthy wouldn't take him out of the lineup even though we won the American League pennant easily. We ran away from the rest of the league. The Red Sox finished second, but they were seventeen games behind us. We got back into the hundred-victory groove, too, with 106 wins.

"If I take you out," McCarthy told DiMag, "they'll say I did it to make you a .400 hitter, and they'll call you a cheese champion."

Joe D.'s average dropped twenty-eight points to .381, still tops in both leagues, thirty-two points higher than Johnny Mize in the National League. He was fourth in the league in home runs with 30 and second in runs batted in, and he would have finished second in a category added later, slugging average. In recognition of it all, the Baseball Writers' Association of America selected him the American League's Most Valuable Player, the first of three times he won the award.

As always, Joe wasn't winning games for us only with his bat. He was playing the best center field in baseball, too. In '39 I saw him make the greatest catch I've ever seen. You can talk about Willie Mays and the catch he made off Vic Wertz in the 1954 World Series, or name any other catch you like, but the one Joe made off Hank Greenberg at Yankee Stadium in 1939 was the greatest anyone who was there ever saw, including the home-plate umpire, Bill McGowan.

I was playing right field and Joe was in center when Greenberg hit a long fly ball into the monuments in deep center field. DiMag was off with the crack of the bat, maybe even a split second before. Good outfielders can do that because they know every hitter's tendencies and also pay close attention to what the pitcher is throwing and where the catcher is calling for the pitch.

Joe set sail for the outfield wall with his back to the plate, flying over the grass and not looking back until he was almost out of the stadium. Then he leaped, made a half-turn, reached up, and caught the ball. He banged into the wall—before they started putting padding on outfield walls—but held onto the ball.

There's another part to that story. It was not only the greatest catch any of us ever saw, it was also the only time I ever saw Joe make a mistake in eleven years as his teammate. As soon as the play was over, he started to trot off the field, but his catch was only the second out. Earl Averill, who was on first base when the play started, was around second and headed for third when Joe made the catch. Joe's slight hesitation before realizing it was only the second out gave Averill just enough time to make it back to first.

Any man who plays center field in the major leagues for thirteen years is entitled to one momentary lapse, especially one that doesn't cost his team a run. That was the only one I ever saw Joe make, and no one else ever saw him make another one, either.

The next day, one of the papers compared Joe to Tris Speaker, the all-time outstanding center fielder for the Red Sox, Indians, A's, and Senators from 1907 to 1928. The story said Joe was like Speaker in his ability to play a shallow center field and pick off line drives for outs because he knew he could catch almost anything hit over his head if he had to go back on a ball.

Gomez was pitching that next afternoon, and Rudy York hit two shots over Joe's head for extra bases. Lefty asked Joe later why he was playing so shallow. Joe, with his deadpan humor, said, "Didn't you see the paper? I'm going to make the fans forget Tris Speaker."

Lefty said, "Just be sure you don't make them forget Lefty Gomez."

Greenberg hit us well that year, as he did every team every year. Even our ace relief pitcher, Johnny Murphy, had trouble getting him out with curveballs and his pinpoint control. Finally Joe D. became so frustrated he said to Murphy, "Why don't you fastball this guy once?"

Joe knew that Greenberg, a good guess hitter, might be guessing curveball in a certain situation because he knew that was Murphy's out pitch, and we could surprise him with a fastball.

The next day, Murphy is in the game in the late innings and throws Greenberg a fast ball, which Hank promptly knocks deep into the Bronx, and we lose the game.

Murphy's locker was a few down from Joe's and across the room. After the game, Joe gets up off the stool in front of his locker, walks across the room to Murphy, and says, "Don't you *ever* listen to anything else I say the rest of my life."

Some of the people who were around in 1939 will tell you that you could see Gehrig fading the year before. They say he didn't have a good year. That's not true. Lou played in every game in 1938, extending the streak of consecutive games that won him the name "the Iron Horse" to 2,122. He hit .295 with 29 home runs, 115 runs scored, and 114 runs batted in. And he led the American League first basemen by making 157 double plays. In the World Series, he hit .286.

That doesn't sound to me like someone whose performance would be cause for concern. There was never any talk among us that something might be happening to our teammate and leader, because there was no reason for such talk. As far as any of us knew in 1938, Lou Gehrig was still Lou Gehrig.

But 1939 was a different story.

Bill Dickey noticed in spring training that Lou suddenly wasn't able to get out of the way of pitches in batting practice. The reflexes just didn't seem to be working fast enough. In an exhibition game in Clearwater, Florida, against the Phillies, Gehrig hit a long fly ball off the wall in deep right-center field, the kind of hit that was a triple for the man who stole 102 bases and was fast enough to steal home 15 times, only four times fewer than Jackie Robinson.

I watched Lou running out that hit, and I was having trouble believing what I was seeing. Between second and third he just didn't seem to be getting anyplace. It looked as if he were running uphill. The Phillies threw him out at third. In the dugout, I sat in silent shock. No one said anything. But each of us knew what the rest were thinking.

Lou started the season and played in our first eight games, extending his astounding streak to 2,130 consecutive games, something that Cal Ripken of the Orioles, with over fifteen hundred straight games, can break only if he plays in every game between now and 1995. Lou got only four singles and no extra-base hits in 28 trips to the plate. He scored two runs, batted one in, drew five walks, and struck out once. His batting average was .143.

Lou Gehrig was finished. We knew that. But we didn't know how this situation was going to affect the rest of us. In the end, Lou did what McCarthy knew he would. He did what was best for his team.

McCarthy was hounded by reporters during those first eight games. They wanted to know when he was going to take Lou out of the lineup. He was done. Everybody could see that. Why keep playing him and damage the team's performance and its chances of winning the pennant and the World Series for the fourth straight time? Here we were trying to extend our *team's* streak while Gehrig was jeopardizing our chances by extending his own.

But McCarthy told the writers the decision would have to be Lou's, not his. He told them he had too much respect for Gehrig to take him out of the lineup for the first time since 1925.

He gave me the same answer during those first eight games. He told me, "If Lou can't play, he's going to have to take himself out of the lineup. I won't do it."

The end came suddenly. We were playing the Washington Senators in Yankee Stadium on April 30. It was a Sunday. Lou went hitless in four trips to the plate and messed up an easy throw. We lost the game. But something else happened in that game, and the story is that it was what convinced the one we called "Biscuit Pants," because of his stocky build and broad rear end, to "hang 'em up," as the players say.

Lou had already suffered the ultimate indignity for a great hitter. In a couple of our games, the pitchers walked DiMaggio to face Gehrig. They were willing to pitch now to the great Yankee who hit 493 home runs, had the third most career RBIs in history, and owned a lifetime batting average of .340, because they knew they could get him out.

The Red Sox did that twice on Opening Day. He hit into a double play both times.

But what convinced Lou to take himself out of the lineup was a routine ground ball to the pitcher. Johnny Murphy fielded it cleanly and made a good throw to first base, but Lou had to struggle to get to the bag for the throw.

After we returned to our dugout on the first-base side of Yankee Stadium for our turn at bat, some of us said, "Nice play, Lou."

Gehrig said later that when he realized his teammates felt that they should congratulate him on the most routine of plays, he knew it was time to go.

We took the train to Detroit the next day, but before the first game of the series, Lou found McCarthy at Briggs Stadium and said to him, "Joe, I always said that when I felt I couldn't help the team any more, I would take myself out of the lineup. I guess that time has come."

"When do you want to quit, Lou?"

"Now."

When the rest of us got the word, Lefty Gomez, with his unique talent for finding humor to lighten a somber time, told Gehrig, "Just think, Lou, it took fifteen years for them to get you out of the lineup. Sometimes I'm out of there in fifteen *minutes*."

Gehrig, in his typical honesty and modesty, offered no excuses when reporters asked him the reasons for his decision. He didn't tell them how bad he felt physically or what an effort it was to do anything any more, much less play major-league baseball. He told the writers and broadcasters simply, "I can't hit and I can't field."

Lou checked into the Mayo Clinic in Rochester, Minnesota, for an examination. On June 20, the entire team, the entire city, and the entire nation were shocked, much like the national disbelief 52 years later when Magic Johnson announced his illness and retirement. Ed Barrow released the report on Lou's condition to the press, signed by Dr. Harold C. Harbein:

This is to certify that Mr. Lou Gehrig has been under examination at the Mayo Clinic from June 13 to June 19, 1939, inclusive.

After a careful and complete examination, it was found that he is suffering from amyotrophic lateral sclerosis. This type of illness involves the motor pathways and cells of the central nervous system and, in lay terms, is known as a form of chronic poliomyelitis—infantile paralysis.

The nature of this trouble makes it such that Mr. Gehrig will be unable to continue his active participation as a baseball player inasmuch as it is advisable that he conserve his muscular energy. He could, however, continue in some executive capacity.

When it was over, Lou could look back on a career filled with achievements that we mere humans could never approach. His streak wasn't remarkable just because it reached the stratospheric number of 2,130 consecutive games, but because of how well he performed throughout that period. He didn't just play in all those games—he dominated them.

He hit more grand-slam home runs than anyone else in baseball history, 23. He still holds the American League record for runs batted in with 184 in 1931, in the seventh year of his streak. In 1934, without a day off for nine seasons, he won the triple crown by finishing first in batting average, home runs, and runs batted in. He is tied with George Sisler for the fifteenth highest career batting average with .340, only two points behind Ruth and four behind Ted Williams—all of this while never missing a game for fourteen seasons.

Then there's this eye-popping statistic: Mickey Mantle, Willie Mays, Hank Aaron, and Reggie Jackson never had one season in which they drove in 142 runs. Gehrig *averaged* 153 RBIs over eleven consecutive years.

He played with broken bones, sprains, pulled muscles, torn tendons, lumbago, and high fevers. During his marathon streak he was hit in the head by the pitch three times. Late in his career, his hands were X-rayed. Doctors found seventeen fractures that had healed themselves. He broke every finger on both hands, some twice, and never mentioned any of this to anyone.

I was there on Lou Gehrig Day at Yankee Stadium, when we played the Senators in the traditional Fourth of July holiday doubleheader. By now the fans and the rest of us knew that Lou was terminally ill with ALS, a disabling, progressive illness. It has killed several more recent notables including Senator Jacob Javits and actor David Niven, but it is still called what it has been called since 1939, "Lou Gehrig's disease."

The fans turned out in dazzling numbers—61,808 of them—to pay tribute to Lou. The Yankees lined up at home plate and presented Gehrig with an engraved cup from all of us. It said:

> We've been to the wars together;
> And we took our foes as they came;
> And always you were the leader,
> And ever you played the game.
>
> Idol of cheering millions,
> Records are yours by the sheaves;
> Iron of frame they hailed you,
> Decked you with laurel leaves.
>
> But higher than that we hold you,
> We who have known you best,
> Knowing the way you came through
> Every human test.
>
> Let this be a silent token
> Of friendship's lasting gleam
> And all that we've left unspoken—
> Your pals of the Yankee team.

All of us were crying—fans, players, umpires, reporters, everyone—as we saw Lou fight back his own tears. He leaned into the microphone at home plate with emcee Sid Mercer and Ed Barrow at his side and said with that Gehrig sincerity:

> You have been reading about a bad break I got . . . Yet today, I consider myself the luckiest man on the face of the earth . . . I might have been given a bad break, but I've got an awful lot to live for. Thank you.

Mel Allen entered our lives in a big way in 1939. He was as

new in town as I was. He came to New York after earning a law degree at the University of Alabama, where he had enrolled as a freshman at fifteen, and quickly won an audition at CBS for a radio announcer's job. He broadcast the 1938 World Series, and in '39 he became "the voice of the New York Yankees," hooking up with Arch McDonald to form the first Yankees broadcast team, brought to you by Wheaties, "the breakfast of champions."

McDonald, who broadcast the Senators' games before coming to New York, returned to Washington after only one year, but Mel stayed and made himself an institution of New York baseball. He became as famous as our players, and so did the battle cry he sounded when one of us would hit a home run: "Going—going—gone!"

Mel coined another broadcasting expression that became a second trademark for him: "How about that!" He exclaimed it every time one of us got a key hit or made a big play. He says today he started using it when Joe D. came back off the disabled list after sixty-five games in 1949 and launched us toward the pennant by hitting four home runs and driving in nine runs in three games against the Red Sox in Boston.

By the time Mel left the Yankees in the mid-1960s, he had broadcast the greatest moments of the Yankees over a quarter of a century: Lou Gehrig Day in 1939, Joe DiMaggio's 56-game hitting streak in 1941, the bid by Bill Bevens in 1947 for the first no-hit game in World Series history, Don Larsen's perfect game in the '56 Series, and the 61 home runs in 1961 by Roger Maris.

One of his most poignant memories is of Gehrig, not when he was standing at home plate in 1939 but when Lou paid a visit to us in 1940. "The year after he retired," Mel remembers, "I was sitting on the bench when someone came running up and said, 'Lou's here.' He couldn't walk by then. He shuffled." All of us greeted him as if there were nothing wrong.

Then we took the field for practice, and Mel found himself alone on the bench with him. Mel remembers, "Gehrig leaned over, patted me on the leg, and said, 'You don't know how important your radio broadcasts are to me. They keep me going.'

"I thanked him, excused myself, walked down the runway, and began to bawl."

Allen was good enough to adapt his broadcasting to television when it came into popularity ten years after he began his radio career, an adjustment not every radio performer was able to make.

He had his critics. Some of the fans in other cities didn't like him simply because he was the Yankees' announcer. When he was the broadcaster for a World Series, they identified him with us, and they grew to dislike us because we were winning all the time, so they disliked him, too. It was understandable, but it wasn't Mel's fault. He wasn't winning a hundred games a year—we were.

In 1950, the people of New York held Mel Allen Day at Yankee Stadium. He got the usual deluge of gifts plus $14,000, a hefty sum in any year and especially forty years ago. He used the money to establish two scholarship funds, one at his alma mater and the other at Columbia University.

He named them in honor of Babe Ruth and Lou Gehrig.

I injured my knee again in 1939. I played only 89 games in the field and appeared as a pinch-hitter in 11 others. With that much time out because of injury, my numbers for the year were down— only 9 home runs and 57 RBIs—but my average went up seven points to .277. I was hitting with consistency, and I was confident that I would raise my average even more in 1940.

In the process, I was convincing myself during my third year in the big leagues that I was going to stick. I began to feel like an established major-league baseball player. That's how hard it is to make it. It takes some players that long or longer to feel that way, because they know the competition is so tough.

I once asked Birdie Tebbetts, an outstanding catcher in the majors for fourteen seasons, if there was one particular point early in his career when he was convinced he had made it. He said yes, and, like mine, it didn't come until his second or third season.

"I was with the Tigers," he said. "After a game in one of my first seasons, a regular on our team invited me to go to dinner with several teammates. I thanked him but said I couldn't make it. Then it dawned on me: If I can turn down a dinner invitation from one of our starters, I must feel sure of myself as a big leaguer."

I asked Yogi Berra the same question, wondering at what point this Hall of Famer and triple winner of the Most Valuable Player Award felt certain he would make it. His answer was a classic of confidence. "Aw," Yogi said, "I *always* knew I would be a major leaguer."

While I was forced to the sidelines for the last part of the season and the World Series, Charlie Keller was playing every day and scoring big in his first year up from Newark. To say Keller had an outstanding rookie season is putting it mildly. He outhit another 1939 rookie, Ted Williams, by seven points, .334 to .327, something he was proud of for the rest of his life.

Charlie was another McCarthy-style player, one who would do anything his team asked of him. He made one of the greatest and least-known sacrifices over his entire career of any player I've heard of.

The Yankees in those days wanted their left-handed hitters to "pull" the ball around to right field because the wall there was only 296 feet away. They wanted home runs. They didn't have to convince me, because I was already a pull hitter. But not Keller.

Charlie was a line-drive hitter at the University of Maryland and all through his minor-league career, spraying his hits all over the ball park. And he hit the ball hard, even his grounders. Each hop of his ground balls seemed to bounce faster than the one before. His grounders handcuffed infielders because the balls shot past them faster than those from other hitters.

Keller became a Yankee because George Weiss had good intuition and a commanding knowledge of young talent and where it was. He was talking to McCarthy in St. Petersburg in the spring of 1937 when Joe began insisting that our team would need another left-handed hitter in a year or two, with Gehrig already getting along in years and Selkirk and others due to be in their thirties before too much longer.

"On a hunch," Weiss said in later years, "I said we probably could get one at the University of Maryland if we paid his way through a remaining year of college."

The two agreed to offer Keller a contract, and when they did, Charlie didn't even wait for the school year to end. "I don't think he waited to pack an extra shirt," George said. "He reported to the Newark club almost immediately. From his first time at bat, we knew we had something. Keller was a natural as a college boy."

They were even more confident of their choice when Charlie, in his only two years in the minor leagues, hit .353 and .365 at Newark.

He could have had a lifetime average thirty points higher in the major leagues than his .286, which is a highly respectable average itself, if they hadn't changed him into a pull hitter. The evidence is right there in the numbers. As a rookie, he hit only 11 home runs but had that .334 average. As a second-year man, he hit ten more home runs than in '39, but his average dropped forty-eight points to .286.

They say everyone is allowed one mistake. Maybe Charlie was McCarthy's. If the Yankees had let him use his natural batting stroke, and if he hadn't been plagued by chronic disk problems in his back, Charlie Keller would be in the Hall of Fame today.

Charlie was quiet, shunning the bright lights of the big city and preferring the company of his best friends on our team, Marius Russo, another rookie that year, and Red Rolfe. He took some ribbing for his quiet, country preferences that stemmed from his roots in Middletown, Maryland, but he was able to defend himself against his tormentors, especially one night in Dallas in 1939.

We had just finished our spring training and were playing exhibition games on our way back to New York for the start of the season. After a game in Dallas, a friend of George Selkirk named Thurmond Randolph, a national rifle champion, invited our whole team to his farm for dinner.

The rest of us had been there a while when the two rookies, Keller and Russo, arrived with Rolfe. Right away Charley Ruffing, one of the best—or worst—players on our team when it came to needling someone, offered to get Keller a drink.

Charlie declined, which, or course, led to more needling from Ruffing. Eventually Keller gave in, and Ruffing fixed him a glass of Southern Comfort and tonic.

After his first sip, Keller said, "It tastes like lemonade."

Ruffing said, "Sure, Charlie. Have some more."

After finishing his first glass, Keller decided to have a second. The rest of us could see his shyness beginning to fade. Ruffing continued to kid Keller, joined by another one of our needlers, Johnny Murphy.

That never sat well with Keller. He didn't care for Ruffing because of a couple of tricks he pulled on him, and because he got the impression that Ruffing was singling him out for special roastings just because he was a rookie.

As Keller started to open up and join in the conversation while enjoying his second Southern Comfort, Ruffing couldn't resist the temptation to get sarcastic with him.

"Well," he said, "listen to ol' King Kong."

His sneering tone was offensive by itself, but it was a double insult because Ruffing knew that Keller hated to be called "King Kong," a reference to his strength and his hairy arms.

Keller, to the astonishment of everyone, turned on Ruffing and says, "I don't want to hear anything out of you, Grizzle Puss."

Bill Knickerbocker, a utility man who had just been traded to us by Cleveland, was enjoying it with the rest of us. Knickerbocker, who was beginning to show more skin and less hair on his head at that point in his career, said to Ruffing, "Man, Charley, did he lay into you!"

Keller snapped at Knickerbocker, "That goes for you too, Hair-and-a-Half."

I don't know where Keller came up with that nickname. None of us had heard it before. I think it was a spur-of-the-moment inspiration, compliments of Southern Comfort.

Frankie Crosetti, who had even less hair than Knickerbocker, was laughing harder than any of us, so Keller said to him, "You too, Skinhead."

Charlie felt bad about the incident later. After a few days he told me, "I shouldn't have said those things."

I told him, "The heck you shouldn't."

As for that other rookie, Williams, the word was flashing around the league in a hurry that this skinny kid from San Diego might outhit all of us. On the day of our first series in Boston that year, Joe Gallagher, one of our outfielders, who saw Ted in the minors the year before, told our pitchers in a team meeting, "Pitch him high and tight, then low and away."

There wasn't a surprised player in the room when Gallagher

said that. It's the advice pitchers always get—high and tight, low and away. By the time he said it, I'm sure every one of our pitchers was hearing it for the fifteen thousandth time.

Spud Chandler was pitching for us. Williams roughed him up for a couple of hits, so McCarthy asked Chandler in the clubhouse after the game, "Well, what did we learn today about pitching to Williams?"

Chandler said, "I'll tell you what I learned—high and tight is ball one, and low and away is ball two."

By the time the series was over, Williams had made believers out of all of us. Dickey, the man who played every day with Ruth and Gehrig, said, "I'll tell you what I think about him. I think he's just a damn good hitter."

Throughout his career, Williams preached the importance of waiting on the pitch and getting a good pitch to hit. He's right about everything, including his opinion that the currently popular style of hitting by letting your top hand fly off the bat during your follow-through is a bunch of baloney. It accomplishes two things: It takes away your power, and it messes up some promising hitters.

I was talking hitting with Ted during spring training at Phoenix in 1951, my first year as a coach. His career had almost ten years to go, although it would be interrupted when he was called back into the Marine Corps to fly a jet fighter during the Korean War. He kept emphasizing the importance of several elements, including waiting on the pitch and unlocking your hips early so you can really tie into the ball.

I told him I agreed with all of that, but he had an unfair advantage over the rest of us: his eyes. It's well known that Ted was gifted with exceptional eyesight, and my contention was—and is—that good eyesight is the biggest asset a hitter can have.

I used an exaggeration for illustration: "How would you like to hit at midnight with the lights out? You wouldn't, because you can't see the ball. Well, I can't see it as well as you can. So my timing is thrown off just a fraction more than yours by changeups and curveballs. It takes me that much longer to figure the pitch out and then react to it than it does you. It all starts with the eyes. Eye-to-hand coordination is the key to hitting."

Stan Musial, who was also blessed with keen eyesight, supposedly said that he could spot a curveball only four feet after it left the pitcher's hand. No wonder he was the National League batting champion seven times.

We made McCarthy's wish come true. We won our fourth straight pennant and World Series. And we did it his way—with teamwork. It helped that DiMag hit .381 and that Red Rolfe led the league in hits, doubles, and runs scored. Babe Dahlgren, taking Lou's place at first base, chipped in with 15 home runs and 89 runs batted in, not exactly Gehrig-like figures but enough to contribute to our success.

It also helped that we were displaying the same kind of dazzling Yankee power that Ruth and Gehrig boomed into a tradition in the 1920s. We reached one of the eye-popping peaks of any Yankee team one day in 1939 when we hit thirteen home runs in a doubleheader against the A's in Philadelphia.

Babe Dahlgren, Joe D. and Joe Gordon each hit three homers, if you can believe that: three players on the same team hitting three home runs each on the same day. I've never heard of that before or since, even with more players and more teams today.

I hit one that day, too, but I felt like a piker. We hit eight in the first game, which set a record for one game, and five in the second, which set a record for two games. The next day we needed only one to break the record for three games.

We never came close.

Our chances that year were also helped by Johnny Murphy's achievement of leading the league's relief pitchers with 19 saves. Johnny was one of our most intelligent players and a team leader while making himself the premier relief pitcher of his day. In doing so, he was bringing relief pitching far greater respect than ever before. The men in the bullpen were beginning to enjoy more recognition—and salary—than before, starting with Johnny himself.

Our defense was just as important that year as our offense. Joe Gordon, Frank Crosetti, and Bill Dickey led their positions in putouts. The Crow, Dickey, and George Selkirk led their positions in fielding averages. With a defense that tight, strong relief pitching, and the league's leaders in hits and batting average, plus the most successful manager in baseball, nobody in the American League could catch us.

In the World Series, we took on the Cincinnati Reds and their manager, Bill McKechnie, who was in his eighteenth year as a big-league manager after eleven years as a player and was managing in the World Series for the third time. He had more years of experience than Joe, who was completing his fourteenth season as a "skipper," as the players call their manager. In World Series experience, though, the reverse was the case. Joe was managing in his sixth—and he had won all but one. McKechnie had lost two of his three.

On paper we were a close matchup. The Reds were solid in every phase of the game. They beat out the Cardinals by four and a half games with the hitting of first baseman Frank McCormick, who led the National League in hits and runs batted in, and a strong pitching staff that included Bucky Walters and Paul Derringer. "Strong" is the right word. Walters and Derringer finished one-two in complete games that year and in innings pitched. They were stingy, too. Bucky led the league in fewest hits per nine innings, and Paul led it in allowing the fewest walks.

With strength in every department, the Reds were not going to be pushovers. But in fact, they almost were. Our pitchers shut down their hitters: McCormick, Ernie Lombardi, Billy Werber, and the rest. The Reds scored only eight runs in the entire series. We won it in four straight.

In fact, neither team wore out the opposing pitchers. Cincinnati's team batting average was anemic—.203—and ours was only three points higher.

Charlie Keller showed the world that a rookie can lead the World Series in hitting. He did, with a .438 average. He also drove in the most runs and scored the most—eight—equaling the whole Cincinnati team.

Charlie, doing what management wanted him to do in Yankee Stadium, tripled past Ival Goodman in right to lead off the ninth inning of the first game and scored on Dickey's single after Derringer walked DiMaggio intentionally to pitch to Bill. It gave us a 2–1 win on a four-hitter by Charley Ruffing. Derringer allowed only six.

Derringer showed class in defeat. After the game, he told the home-plate umpire, Bill McGowan, "Mac, that was the best job of umpiring I have ever seen."

The second game was a preview of the Bill Bevens World Series game eight years later, when Bevens had a no-hitter in the ninth inning of the 1947 Series against the Dodgers. In this game, Monte Pearson pitched a no-hitter for us for seven and a third innings before Lombardi broke it up with a single. Monte finished with a two-hitter and won it, 4–0, with the help of a double and homer by Dahlgren.

After two games, neither team had used a relief pitcher. That changed in the third game, when we moved to Cincinnati and beat the Reds, 7–3, with Keller hitting two home runs, each with a man on, and scoring three times himself. Cincinnati got ten hits to our five, but the difference was obvious: All of the Reds' hits were singles. Four of ours were home runs, with DiMag and Dickey adding to Keller's two with one each. Bump Hadley, who relieved Gomez in the second inning after Lefty developed arm problems, slammed the door on them by allowing only three hits after that.

The final game was a strange one. Keller continued his pace with another home run, and Dickey did the same, but after nine innings we were tied, 4–4. Both teams were throwing their best pitching into the game. The Reds were desperate to extend the Series, and we wanted to win it right there while the opportunity was so great. The game went into extra innings. Johnny Murphy, baseball's best relief pitcher in those years, was on the mound for us, going against Bucky Walters.

The Reds simply collapsed in that tenth inning. Crosetti led off the inning by walking on five pitches. Rolfe sacrificed him to second on the first pitch, bunting to Frank McCormick unassisted at first base. Keller hit the first pitch on the ground to Billy Myers, Cincinnati's shortstop, near the bag at second, but he booted it for an error, allowing Crosetti to advance to third.

DiMaggio fouled the first pitch to him down the third-base line, then singled to right to score Crosetti. Ival Goodman let the ball roll through him for another error, allowing Keller to score by sliding into Lombardi and under his tag. While Goodman, McCormick, and Lombardi were making the play on Keller, DiMaggio took third.

But the play wasn't over. Lombardi seemed stunned from Keller's slide into him and was literally sitting on the ground near the plate, the ball just out of his reach, when Joe saw no one was covering home. Joe, who was always alert to take every advantage he could, bolted for home and made it with another slide under an attempted tag from Lombardi.

We scored three runs on one single. When the inning was over, the totals read 3 runs, 1 hit, 3 errors.

In our clubhouse, bedlam broke out. Art Fletcher, the most serious member of our team on the field and always the most elated when we won our championships, led a team sing-along in our unique choral rendition of "Roll Out the Barrel." Paul Derringer, who deserved so much better, came over and congratulated us. The president of the American League, Will Harridge, tried to do the same thing, but we shouted him down and he left. And we had the most special visitor we could ask for: Lou Gehrig. He came into the dressing room and told us we put on "the greatest finish I've ever seen."

Fletcher was ecstatic in his ravings about DiMaggio's base running. He said that when Joe streaked into third base, "I told him nothing but 'watch the ball,' and boy, he did. He gave us one of the greatest pieces of sliding I've ever seen. He had to slide over Lombardi's hand and then dig down and touch the plate, and he did it to perfection."

DiMaggio's legs and hips were covered with bruises from his heroic run.

In the Cincinnati dressing room, Bill McKechnie, having lost in his bid to win his second World Series as a manager, told the press, "You can't explain that tenth inning. There is just nothing to explain it. It's just one of those things."

But on the Yankees, we knew the explanation, and it wasn't "just one of those things." The explanation was Joe DiMaggio.

John Drebinger captured the drama and its significance in the opening paragraph of his article in the New York Times:

> Marse Joe McCarthy's mighty Yankees, beyond question the most amazing club in the 100-year history of baseball, inscribed another brilliant page upon the records of the game today when they crushed the Cincinnati Reds in ten innings, 7–4, to close the 1939 World Series in a whirl of statistics that attested still further to their greatness.

Drebinger told his readers that for the first time, a team won its league's pennant and the World Series four years in a row, we won our ninth straight World Series game, and we scored our second straight four-game sweep. The cry that was sounded across the land during the Ruth-Gehrig dynasty ten years earlier was being heard again: "Break up the Yankees!"

The next morning, we returned to New York's Grand Central Station from Cincinnati, joined by Mayor La Guardia, as conquering heroes aboard a private train that was twelve cars long.

The Yankees never were the only show in New York, especially in 1939. That was a banner year for new movies, and I made sure I saw them all: "The Wizard of Oz," "Gone with the Wind," and "The Grapes of Wrath." If you wanted to enlarge your social circle, you could now take dancing lessons at the Arthur Murray studio on 43rd Street, where, according to the newspaper ads, the lessons "cost very little." That was as specific as they got.

If you took Mr. Murray up on his offer, you could dance to the music of America's newest "big band" favorite, Glenn Miller, who seemed to have as many hits in 1939 as DiMaggio: "Moonlight Serenade," "Sunlight Serenade," "Little Brown Jug," "Johnson Rag," and "In the Mood."

At the movies—the "photoplays," as the listings in the New York Times were called—you could see *All Quiet on the Western Front* at the Rialto, the "uncensored version at last!" At the Roxy they were showing a comedy, *Eternally Yours,* starring Loretta Young and David Niven. Leslie Howard and Ingrid Bergman were in *Intermezzo* at Radio City, whose newspaper ads said you could also see "a clever new revue" on stage called "The Clocks."

Dust Be My Destiny was playing at the Strand, with John Garfield and Priscilla Lane. Onstage: Ted Weems and his orchestra, with Ann Sheridan.

For something different, you could take in a floor show, have dinner, and enjoy an evening of dancing, all at Billy Rose's Diamond Horseshoe in the Hotel Paramount, just off Broadway. Not only that, the place was "comfortably air-cooled," something you didn't find in every restaurant/nightclub in 1939. It wasn't cheap, though. Like most fancy places, they had a minimum charge: a dollar.

The World Series share for each member of the Yankees was $5,542, only $241 short of the record for a four-game Series, which we set the year before. And there were some tempting possibilities for spending it. We could take our World Series winnings and travel on a two-week boat cruise to Miami Beach if we felt like spending $81, traveling aboard the Clyde-Mallory Lines. If we wanted to spend another $24, we could go to Havana on the same cruise.

At the same time that we were winning the World Series, Detroit was introducing its 1940 model automobiles, something else to make the World Series money burn a hole in our pockets. The New Ford V-8 had a sixty-horsepower engine. The Lincoln-Zephyr featured a "one-piece windshield" and a twelve-cylinder engine, and "running boards have been eliminated."

The new Oldsmobile didn't have a clutch. The engineers at Olds came up with something called "Hydra-Matic Drive," which was an automatic transmission. The gears actually shifted by themselves. A newspaper review of the car said this innovation worked "through oil control." The article said, "Driving ease and smooth power application reach a new high."

Pontiac was introducing seventeen models, and Studebaker was joining some of the others by using the new sealed-beam headlights. Studebaker even had a hood on the engine that locked.

I made sure I took in New York's newest tourist attraction, the World's Fair, with its sparkling displays about life in the future including an amazing invention in a box called "television."

The future was the Number One item of discussion, and not because of the World's Fair. Adolf Hitler's troops invaded Poland on September 1. World War II began, even though most of the fighting was restricted to Europe until we jumped in two years later.

Nevertheless, the handwriting was on the wall. Some Americans opposed our involvement, but many more felt that we either should get into it or would be drawn in. On the other side of the world, things weren't much better. Japan was making noises about American interference in the Pacific, so international tensions were increasing there, too.

On our train rides and while sitting in hotel lobbies cooling ourselves with straw fans, we were talking about more than just baseball. It was almost a Dickens-like season—the best of times and the worst of times: our fourth straight World Series victory but Lou Gehrig's terminal illness, my growing confidence but my knee injury, the improving economy as America struggled out of the Great Depression but the scary happenings in Europe and Asia.

On the same day that we defeated the Reds, the British shot down a German war plane over the North Sea, a month after Hitler's invasion of Poland. And on the same front page that carried Drebinger's story of our championship, a "wireless" article sent from Paris by P. J. Philip left no doubt about the outlook for war or peace:

> Chancellor Hitler's much advertised peace offensive has misfired, in the opinion of all those here whose task it is to study hour by hour the diplomatic and political aspects of the war. He has failed to find anyone among the neutrals to push his claims or even suggest that peace might be still possible.

Baseball, with its long season of ups and downs and its unrelenting demand that you play your way through times of difficulty and uncertainty, is the great conditioner for times like 1939. Those of us who were major-league baseball players that year knew what was going on in the world. We also knew that millions of Americans were looking to us for their fun and relief from the tensions of the times.

Six

That Empty Feeling

As the world entered a new decade, the Yankees entered a new era. We started the 1940 season without either Babe Ruth or Lou Gehrig, the first time in twenty years that we didn't have one of them in our lineup.

We wanted to go for five in a row, but we didn't get the years that we needed out of several of our key players. Ernie "Tiny" Bonham, our six-foot-two right-handed pitcher who weighed 215 pounds, a big man in those years, led the American League's pitchers with the best earned run average, but the most wins on our staff were Charley Ruffing's 15. That's not enough for a team that wants to win a pennant.

Our hitting fell off badly in some cases. Joe D. was still one of the terrors of baseball, and he won the batting championship for the second straight season, this time with a .352 average, but he and I were the only two .300 hitters in our everyday lineup. George Selkirk's average dropped to .269, down thirty-seven points from 1939. Dickey's drop was even worse: fifty points to .247. His homers went down from 24 to 9, and his RBIs dropped from 105 to 54. Keller, the .334 hitter in his rookie year, helped us with his increase of ten homers over '39, but that forty-eight-point drop in his average didn't do much for us.

Despite these dropoffs, we were in the race all the way and were not eliminated until the last day of the season. We finished third, but we were only two games behind the pennant winners, the Tigers. Detroit won 90 games, the Indians were second with 89, and we won 88.

It didn't help us at all that Johnny Babich beat us five times that year. He was a former Yankee minor leaguer, pitching at Kansas City and unhappy that he wasn't being called up to the big club, when the Yankees traded him to the A's. He won only thirty games in his entire career, and those five over us in 1940 killed us.

McCarthy was livid in the clubhouse after the fifth loss to a pitcher we could have had on our team. He said out loud, "Johnny Babich! Who ever head of Johnny Babich?"

Joe Gordon gave one answer: "It's a cinch our scouts haven't."

But Mr. Dimaggio was destined to even the score with Mr. Babich in 1941.

There was far worse news involving Lou Gehrig. He was failing. My brother Eddie came to town for a visit that summer, and we went to see Lou at his home, along with three of the best writers of that day or any other day—Red Smith, Grantland Rice, and Henry McLemore.

We found Lou in bed. He was in a good mood—Lou was always in a good mood—feeling confident and telling us, "I'm going to beat this."

But we knew from looking at him that he wasn't going to win this one. He couldn't have weighed more than 125 pounds. I didn't see how he could still be alive.

Eleanor, his wife, told us as we prepared to leave, "The doctor's report shows Lou is getting better, but I don't think so. I think he's saying that just to cheer us up."

The Tigers proved they were good enough to break our string of pennants and World Series victories. They were a solid ball club behind the quiet leadership of Hank Greenberg, who led the league in home runs with 41 and RBIs with 150 and hit .340. He wasn't the only .340 hitter on that club. Barney McCosky, the Tigers' center fielder, had the same average on his way to a .312 lifetime batting average in eleven seasons, with three years lost due to military service in the war.

The Tigers had Rudy York at first base, and he gave them another power hitter: 33 homers, 134 RBIs, and a .316 average. They had Charlie Gehringer playing second and hitting .313, plus other capable veterans like Dick Bartell, Pinky Higgins, Pete Fox, and Birdie Tebbetts.

The Tigers had a 20-game winner on their pitching staff, almost a requirement if a team is to win a pennant, with Buck Newsom, who won 21 and lost only 5. Schoolboy Rowe, their six-foot-four right-hander, had an even higher winning percentage than Newsom. He won 16 and lost only 3 and had the best won-lost percentage in the league. Tommy Bridges gave Detroit even more savvy on the mound. Once the possessor of baseball's best curveball, he was thirty-three years old that season, but he still chipped in with 12 wins.

As good as Newsom and Rowe were in 1940, they were a long way behind the man who was the best pitcher in baseball that year and many more, Bob Feller. He was in his fifth major-league season. He led the American League in wins in 1939 with 24, and in '40 he led both leagues with 27. By the end of that season he had won 82 games in his first five seasons, led both leagues in strikeouts for the past three years, and led the American League in complete games and innings pitched for the last two.

There's another statistic that makes all of that even more amazing: When the 1940 season ended, Bob Feller was twenty-one years old.

Greenberg said there was another reason that the Tigers won the pennant in '40. He said it was because Del Baker, their manager, was masterminding a system for stealing the opposing catcher's signals to the pitcher. In his autobiography, he also wrote that we were doing the same thing from the scoreboard in Yankee Stadium and that this was one reason we had a certain amount of success against Bob Feller in New York.

Hank was only partially correct. We were stealing signs, all right. We did it for years, but his statement that we were getting them from the scoreboard showed how slick Fletcher and Combs were at it. And because our sources were our coaches and not the scoreboard at Yankee Stadium, we were stealing signs in every city, not just when we played at home.

Greenberg attributed the Tigers' success in 1940 to the outstanding seasons that he and York had at bat, and he linked that to the advantage they had in knowing that the next pitch was going to be. He wrote in his book, "I think it was picking up those signs that was instrumental in enabling us to win that 1940 pennant."

I was able to come back from my knee problems long enough to hit .307 before I developed more trouble. That was a jump of exactly thirty points in my average. My totals included 28 doubles, 5 triples and 10 home runs. I belonged in this league. I was sure of it now.

Still, the season had a kind of an empty feeling at times. Losing the pennant after you've won it four times in a row, especially when you lose by only two games, leaves you with a letdown of sorts.

You don't want to be greedy about winning the pennant every year, but with the Yankees, when we didn't, we knew we had to come back and do better the next season, especially with Ed Barrow telling us that he wouldn't give us a raise because "playing in the World Series is your raise." That's why all of us on those Yankee teams of the late 1930s and '40s felt we had to keep winning. On the field, the Yankees used to lead the league in victories, but in the front office they never led it in generosity.

The knee went out on me again on the last day of August when I tore some ligaments in Boston, but you can always find a plus side if you look hard enough. In this case, I went down with an injury, but I came up with Eileen O'Reilly.

I was admitted to St. Elizabeth's Hospital in upper Manhattan and was a guest of the management for twenty-eight days. Eileen was one of the nurses on my floor. She was new to the city and even to the country, a young colleen from her native Ireland who was making her way in the U.S.A.

My best friend in New York, Eddie Hoffmeister, ran a restaurant in a small apartment hotel on 58th Street between Sixth and Seventh avenues next door to the Essex House. He visited me twenty-seven of the twenty-eight days I was in the hospital, and on the one day when he couldn't make it, he sent his partner. Each visit included the best items from the restaurant's menu— roast beef, the soup of the day, even beer. One of the orderlies, a German named Martin who still had his sharp accent from the old country, found out about the beer and all of a sudden told the nurses he would take over the responsibilities for my rubdowns. I knew his motive. He wanted a beer bonus.

He brought this cute little Irish girl into my room one day, and we hit it off right away. When she was nice enough to fluff up my pillow, I made some smart remark, and she kiddingly threw the pillow at me, for which I gave her a gentle slap across her south side.

She said, "Fresh!" Then she left the room—but she came back, because she liked my food. She used to come into my room and listen to the radio with me, the greatest form of entertainment in 1940 and one I still enjoy today. Classical music, including some of the best-known symphonies, were a favorite with both of us, plus the pop hits in 1940: "Star Dust," "Tuxedo Junction," and the Pennsylvania Hotel's phone number turned into a hit song by Glenn Miller, "Pennsylvania 6-5000." We sat there for as long as Eileen could get away with it.

She didn't bother to come in if I had a ball game on the radio. She told me she hated baseball. Fifty years later, Eileen is still listening to the radio with me—except when I have a ball game on.

While I was recovering from my torn ligaments in the hospital, a fateful thing happened in St. Louis. We lost a game to the Browns, one of the worst teams in baseball, who lost twenty games more than they won that year. Some of my teammates told me a factor in our loss was a mental mistake by Babe Dahlgren, who either missed a sign or made some other kind of mental error. It doesn't make any difference what Dahlgren's lapse was. Mc-Carthy would not tolerate any kind.

To make matters worse for Dahlgren, the loss came at a point in the season when every game was crucial to our chances of repeating. If we had won that game and Babich had lost one of those five games to us, we would have tied the Tigers for the pennant.

McCarthy knew how much every game meant. To lose a key game on a fielding error or a wild pitch or a strikeout with the winning run on base would have been bad enough, but for the Yankees to lose on a mental error was simply unacceptable to McCarthy. You couldn't offer any excuses to Joe for something like that. To him, there were none.

The Yankees had trouble finding a replacement for Gehrig for years, and our problems with the position began with that incident. McCarthy never forgot that mistake and never forgave Dahlgren for it. Before the 1941 season began, the Yankees got rid of him. They sold him out of the league to the Boston Braves. You didn't need 20–20 vision to see the fine hand of Joe McCarthy in that sale.

The face of the Yankees was changing. In addition to the absence of Ruth and Gehrig, two of our other mainstays, George Selkirk and Lefty Gomez, were getting along in years, and their numbers in 1940 were cause for concern. Selkirk had that thirty-seven-point drop in his batting average. Gomez, a 20-game winner for us four times in the 1930s, missed most of the season with arm trouble and won only three games, pitching only 27⅓ innings. The Yankees talked to the Dodgers about making a trade for him, but it didn't happen. When he was asked how much longer he could pitch, his answer was, "As long as Murphy's arm holds up." He was thirty-two that November, not the best age to try to come back from an arm injury.

Selkirk, the one we called "Twinkletoes," was another McCarthy favorite. He was equal to any pressure, and he was a joy to have on your ball club. George was a Canadian, born in Ontario, but he could play our American game with the best of them. He hit over .300 five times and ended with a lifetime average of .290 over nine seasons, his career cut short by World War II.

George was six-foot-one and 182 pounds, but he was much stronger than he looked. Gehrig was as strong as any man in baseball, but Selkirk was able to wrestle with him when they were horsing around and hold his own, even though Gehrig outweighed him by twenty pounds.

Twinkletoes wasn't above providing comic relief. I saw him hit a screaming line drive to dead center field in Yankee Stadium, one that looked like a double at least. He wasn't halfway to first when he saw the center fielder make a leaping catch of his drive. Without a split second's hesitation, Selkirk jumped into the air, whirled, ran back down the first-base line, and slid into home plate.

Gomez was one of the star pitchers of the 1930s. From '31 through '38, he won 151 games, almost twenty a year. In '34 he led the league in almost every pitching department: 26 wins, most strikeouts, lowest earned run average, most shutouts. He was the American League's starting pitcher in five of the first six All-Star Games. Under the greatest pressure in baseball, the World Series, he was perfect: 6 wins, 0 losses. Remembering his greatness, the writers elected Lefty to the Hall of Fame in 1972.

Lefty also had baseball's quickest sense of humor. When he received word he was to be enshrined forever in Cooperstown, he told the reporters, "It's only fair. After all, I helped a lot of hitters to get in."

He was at his best and his funniest in pressure situations. In one game, he faced Jimmie Foxx when the Red Sox had the bases loaded. He kept shaking off Bill Dickey's signs, until Bill finally asked for time out, went to the mound, and asked what the heck Gomez wanted to throw.

"Nothing," he said. "Let's wait a while. Maybe he'll get a phone call."

His boldest delaying tactic came in the World Series against the Giants in my rookie year. We were playing at the Polo Grounds, in what proved to be the final game. The Giants had a rally building when Mel Ott, their home-run-hitting outfielder, came up as the potential winning run. He had already hit one home run off Lefty in this game, and this was no time for another.

Lefty was a nut about aviation in those romantic early days of flying. Just as Ott stepped into the batter's box, a plane flew low over the ballpark. Gomez asked for time out and then just stood there and held up the World Series while he watched the plane fly over.

Even the best hitters had trouble hitting Lefty, including the great Al Simmons. Simmons once complained to Bill McGowan behind the plate that Gomez was throwing spitballs. When

McGowan relayed the Simmons complaint, Gomez said, "Tell him to hit the dry side."

Lefty could get his point across to umpires without saying a word, like the day when he thought Bill Summers should call time in Cleveland because it was getting so dark with storm clouds rolling in over League Park from Lake Erie. When he walked up to the plate for his turn at bat in the late innings, he held one hand behind his back. As he stepped into the batter's box, he held out that hand—holding a lantern. Summers took the hint.

Lefty had his own psychological techniques that he applied on himself. Maybe the most original of all was the one we heard about the time in Boston when Joe McCarthy found him dressed in uniform inside a phone booth at the top of the grandstand in Fenway Park.

Left-handers don't fare well in Fenway, with its short left-field wall, "the Green Monster." With the added advantage of a right-handed hitter facing a left-handed pitcher, those confining dimensions seem even smaller. When McCarthy asked Lefty just what the devil he was doing in a phone booth on top of the ball park, Gomez told him he was staying in there until game time as a confidence builder because by the time he got out, the dimensions of Fenway would look twice as big to him.

To which McCarthy responded, "That will cost you a hundred."

When Mark "the Bird" Fidrych burst on the scene with 19 wins for the Detroit Tigers in 1976 and captured the fancy of the fans with a variety of eccentricities like talking to the ball, a writer asked Lefty if he ever did that.

"Sure," he said. "Lots of times."

The reporter asked what Lefty told the ball. His answer: "Go foul! Go foul!"

The word on Lefty to this day is that he was the world's worst hitter. Not so. I once saw him get four hits in one game. He drove in the first run in the history of the All-Star Games. In the '37 Series, I saw him drive in Lazzeri with a single that put us in front, then score the final run in our 4–2 win.

But he always used his hitting as another source of making fun of himself. He doubled once, only to get picked off second. When he got back to the dugout, McCarthy, as he always did, asked, "What happened?"

Lefty said, "How should I know? I've never been there before."

Our bat boy, Timmy Sullivan, joined in the ribbing. When Gomez would ask Timmy for his bat, Sullivan would say, "What are you planning to do with it?"

Lefty not only roomed with the great DiMaggio—before that, he roomed with the great Ruth. The two became fast pals, and they had a standing bet every season that Lefty wouldn't get ten hits for the year. Babe even gave him odds—his $250 to Lefty's $50.

"One year," Lefty remembered, "I beat out a roller to third on the final day and kept running. I rounded first. Babe came rushing off the bench like a madman and started arguing violently that I missed first.

"He was trying to save this $250, but the umpire said I was safe. I was so happy I couldn't stop running. They threw me out by forty feet at second."

When it came time for Lefty to hang up his spikes, Wilson Sporting Goods hired him to do promotion work and act as the company's goodwill ambassador. When he filled out the employment form and came to the question about the reason for leaving his last employer, Lefty wrote, "I couldn't get anybody out."

And when folks asked him in later years what he owed his success to, he always told them, "Clean living, a fast outfield, and Johnny Murphy."

Despite the laughter he brought to everyone and the joy he spread with his always positive attitude toward life, Gomez was a deadly serious and gifted competitor—and one who could be counted on when the chips were on the table.

McCarthy told me in later years how much respect he held for Lefty as a pitcher. "If there's one game I have to win," he told me, "I wouldn't be afraid to give the ball to Gomez."

Another DiMaggio entered the major leagues in 1940, the third center fielder by that name playing in the big leagues at the same time. His brother Vince was hitting home runs for the Reds after breaking in with the Braves in 1937, his brother Joe was tearing up the American League in Yankee pinstripes, and now Dom, the baby of the family, broke in with the Red Sox. The Yankees were sorry that Dom, if he couldn't play for us, hadn't gone to a team in the National League. We didn't want to have to play against anybody named DiMaggio.

Dom added to the DiMaggio reputation for greatness right from the start. He hit over .300 in his rookie season, did it again three more times, was voted to the American League All-Star team eight times, and ended his career with the same lifetime batting average as Mickey Mantle, .298.

He was as fast as any of the DiMaggios. If he hadn't been the leadoff hitter in a lineup that had Ted Williams coming up behind him, the Red Sox would have given him the green light to steal more bases. He was fast enough to steal forty or more any year they let him try, but they never did. He led the league in stolen bases once, but he could have done it every year.

The public considered him small, but he wasn't any runt. He was five-feet-nine, but we were used to seeing Joe, who stood six-feet-one, and Vince, who was only a half-inch shy of six feet.

Dom defied the odds by making the grade while wearing glasses back in the days when scouts didn't give you a second look if you wore them. The thinking was, you could get hurt too easily if you were hit by a pitch or a bad hop. Dom helped to destroy that prejudice, even while being called "the Little Professor" because of his size, the glasses, and his serious expression.

Many people rated Joe and Dom one-two in their ability as center fielders, both better than Vince, and some good judges of baseball talent said it was a tossup. Joe was and is the greatest all-around baseball player, offensive and defensive abilities combined, that I ever saw. But those who say the difference in outfield ability between Joe and Dom was too close to call won't get an argument from me.

No center fielder, including Joe, was better on ground balls hit to the outfield than Dom. Both of them started as shortstops on the sandlots of San Francisco, but with their great speed and ability to cover long distances, plus their unusually strong and accurate throwing arms, they both were switched to center field for the start of their professional careers with the Seals.

They were close in their relationship, but it never showed on the field. Players congregate around the batting cage during batting practice, and as the visiting team's time expires and the home-team players are showing up to hit, there is the visiting and banter that baseball players enjoy, the "camaraderie" that means so much to them.

But not with Joe and Dom. I never saw them talking to each other around the cage or at any other time before or during the game. They would have dinner at each other's place when the Red Sox and Yankees were playing each other. Away from the field they were brothers. But on the field they were opponents.

Dom was every bit as competitive as Joe. We were playing the Red Sox during the years that Bobby Brown was our third base-man in his first career. Later he became a physician, then owner of the Texas Rangers, and now he's president of the American League.

Dom was always able to take big leads off the bases because he was so quick and fast. He could get back to the bag in a hurry if the other team tried to pick him off. If that didn't happen, he had that much of a head start when the ball was hit.

He was taking one of his extra-long leads off third one day, and Bobby started to look at him as if he felt insulted. Brown used to be good at trying to figure out why people were doing certain things, a diagnostic ability that must have served him well as a doctor. On the field, in that kind of situation, he would start to stare at you and keep right on staring—and staring and staring.

After each pitch, Dom would head back to the bag, only to see Brown staring at him. After the third time, Dom decided that was enough. With hands on hips, he stared right back at Bobby—then spit at him. It had to be the only time in his life that the gentle-manly Dom DiMaggio ever spit at anybody.

That competitive fire and his excellence as an athlete produced a career that could have won Dom a spot in the Hall of Fame if he had been able to play longer. But like so many other players of our time, he lost three years, prime ones, because he enlisted in the armed forces during World War II.

One of the favorite eating places in New York for all of us was Toots Shor's restaurant. Toots was New York's most prominent sports fanatic. He catered to so many members of the city's sports community with his restaurant in midtown Manhattan that it looked like a New York Sports Hall of Fame any time you walked through its doors.

Toots was as well known as his establishment. He was one of Joe DiMaggio's best friends, and Joe was a frequent visitor there, especially in the prewar days, when the New York gossip columnists tried to link him romantically with every showgirl in Manhattan including the entire line of the Radio City Rockettes.

New York's other notables were there too, and one of them, Walter Winchell, was on the scene every day. He had his own reserved table in the center near the entrance, where he gathered juicy items for his syndicated Broadway gossip column and his Sunday night radio show. From his strategic position, Winchell, who fit the Hollywood stereotype of the cigarette-smoking, brash-talking newspaper reporter and kept his hat on indoors, maybe because he had a bald head, could see and be seen, with an emphasis on the latter.

Reporters, columnists, magazine writers, show business personalities, and celebrities from every other field graced Shor's tables, but the ones Toots loved the most were the athletes, especially the town's baseball players. A clue to the Shor order of importance came the day that Toots was entertaining one of the most distinguished celebrities in any field, Sir Alexander Fleming, when Fleming was at the peak of his fame as the discoverer of penicillin.

A waiter came to their table and informed Toots that Mel Ott of the Giants had just arrived, after becoming the first National League player to hit 500 home runs in his career. Toots told Sir Alexander, "Excuse me—somebody important just came in."

As young men in our twenties, we were aware of what was going on in the world outside America's baseball parks. On our trains and in our hotels, when baseball wasn't the topic, two men and what they might do were: whether Hiltler would stop his aggression, and whether Franklin Roosevelt would become the first president to run for a third term.

Hitler wasn't going to tell us what he was going to do, but while the Reds and the Tigers were playing the World Series, FDR was defying tradition and opposing Wendell Willkie. Roosevelt did something else that fall of far more direct importance to every young man. Twenty-one days after the World Series ended, he and his Secretary of War, Henry Stimson, met in Washington on October 29 and pulled a capsule out of a large bowl filled with other capsules. To be prepared for war, the United States drafted its first man into the army.

We didn't sit around in 1940 sucking our thumbs and shaking at the knees because of the growing possibility that we would be wearing a different kind of uniform in the immediate future. There was so much to enjoy.

We spent countless hours listening to the radio and laughing at Jack Benny, Bob Hope, and Edgar Bergen with Charlie Mc-Carthy, trying to answer the questions on "Dr. IQ" and Phil Baker's "Take It or Leave It." We shared the suspense of "I Love a Mystery" and "The Shadow" and "Inner Sanctum." We tapped our feet to the sounds of Glenn Miller, brought to you by Chesterfield cigarettes. We sang along with Kate Smith and Rudy Vallee, and we didn't have to wait for their shows to come on the radio. We could play their records on the new victrolas.

War or no war, it was a time for the young.

Seven _____

That Special Season

America's young men made different types of history in 1941: the happy kind if you were a Yankee or one of our fans, the heartbreaking kind if you were from Brooklyn, and the tragic kind if you were stationed at Pearl Harbor. I was among the lucky ones; I had a hand in the happy kind.

The year started the way it always did for every Yankee player, with a cold, harsh letter from our team president, Ed Barrow, dated February 10:

My dear Henrich:
Just received your letter of February 8th, returning your unsigned contracts.
I brought up the question of your 1941 contract at the Board of Directors' meeting this morning and, after quite a little discussion, I was authorized to make your salary $12,000, the same as you received last season, with a bonus arrangement. The increase was granted to you with the understanding that you sign and return your contracts to this office without any further argument or delay.

You are being very well-treated under the circumstances, as the uncertain business conditions and the possibility of war make the outlook for baseball this summer rather discouraging.

Am returning the contracts to you, with the figures changed as per the above, and if you are smart you will not waste any time in signing and returning them to this office.

I don't know how smart I was, but I signed them. I didn't have any argument with the amount, but that bonus trick wasn't the ideal arrangement for me. Any employee who gets a raise wants it established in his annual salary. By giving me more money in the form of a "bonus," the Yankee management could always decide against a bonus the next season, and I'd be stuck arguing just to keep my old salary. I wasn't getting a raise. I was just getting a bonus.

It was that kind of treatment of their employees that caused so many problems for the owners in later years and has led to today's astonishing salaries and multiyear contracts. If baseball's owners hadn't treated their players like slaves in denying them their freedom to change employers and keeping them under their thumbs in so many other ways, the pendulum would not have swung as far in the other direction as it has.

With Dahlgren gone, we began the '41 season with a vacancy at first base. McCarthy decided to fill it with the help of not one new player but two.

A new double-play combination was formed on the Yankees that year: shortstop Phil Rizzuto and second baseman Jerry Priddy, both up from our Kansas City farm team. They attracted attention in spring training with their work around second base and showed they were ready for major-league competition. Their arrival gave Joe McCarthy the opportunity to conduct an experiment. He moved Joe Gordon from second base to first.

Only it didn't work, for two reasons. Gordon played first base for us in thirty games that year, but he never felt comfortable there, and Priddy never got started playing second. He needed more time to make the adjustment than Rizzuto did. McCarthy solved the problem by benching Priddy, moving Gordon back to his natural position as our second baseman, and putting Johnny Sturm on first. Priddy didn't really come into his own until the Yankees traded him to the Washington Senators two years later.

Rizzuto, however, was right at home from the start, in more ways than one. He was a New York native, and he was playing a big-league brand of ball at short and headed for a .307 batting average for his rookie year. He made the adjustment to working with Gordon just as well as he adjusted to everything else that year. They led the league's second-base combinations in making double plays with 109.

Phil, the one we called "Scooter," was only five-feet-six, but he covered all the ground necessary at short and had the fastest hands in the business when it came to getting the ball on its way to first base, especially when he was the middle man on the double play. The ball seemed to be out of his glove before it was in it. He was a magician showing you that his hands were faster than your eyes.

Lefty Gomez made him feel a part of the team right away. Lefty was our pitcher in one of Phil's first games in front of the home folks at Yankee Stadium. In one of the early innings, he called Rizzuto over to the mound from short. Rizzuto was puzzled. There wasn't any crisis going on. It was still early in the game. What could Gomez want?

When Phil got to the mound, Gomez said, "Are your parents here today?" Rizzuto told him yes.

Gomez said, "Then stand here just a minute. Imagine how proud they'll be to see that the great Gomez is asking their son for advice."

Rizzuto indirectly contributed to Priddy's problems. In one of our first games, Priddy, who had a temper, committed an error and then found himself getting a good going-over from one particularly noisy Yankee fan behind our dugout.

After we came in from one of our innings in the field, Priddy told Scooter, "I'd sure like to go into the stands and nail that guy who's riding me."

Rizzuto said, "What's he look like? Does he have black hair?"

Priddy answered, "Yeah, as a matter of fact, he does."

"Kinda curly?"

"Yeah."

"Does he have a mustache?"

"Yeah, that too."

Rizzuto said, "That's my dad."

We soon discovered that Rizzuto had one weakness—insects. He was terrified of bugs. Beginning that year and for the rest of my seasons with the Yankees, and probably after that, Rizzuto would find insects in his valuables box when he went to get his wallet and his watch after a game. We'd all be in on the gag and stand waiting for his reaction.

He became especially antsy—and that's the right word—the day one of the guys put a praying mantis in his valuables box. But another gag made him change one of his habits, back in the days when fielders still left their gloves on the outfield grass while their team was at bat.

Rizzuto trotted out to the edge of the outfield grass behind short-stop to start the next inning and picked up his glove, only to find a dead grasshopper inside. From that inning on, Rizzuto would shake his glove after picking it up, or take it with him to the dugout.

The Yankee players and writers in that era tried to make a lot of fun out of Rizzuto's foibles, but they were underestimating Phil. He was always a cagey person, smart enough to put up with all the pranks and acting surprised or embarrassed as fit the occasion.

What his needlers failed to give Scooter credit for, however, in their excitement was that Phil wasn't really that excited himself. I found out early that Rizzuto is too intelligent for you to make a fool or a sucker of him. You could put him on—or try to—as much as you wanted, but you were never ahead of Rizzuto.

Rizzuto earned a growing amount of recognition over the years as one of the most important Yankees, respect that reached its peak when he won the American League's Most Valuable Player Award in 1950. Even today there are those who will tell you he was more valuable to us at times than DiMaggio.

McCarthy appreciated Phil's importance to us right from the start. George Weiss said that after the Yankees won three more pennants in a row from 1941 through 1943 following our close race with the Tigers and Indians in 1940, McCarthy told him that if we had brought up Phil Rizzuto to play shortstop that year instead of a year later, McCarthy might have won eight pennants in a row. Weiss said, "He was undoubtedly right."

There is no question that 1941 was a season worth writing about, and many people have. It was my pride and privilege to play a role in three of the four historic baseball events of that year.

That was the season of the two greatest individual achievements in the history of American team sports: Joe DiMaggio's 56-game hitting streak and the .406 season by Ted Williams. With the exception of George Brett's .390 season in 1980, no one has come close to either accomplishment in the fifty years since.

I played next to Joe for every game of his streak, and I saw Ted in the twenty-two games we played against the Red Sox. Ted also hit the most dramatic home run in the history of the All-Star Game that year, but I can't claim to have been a part of that; I was on my honeymoon. The season with so much history crammed into it ended with another history-making event in the Yankees-Dodgers World Series, and I played a key role in that dramatic episode—by striking out.

Joe started his streak on May 15, with a single in the first inning off Ed Smith of the White Sox. Joe's hit scored Rizzuto, who led off the inning with a double, but that ended our scoring for the day. We were clobbered, 13–1, and the loss seemed to be a commentary on our season to that time.

We weren't playing well at all. That was our tenth loss in fourteen games, and it dropped us below .500 to a record of 14 wins and 15 losses. The Yankees didn't usually occupy that neighborhood in those days. That was all right if you were used to finishing in the middle of the pack, but we were the Yankees. We knew we were better than that. After our third-place finish of the year before, we knew we had to get hot. We did, and Joe D., "the Yankee Clipper," was the one who ignited our fire.

Joe kept on hitting, and he hit everything hard, including the outs. His ground balls were scorchers, and anything he hit to the outfield was what the players call "a frozen rope," a hard line drive that sometimes prompts the remark, "You could hang your laundry on that one."

We weren't excited until well into Joe's streak. The players didn't talk about it much while it was building, and the writers and broadcasters didn't give it any coverage. One of the first mentions of the streak came after it hit nineteen games, when the last sentence of the story in the New York Times the next morning said, "DiMaggio, incidentally, has hit safely in nineteen straight games."

One of the games in the streak that I remember most vividly was number 38. By that time, people were paying attention, and they weren't just baseball fans. Joe was making the evening news, because Americans everywhere were beginning to ask each other, "What did DiMaggio do today?"

In the thirty-eighth game, we were facing Eldon Auker, a submarining right-hander for the St. Louis Browns, at Yankee Stadium. Auker was holding Joe hitless when we came to bat in the eighth inning. The closest he had come to a hit was a ground ball to Johnny Berardino at short on his second trip to the plate. Berardino, who is now Dr. Steve Hardy on the television soap opera "General Hospital," had trouble handling it, and Joe reached first, but the official scorer, Dan Daniel of the *New York World-Telegram*, ruled the play was an error. The fans groaned, and we looked out of our dugout and up at the press box behind home plate to let Daniel know we disagreed with his ruling against our leader.

In our eighth inning, we were winning, 3–1, so it looked as if we wouldn't get to bat in the ninth, and something was going to have to happen for Joe to get one final chance in the eighth. He was scheduled to be the fourth hitter in the inning. We needed a base runner, and if we got one, then we would have to avoid the double play.

Johnny Sturm led off the inning by popping up. We were two outs away from the end of Joe's streak. But Red Rolfe made a key contribution when he drew a walk. That gave us the opportunity we needed, except for one thing: the possibility of a double play to end the inning in what looked like our last turn at bat, unless the Browns came from behind in their ninth. I was the hitter, and I "owned" Auker. I hit him better than I hit any other pitcher in the American League. I hit him with such consistent success that most people would have considered a double play unlikely.

But there was this additional complication: I hit Auker so hard so often that I might hit a real shot on the ground that could be well hit but still turned into a double play, and there was always the possibility that I might hit a line drive right at one of the infielders, who could double Rolfe off first to end the inning.

I asked for time out and walked over to our dugout. I asked McCarthy for permission to bunt. I knew that if Joe got a chance to hit, Auker was a class guy who would never walk him. He'd never take the coward's way out. He'd pitch to Joe. McCarthy never hesitated. You don't bunt with one out in the eighth inning and your team ahead by two runs, but after I told him the reason behind my suggestion, he gave his blessing immediately.

I laid a bunt down the third-base line and was thrown out at first as Rolfe took second. The inning was still alive, and Joe was getting one last chance to extend his hitting streak to thirty-eight straight games. He hit the first pitch on a line to left center for a double.

Joe's games in which he broke the various records for hitting streaks on his way to 56 games were certainly the most satisfying ones for him, but there was another that gave all of us satisfaction. That came two games after my bunt, in the fortieth game of the streak. It involved our nemesis from 1940, Johnny Babich.

Johnny still had a bug in his craw because the Yankees didn't call him up from Kansas City when he was their property and instead let him go to the Philadelphia A's. So after beating us five times in 1940, he wanted to extract an additional measure of revenge by stopping Joe's streak after thirty-nine games.

That's the attitude of a competitive person, and any athlete would respect that. But some quotes attributed to him before the game made it clear that he was going to stop Joe, and if he had to walk him to do it, he would. No athlete would respect that.

Babich got DiMag out on Joe's first time up, but only after he hit a long drive that went barely foul. On his next time, Joe didn't see anything close. Babich was obviously staying out of the strike zone and was going to walk Joe and stop his streak that way.

Joe told us after the game that he got steamed at Babich for taking the cowardly way out. To McCarthy's everlasting credit, he flashed the "hit" sign to Fletcher with the count three balls and no strikes. Fletch relayed the sign to Joe.

DiMag sent a rocket shot up the middle—right through Babich's legs—for a hit. Babich fell to the ground, scared stiff. Joe says that when he got to first base and looked toward the mound, Babich was "as white as a sheet."

Joe broke George Sisler's modern record of hitting in 41 consecutive games during the first game of a doubleheader in Washington in hundred-degree heat. I didn't play as big a role that game day as I did against Eldon Auker, but my bat did. He tied the record with a double in the sixth inning of the first game against Washington's knuckle ball specialist, Dutch Leonard.

Between games—would you believe it?—a fan stole Joe's bat. Somehow the culprit was able to bolt into our dugout, probably while we were swigging down some cold drinks in the visiting team's clubhouse, and take the bat for a valuable souvenir.

Nobody knew it had happened when I stepped into the batter's box in the first inning of the second game. As I did, Joe called out to me from the on-deck circle, "Hey, Tom! You've got my bat."

I asked for time out, walked toward Joe, and showed him I was using a DiMaggio model, but it was my bat, not one of his.

That's when it dawned on him. He told me, "Somebody stole my bat."

When his turn came, he used somebody else's bat and lined out to Buddy Lewis in right center against Sid Hudson, the tall Senators' righthander who won 17 games as a rookie the year before. As we were trotting to the outfield together for the Senators' half of the first inning, he said to me, "That would have been in there if I'd hit it with my bat."

I could tell he was worried. There he was, trying to set the record, and his bat was gone. In the dugout during Washington's second inning, I said to him, "Use mine. It's like yours anyway." But he didn't want to use it for fear of cracking or breaking it.

In the third inning, Joe hit one of his patented line drives, but it was right at Cecil Travis, the Washington shortstop. Finally, Joe decided to take me up on my offer. I'd like to report that it made an immediate difference, but that's not what happened. In the fifth inning, using my DiMaggio model bat, he flied out to Doc Cramer in center.

Red Anderson relieved Hudson before Joe's next turn at bat, and in the seventh inning Joe hit one of Anderson's fastballs on a line to left for a single. He owned the modern record all by himself, hitting safely in 42 straight games. Sisler sent him a congratulatory telegram and told reporters, "I'd rather see DiMaggio break it than anybody I can think of. The guy is a natural in everything he does and is a great hitter. His streak is no lucky fluke, believe me."

While we were in Washington, the whole team got together at the Shoreham Hotel, where the American League teams stayed, and surprised Joe with a humidor topped by a gold figure of Joe at bat. The signature of every player was engraved on the side.

We toasted Joe with a glass of champagne and sang "For He's a Jolly Good Fellow." Joe told us that the Yankees were his family, and that all of us in that room on the fourth floor were more than his teammates. He told us that each of us was his "friend and brother."

The memory of that private ceremony among us has remained with Joe over the half-century since. At a ceremony honoring him in Chicago in 1991 during the fiftieth anniversary of his streak, he told the crowd, "That was the happiest moment of my baseball life."

After we returned to New York for a series against the Red Sox, Joe's good luck held up. Some of his loyal fans had embarked on a self-authorized investigation to find that bat. They located a kid in Newark, got the bat, and returned it to Joe just in time for the Boston series.

The heat wave that we played in during our series in Washington seemed to follow us back to New York for our series with the Red Sox. We played the first game on July 1, with the temperature in the mid-nineties. There were no air-conditioned clubhouses to duck into in those days, so when you got to the ballpark three hours before game time to begin practice, you were stuck in the heat and humidity—and New York has plenty of both—for five or six hours. If you were playing a doubleheader, and we played more of them than they do today, you'd be sweating through those old-fashioned thick wool flannel uniforms for a drenching eight hours.

The whole nation was excited about Joe's streak by now, so 52,832 fans turned out to see the great DiMaggio. The players all around both leagues were talking about it all the time. We knew we were seeing baseball history in the making, and the longer the streak went on the more likely it became that we were witnessing something that might never happen again.

Yankee players could see something else, and maybe the Dodgers and Giants, too. Joe was exciting the largest city in America. Those supposedly sophisticated New Yorkers who might have thought they had seen everything were as thrilled each day as the folks in Savannah, Peoria, and Boise at the news that Joe got another hit.

DiMag was giving the millions of people in New York something new to be proud of. The World's Fair, the subject of so much local pride in 1939 and 1940, was gone now, and with Joe it was also forgotten. New York had a new distinction being showcased before the world. Joe was making millions of people happy every day. He was giving them something to anticipate at the breakfast table, and something to feel thrilled about at dinner. An entire city was feeling alive, electric with excitement, just because of what one man was accomplishing day by day.

Has any other man or woman in any profession ever affected an entire population like that, sustaining the greatness of his achievement over two full months? No. Only The Great DiMaggio.

Now that Joe had broken Sisler's *modern* record, the talk moved on to whether he could break the *all-time* high of 44 games in a row, set before the turn of the century by Wee Willie Keeler, the man who said the secret of his success was to "hit 'em where they ain't." Dom DiMaggio told Joe on the field before the first game that he thought it was silly to ask him now to break a record set in the 1800s. Dom said he thought it was irrelevant, and maybe the reporters—what today we call "the media"—were just trying to extend a good story for their own benefit.

Dom had a legitimate point. For one thing, Keeler's streak was accomplished under different rules. In his time, the batter was not charged with a strike when he hit a foul ball. Joe might never have been in the position of having two strikes on him under that rule. He might have hit in every game the rest of the season.

Under 1941 rules, Joe popped out foul to Lou Finney, Boston's first baseman, in the first game, and then an interesting thing happened. On his next trip to the plate, he hit a ground ball to third. The Red Sox third baseman, Jim Tabor, was playing Joe deep, the way many of the third basemen in the league were doing now, with Joe's blazing bat and his exceptional ability to get around on the pitch and pull the ball to the left side of the field, thus getting the strength and force of his entire body into his swing.

Tabor fumbled Joe's grounder and then made a poor throw to first, allowing Joe to reach second. In the press box, the official scorer for that game, Dan Daniel of the *New York World-Telegram*, was on the spot. Joe wasn't the only one under pressure during his streak. Every player on the opposing teams was, and so were umpires and official scorers.

For Daniel, the burden was even greater than it would have been for other scorers because of that ruling in Joe's thirty-eighth game, that his grounder to Berardino was an error instead of a hit. On this play, he went the opposite way. He ruled it a hit. Joe's streak was still alive. But knowing Joe, that wasn't going to be good enough. He never liked anything tainted. He was a champion, and he knew it. He always wanted his performance to reflect his stature.

Joe got Daniel off the hook again, this time with another one of his screaming shots to left field in his next time up. Nobody needed a ruling from the official scorer. The crowd went nuts. Once again Joe was proving that he not only had the talent of a champion but the ability to excel under pressure, something that only winners have. Six times during his streak, with the national spotlight bearing down on him, he got his hit on his last time up in the game.

In the second game, Joe was successful right away, and it was a good thing. He lined a single over the head of Boston's player-manager, Joe Cronin, at short in the first inning, and the crowd gave Joe a hero's acclaim again. Now he was tied with Keeler at 44 games, the longest streak in this century or the last. The umpires that day were Joe Rue, Ed Rommel, Bill Stewart, and Bill Summers. After five innings, the minimum amount required to make the game official, they called it off due to darkness.

The next day was just as hot as the day before and the day before that. Lefty Grove, their Hall of Fame pitcher, was scheduled to start against us, but Lefty turned forty-one in March of that year. He was one of the fiercest competitors I ever played against, but he also knew the facts of life. He told Cronin he just couldn't hold up in that kind of heat any more.

For Lefty, that had to be an extra-painful decision. He was trying desperately to reach the immortal level of 300 victories, and he would have loved nothing more than to do it against the Yankees. But he was smart enough to know that the weather could flatten you when you're that age and trying to pitch a baseball game in the big leagues.

He did get his 300th victory, three weeks later, the last game he ever won.

Instead of Grove, we faced Dick Newsome on July 2. Newsome was a rookie, but he was having a strong year. He won 19 games that season, his career high. He won only 8 games in each of the next two years and then dropped out of the big leagues.

But in 1941, Newsome could be hard to beat. Joe went hitless in his first two times up, but on his third trip, Newsome made a pitcher's mistake: He got behind in the count to a great hitter, giving the hitter all the best of it.

The count went to two balls and no strikes, a situation that good hitters yearn for. That's when you know the pitcher has to come to you with a strike or he'll be only one pitch away from walking you. And what's the easiest pitch for most pitchers to control? A fastball. And what's the easiest pitch to hit? A fastball.

Joe hit that 2–0 pitch over Yankee Stadium's left field wall. Forty-five straight games. The all-time record was his. And he did it in such typical Yankee and DiMaggio fashion, a home run, and in Yankee Stadium, famous as "the House That Ruth Built."

In our dressing room after the game, Lefty Gomez was again equal to the occasion. He said Joe broke Keeler's record by using Keeler's own technique. Lefty said, "He hit it where they ain't."

The streak went on, to the next magic-sounding level of fifty straight games. Even now that's hard to comprehend. Just imagine hitting in fifty straight games. For Joe, though, it wasn't anything new. Playing for the San Francisco Seals of the Pacific Coast League on his way up to the Yankees, Joe hit in 61 straight! With the Yankees, he hit in 23 straight in 1940, 21 in a row in

'37, and 18 straight as a rookie in '36. During spring training in 1941, he even gave us a reminder that he was still capable of long consecutive-game hitting streaks. He hit in nineteen straight games in Florida and then opened the regular season by hitting in our first eight.

His 61-game streak with San Francisco was more than just a phenomenal achievement, especially for a kid who was still in his teens. It was also the best kind of personal preparation for breaking a major-league record at the tender age of twenty-six. His conduct never changed. He handled everything that came along. He was winning games for us with his bat, and also with his glove, his arm, and his speed in the outfield, and on the bases, too.

And winning is putting it mildly. The same Yankee team that was one game under .500 and struggling badly when Joe started his streak was in first place as the streak grew out of the forties and into the fifties. Joe singlehandedly turned a losing team into a winner, and over a sustained period of time. This was a star who wasn't just having an unforgettable week or ten days, which is an achievement in itself. He was maintaining a superhuman level of performance for two months.

He was hitting the ball hard and consistently. He wasn't getting by on anything cheap. The only infield hit in his entire streak was a grounder to Luke Appling that Joe beat out, but he got a solid hit to the outfield his next time up. The only thing that looked even slightly lucky was a blooper—we used to call them texas leaguers—that he hit off his ear against Thornton Lee in Chicago.

Through all those days and weeks, Joe was the same Joe, usually quiet, always polite with the press, enjoying his spare time with Lefty Gomez, visiting Toots Shor's, and never, never showing any signs of cracking under the unrelenting national publicity.

They even wrote a song about him that became a big number on "Your Hit Parade." It was recorded by Les Brown and His Band of Renown, "Joltin' Joe DiMaggio." It became as popular as the Glenn Miller hits of 1941: "Chattanooga Choo-Choo," with the vocal by Tex Beneke and the Modernaires, "Elmer's Tune," with the Modernaires joined by Ray Eberle on the vocal, and "String of Pearls."

Through it all, Joe maintained his composure as an athlete and his dignity as a champion. His friend Hemingway defined courage as "grace under pressure." That also defined Joe DiMaggio.

When the end came, it was vintage DiMaggio. His streak was stopped, but he wasn't. He went 0-for-3 on the night of July 17 against the Indians in Cleveland's Municipal Stadium, and he never hit the ball harder in his life.

Joe and his pal Lefty Gomez might have come across a bad omen about that night. On their way to the ballpark in a cab, the driver, in a fit of home-team loyalty, predicted to Joe that his streak would be stopped. Lefty, ever loyal and protective of Joe, snapped at the driver from the back seat, "What are you trying to do, jinx him?"

He hit his patented rocket shots, two of them near the third-base bag and another to short. Cleveland's All-Star third baseman, Ken Keltner, made two spectacular plays, and Lou Boudreau, their Hall of Fame shortstop, made a third, turning a sharp grounder into a double play.

Keltner's plays are the ones everyone remembers. On both shots, he turned swiftly to his right, backhanded the ball, being carried across the foul line both times by the force of the blows, and threw a strike to Oscar Grimes at first base while standing in foul territory behind the third-base bag. They had to be two of the greatest plays Keltner ever made, and he made a ton of them.

Keltner wasn't just good; he was smart, too. Earlier in the streak, he started to play Joe closer to the third-base line. He knew Joe was a dead-pull hitter, and that in this streak he was doing what every hot hitter does, pulling the ball even more because he was seeing it better and getting around on it quicker. He knew, too, that Cleveland's pitchers that night, starter Al Smith and reliever Jim Bagby, were not fastball pitchers. Joe would be getting around on them with even better success.

What was Keltner's reaction when Joe hit those two ground balls? "They were hit like bullets," he said. He called his plays "unconscious," but it was more than that. Keltner had great reflexes at third. Other third basemen couldn't have made either of those plays, much less both, and Joe's streak would have been alive. That's significant, because Joe started another streak the next night, against Bob Feller no less, and hit in another sixteen straight games. Without those plays by Keltner and Boudreau, Joe's streak would have lasted seventy-three games, virtually half of the Major League schedule of 154 games.

The story doesn't end there. In the ninth inning of that game, we were leading, 4–1. Gomez was our starting pitcher, but McCarthy brought in Johnny Murphy to finish the game. The first two hitters reached base, and Larry Rosenthal pinch-hit and tripled to cut our lead to one run, 4–3.

Hal Trosky, Cleveland's big-slugging first baseman, who drove in more than 100 runs six years in a row and once led the league with 162, couldn't hit a sacrifice fly to drive Rosenthal in with the tying run. Instead he hit a one-hopper to Johnny Sturm at first base, and Rosenthal had to hold at third. One out. Soup Campbell hit a grounder back to the mound, Murphy trapped Rosenthal off third, and we got him out in a rundown. Two outs. Roy Weatherly grounded out to end the game.

If Rosenthal had been able to score, the game would have been tied, and Joe might have gotten another chance in extra innings. Sturm or Murphy could have let one of those grounders go for a hit to tie the game so Joe could come to bat again in extra innings. We could have taken our chances on winning the game then, and even a loss wouldn't have made any difference in our record. We were beginning to run away with the pennant anyhow. I think the fact that the thought of actually doing that never even entered anyone's mind is a convincing illustration of the honesty of baseball.

I loved Ken's reaction after the game. People were congratulating him for his key role in stopping Joe's streak, but that wasn't the important thing to him. He reminded his admirers, "We lost the game, didn't we?"

Two other reactions bear quoting here, too. Joe was always as much of a champion in defeat as he was in victory, and that night was no exception. With all the pressure of the previous two months, and with the disappointment that surely was his, Joe congratulated Keltner through the reporters, saying he made two great plays, said the streak was over and he had no complaints, and that was that.

When Pete Rose made a run at Joe's streak and was stopped

after forty-four games, the papers quoted him as saying, "What a way to stop a streak—with a changeup." What's wrong with that? Is the pitcher supposed to throw you a fat pitch just so you can keep your streak going? I thought you were supposed to *earn* those things instead of having them handed to you.

Joe always thought so, too.

By himself, Joe was keeping the pressure off the whole rest of our team. He was carrying us, to a degree that a single player has seldom carried an entire team in any sport. In baseball, only Grover Cleveland Alexander's record of 16 shutouts for the Philadelphia Phillies in 1916 rivals what Joe was accomplishing in leading his team to victory in 1941.

The Yankee team that was playing under .500 ball when Joe started his streak was leading the league when Keltner ended it. From a record of 14–15 we slugged our way into first place thirty-seven games into Joe's streak and stayed there the rest of the year, finishing with 101 wins. The second-place team, Boston, was seventeen games behind us. We won forty-two times during Joe's historic fifty-six games, with two other games ending in ties because of rain.

By being able to play relaxed, we were able to play better. That's especially true when it comes to hitting. You can't be tense and be a good hitter because your muscles tighten up and don't respond to the pitch as quickly as they do when you're concentrating but relaxing at the same time. It's not an easy combination to achieve, but it's essential if you're going to be a good hitter.

With Joe D. taking all the pressure himself, the rest of us were able to swing in loosey-goosey fashion, and we did. We hit home runs in 25 straight games, which is still the major-league record. I had the honor of hitting what turned out to be the last home run in that streak, in Griffith Stadium in Washington against Alex Carrasquel.

Many of the home runs in that streak were in the late innings, when we would put on one of our patented rallies to pull out another win. We played mostly day games in those years, and those late rallies of ours often came around five o'clock. It happened so many times during that stretch that Rizzuto called our late-inning power "five o'clock lightning."

In the middle of our glory, tragedy stepped in to cast a temporary pall over our team. Lou Gehrig died. He was thirty-seven. The end came on June 2, on the same day that Joe's streak, still in its early stages, reached nineteen games when he hit a single and a double against Bob Feller in Cleveland.

We knew Lou was in bad shape, but we didn't realize he was near death. He aged rapidly after retiring from the Yankees. His hair turned white almost overnight, he soon developed trouble walking and talking, and we were watching a recently vigorous, healthy human life deteriorate before our very eyes.

The news of his death was depressing for every New Yorker, every baseball fan, and every American. It was doubly depressing for us as Lou's teammates, and I felt it as keenly as I know Joe D., Lefty, his roommate Bill Dickey, and Joe McCarthy did. We worshipped the man. Lou had been a star for ten years by the time DiMag and I came up. When he dazzled baseball with those 184 RBIs and 46 home runs in 1931, DiMag and I were still teenagers. Lou Gehrig was one of our boyhood heroes.

To become his teammate and play in the same starting lineup with him was every boy's dream come true. After Babe Ruth made me a Yankee fan with his home runs and Gehrig came along and started doing the same thing, I used to dream what it must be like to be Lou Gehrig. Then, in 1937, I was blessed as few American boys could ever be. I was a New York Yankee, and Lou Gehrig was my teammate.

Mayor Fiorello La Guardia, "the Little Flower," did a nice thing after Lou retired from baseball. He appointed him a city parole commissioner. For as long as Lou could walk, even after he needed others to help him, he went to his office, listened to the cases, studied the paperwork connected with them, and made his decisions concerning parole for those before him. They say he always showed the same dignity, kindness, and understanding that we respected him for when he was on our team.

One tough New York kid who came before him later credited Lou with being a key influence in pointing him away from more crime and toward the right kind of life. He was a strong, stocky Italian kid named Rocco Barbella. Later he changed his name to Rocky Graziano and became the middleweight champion of the world.

Public ignorance about ALS in 1941 when it killed Lou caused a problem involving our team. Its symptoms resembled those of polio—infantile paralysis—which was a dreaded health threat every summer, with epidemics affecting mostly the young, paralyzing them and causing them to be hospitalized in long, heavy, tubular machines called "iron lungs" to help their breathing.

Young adults could come down with it, too, and did, including Franklin Roosevelt. He spent the rest of his life in a wheelchair, including his terms as governor of New York and president, and every year he spearheaded a fund drive, the March of Dimes. Its purpose was to raise money for research that could help to treat polio and eventually prevent it, the great accomplishment achieved by Dr. Jonas Salk with his vaccine in 1955.

But fifteen years earlier, polio was still one of the great fears in the United States, and it struck terror in our hearts every summer. Against this background, Jimmy Powers of the *New York Daily News* wrote a column in 1940 saying that several of Lou's teammates on the Yankees, including Dickey, had been infected with infantile paralysis. He wrote that this was one of the reasons we slumped in mid-August and failed to win the pennant for the fifth straight year.

Lou, the most mild-mannered of men, was furious. He sued the paper for the staggering sum of a million dollars for libel. The *News* withdrew the claim, printed an apology to Lou, and told its readers that Lou's disease was not communicable. Then Lou dropped his lawsuit.

When Lou died, we needed something to sustain us as a team. After all, he was one of us only two years before. Almost every man on the Yankees had been his teammate. That was another achievement of Joe and another benefit of his streak. It kept all of us going. It helped to hold the Yankees together through our grief over Lou's death. Lou would have liked that.

Eight

Our Sweetest Series

Ted Williams was the other larger-than-life baseball story in 1941. He accomplished things in hitting a baseball that no man has since. He hit over .400, and he did it like a man. He was hitting .39955 going into the last day of the season, a doubleheader against the A's in Philadelphia, and Joe Cronin offered him the opportunity to take the day off, thus insuring an average that would be an even .400 when rounded off.

It was just the opposite of McCarthy's attitude when Joe was burning up the league with his .400-plus average in mid-September of 1939, and Cronin might as well have had the attitude that McCarthy did. Ted turned him down flat, got six hits in the doubleheader, and raised his average six points to .406.

No player in the American League was surprised that Williams was the first man in the league to hit .400 since Harry Heilmann hit .403 for the Tigers in 1923. Ted was closer to perfection with a bat than any hitter I ever saw, then or now.

You can name them all. Pete Rose? His best year was fifty-eight points lower than Ted's, and his lifetime average is forty-one points below. George Brett? A great hitter, but the best he could do was .390 in 1980. He'll probably end his career with a .300 lifetime average, but he won't be close to Ted. José Canseco? He's baseball's only "40–40 man" (40 home runs and 40 stolen bases in the same season), but he's no Williams with the bat. He has "holes" in his swing and can be pitched to, but you won't find a pitcher alive from our era who would tell you that he knew how to pitch to Ted Williams. As for holes in his swing, every hitter has them, but I have never heard or read that any pitcher found out where the holes were in the Williams swing.

Ted was born with uncommon ability and the keenest eyesight a human being could hope for, but the reasons behind his superiority as a hitter went beyond that. He was respected so much by his peers that when he stepped into the cage during batting practice, the rest of us would stop warming up for the game as long as he was swinging, just so we could watch the Master. He wasn't just satisfied with his natural ability as it was. He kept developing it to new levels. In other words, he worked hard.

Williams would take more batting practice than any other player. And it was never enough. He'd wait for the fans to leave after a game, drag a pitcher out with him, and go back onto the field for another half hour or forty-five minutes of hitting. That's a long time to be hitting without interruption, but Ted would do it for periods so long that the rest of us would have dropped from exhaustion.

His brain, which made him a respected fighter pilot in two wars and might have made him the world's leading brain surgeon or nuclear scientist, told him that hitting a baseball is an inexact art form that requires the artist—the hitter—to pursue his work with unwavering diligence. That's precisely what he did.

He did more than out-practice everyone in the physical end of it. He out-thought the rest of us, too. He swung a lighter bat than most of us, 32 ounces compared to anything from 34 to 40 ounces for the rest of us, because he said bat speed was more important than a heavier bat that might give you distance. He said if you have enough bat speed, the home runs will come anyhow, and the lighter bat will give you more singles and doubles than a heavier bat, which can slow your swing down and reduce your ability to make contact.

He was also more disciplined at the plate than the rest of us.

Just as he did throughout his playing career, to this day, as a hitting instructor for the Red Sox during spring training, he insists that most hitters are simply too content to swing at balls that are not in the strike zone. He has said it a million times, maybe ten million: "Get a good pitch to hit." And when you went for something that wasn't a good pitch, you'd hear it from him, usually at the top of his voice: "Don't be so damn dumb!"

Ted was never a contact hitter in the normal definition of that term, but he always emphasized that you had to make contact before you could expect to accomplish anything else with the bat. Whenever we'd talk hitting before the game or in social settings, he'd say, "When you make contact, things start to happen."

He was one of those rare combinations, a man who could hit with exceptional power and for exceptional averages at the same time. People forget that in his historic season in '41, he also led both leagues in home runs with 37. As for his insistence that you have to "get a good pitch to hit," there is the amazing testimony to his greatness: While accomplishing all those things in 1941, he struck out a total of only 27 times.

That was no fluke. In this age when .240 hitters swing for the fences and strike out 125 times a year in the process, Ted's highest strikeout total was 64, and that came in his rookie season. After that, he never struck out more than 54 times—and that was the next year. In fifteen seasons after 1942, when he struck out 51 times, Ted never had fifty strikeouts again.

That's helping your team in a way that is lost on the players of today. Ted Williams was always more of a team player than he was given credit for, mainly because his individual statistics were so overpowering that people tended to overlook his contributions to his team. They never gave him credit for his skill in playing left field in Boston, but Dom DiMaggio, the man who played next to Ted, will testify to it. And they never gave him the credit he deserved for avoiding strikeouts and for drawing walks.

Getting on base by walking was another thing Ted did better than anyone else, because of his strict self-discipline in the batter's box. He led the American League in walks six years in a row and eight times in all. The lowest number in any of those seasons was 126.

Casey Stengel, with a touch of his mumbo-jumbo that came to be called "Stengelese," said Ted "had the best judgment of a

strike of any man in the game, and he's well over six feet, which
gives him a bigger stroke zone than most hitters, and he could still
judge a pitch better than the umpires who were seeing the ball
from straight-on while he was up there standing sideways.''

In 1947, when he led the league in hitting with a .343 average,
he walked 162 times to lead both leagues. Pee Wee Reese and
Hank Greenberg led the National League, but Ted outwalked
them by fifty-eight. Combined with his 181 hits, he reached base
for his team 343 times that year. That's applying your individual
skills to help your team. Maybe he could have hit a few more
home runs by swinging for the fences with some wild cuts, but he
helped the Red Sox more by being so disciplined and reaching base
that many times.

There is additional evidence that reveals the dual greatness of
Ted Williams as both a long-ball hitter and a high-average hitter:
He hit 521 home runs in his career, the tenth most in history, and
yet he also hit over .340 eleven times. At the age of thirty-nine,
long after most of us retire from major-league baseball, Ted led
both leagues in hitting with a .388 average. In the last season of
his career, at age forty-two, he had a batting average of .316 and
hit 29 home runs.

When it was all over for him, after he hit a home run in the
last at-bat of his life, he said he could even have practiced more
than he did. He said he had one regret: ''I wish I had hit more
baseballs.''

I have one vivid memory of playing against Ted in 1941: I don't
think he ever hit a fly ball to me. He hit plenty of shots to me, all
right, because he was a left-handed pull hitter and I was the right
fielder, but the only fly balls in my general direction were over my
head and into the seats.

Everything else was hit hard: line drives that landed in front of
me for singles, drives up the alley in right center between Di-
Maggio and me for doubles, and ground balls that scorched the
earth on their way between Gordon and Sturm for more singles.
Between DiMaggio's rocket shots and Ted's, 1941 was no year to
be a baseball.

When the World Series started at Yankee Stadium on October
1, we knew we were facing a strong team in the Brooklyn Dodgers.

They beat out the St. Louis Cardinals by two and a half games in a race that was close all year. It was the first appearance by the Dodgers in the Series since 1920, but they proved over the course of a tight pennant race that they could win when the heat was on, and they had the established stars who were capable of winning a World Series for them.

Their lineup included Pete Reiser, the National League batting champion that year, Pee Wee Reese, Dixie Walker, Ducky Medwick, Dolph Camilli, Cookie Lavagetto, and Billy Herman. They were strong in pitching, too, with a staff that included Whitlow Wyatt and Kirby Higbe, who tied for the most wins in the National League with 22 each, the veteran Freddie Fitzsimmons, Curt Davis, and Larry French. In the World Series, when you play a maximum of seven games, pitching can win it for you, and those Dodger pitchers were good enough to do that.

The Dodgers also had a talented catcher, Mickey Owen, who had a reputation for being able to handle any kind of a pitch thrown to him. Over the course of the 1941 and '42 seasons, he set a National League record for catching excellence by handling 507 straight chances without an error.

Two of the most successful Major League managers in history were opposing each other. Joe McCarthy, who never played one inning in the majors but knew the game inside and out and knew even more about how to handle a team of professional athletes, has the highest winning percentage for his career of any manager in history, both for his twenty-four seasons and for his nine World Series teams.

The Dodgers' manager, Leo Durocher, who also managed for twenty-four years, has the sixth most wins of any manager, only 117 behind McCarthy and 103 more than Casey Stengel. They're both in the Hall of Fame. Makes you think that Leo should be in there, too, doesn't it?

He was considered a brassy kid when he came up with the Yankees as a shortstop in 1925, but he was good enough to last seventeen years as a player. He was a flashy shortstop, but he couldn't hit. He had a career lifetime batting average of only .247. Babe Ruth called him "the All-American out," but when you played on some of the powerhouse teams that Leo did, especially the Yankees and Cardinals, you could afford an average like that because everybody around you was hitting.

As a personality, though, Leo was in a class by himself. He was a splashy dresser, a kid from West Springfield, Massachusetts, who was nicknamed "Fifth Avenue" by his Yankee teammates and was always getting into scrapes on the field and off. He married a popular movie actress, Laraine Day.

He was thrown out of so many games by umpires that he won another nickname, "Leo the Lip." And he was thrown out just as often by his own boss, the Dodgers' general manager Larry MacPhail, whose fiery personality matched Durocher's and sometimes exceeded it. "MacPhail fired me sixty times," Leo has said, "but I was there when he left."

McCarthy and Durocher were opposites on the field as well as in their personalities. Joe would stay in the dugout, telling his coaches where to position us on defense, flashing his undetected signals to Art Fletcher and Earl Combs when we were up, and running a thoroughly businesslike operation.

Leo, on the other hand, would be ranting and raving, dashing onto the field to argue an umpire's call as often as he could, and yelling at his pitchers to "stick it in his ear! Let's see how he hits when he's on his back!"

He could be a real entertainer, like the time they played a charity softball game at the Polo Grounds starring a collection of celebrities from show business against New York's biggest baseball names. The show biz lineup included Ernie Kovacs—who was a skilled baseball player and got a single and a double that night—in center field, Phil Silvers, and Frank Sinatra, who came to the plate swinging three bats and fell down under the weight of his load, just to keep the folks laughing.

When Durocher came to bat, he intentionally got into an argument with the home-plate umpire and challenged him to a fight, while the crowd ate it up. What delighted them so much was that the umpire happened to be the heavyweight champion of the world, Joe Louis.

Durocher yelled at Louis, "Take the mask off and I'll pop you one."

Louis, always quiet and low-keyed, had only one condition: "Put the bat down."

Durocher held onto the bat, Louis kept his mask on, and they went back to playing ball.

That was Leo. And that was why we wanted to beat the Dodgers in the worst way in 1941. We didn't have anything against their players, or against Durocher for that matter. They were in "the other league," so we didn't have that much contact with them. As a result, we didn't know that much about them.

But this much we did know: We didn't want to lose to a team managed by Leo Durocher.

Judge Landis threw out the first ball as a last-minute substitute for President Roosevelt, who was confined to the Oval Office in the White House because of the worsening international situation. The papers the next day said Roosevelt listened to the game while he worked, on one of those new "portable radios" that Lou Gehrig introduced me to in my rookie season four years earlier. Landis for Roosevelt was an ironic substitution, because Landis detested FDR, and the feeling was mutual. He opposed the idea of a third term for FDR and disagreed with Roosevelt's policies in general.

Even without the president and "Ruffles and Flourishes" and "Hail to the Chief," there was a star-studded atmosphere as we finished our warmups. Two of New York's most prominent politicians were on hand, La Guardia and FDR's postmaster general, Jim Farley. Whoever heard of playing a World Series without the politicians showing up? Babe Ruth was there, too, and so were the two opponents in the heavyweight championship fight three months before, Joe Louis and Billy Conn.

Louis knocked out Conn in the thirteenth round of their famous fight in Yankee Stadium in June of that year, and he defeated Lou Nova two nights before the start of the World Series. But he wasn't without concerns of his own. He had just been drafted into the army.

Red Barber, Bob Elson, and Bill Corum were at the mike for Radio Station WOR, the Mutual station in New York, sponsored by Gillette razors, and Charley Ruffing, our best, was on the mound ready to take on the Dodgers before a sellout crowd of 68,540 fans, double the size of the crowd that we would play in front of when the Series moved to Ebbets Field for the third game.

Durocher made an intriguing pitching selection for the opening game. Instead of pitching Whitlow Wyatt against us, he went with Curt Davis. Davis won 13 games for Brooklyn that year, but Wyatt tied his teammate, Kirby Higbe, as the National League's leading pitchers with 22 wins.

Davis avoided any criticism for Durocher by combining with Hugh Casey and Johnny Allen to pitch a six-hitter. But Ruffing pitched a six-hitter, too, and we beat the Dodgers, 3–2, thanks in part to a home run by Joe Gordon.

It was the sixth World Series victory of Red Ruffing's brilliant career. He won another Series game the next year, and his seven wins are tied for second on the all-time list of World Series winners.

Davis wasn't so lucky. It was the only World Series game of his career.

In the second game, Durocher threw Wyatt at us. We knew we were going up against a veteran, one who had been pitching since 1929, all of those years in the American League with the Tigers, White Sox, and Indians until he joined the Dodgers in 1939. He was never a big winner until 1941. Before that, his only season with more than nine wins was the year before, when he won 15 for Brooklyn.

In '41, he had his career year: tied for the most wins, second in earned run average, second in strikeouts, tops in shutouts, second in complete games, third in innings pitched, second in fewest hits per nine innings, and third in most strikeouts for each nine innings.

In 1942, Wyatt came close to another 20-game season, winning 19, but he never again came close to his performance over those two years in a career that covered sixteen seasons.

In '41, though, he was a star pitcher, so we had to beat the National League's best. To help us do that, McCarthy chose Spud Chandler as our starting pitcher. Chandler, Luke Appling's hunting pal, was finally getting into a World Series. He was finishing his fifth season with the Yankees, having come up in '37 when I did, but he had never appeared in a Series game until this one.

Spud's long-awaited dream had an unhappy ending. It was another 3–2 game, but this time we were on the short end. Two all-time Brooklyn favorites, Dolph Camilli and Dixie Walker, teamed up to get the winning run for the Dodgers, with Camilli singling Walker home in the sixth inning. It was the first World Series game we lost after winning ten in a row.

Fate made Chandler wait but eventually treated him more kindly. He won two games in the '43 Series.

The Series moved to Brooklyn for the third, fourth, and fifth games in what we used to call a "subway Series" or a "nickel Series" because the hometown fans of both teams could travel to their team's away games as well as the home games simply by hopping on the subway for a nickel.

I made it my business during batting practice before the first game in Brooklyn on October 4 to check the right-field wall at Ebbets Field. I had played only a few exhibition games there. I was always an analytical sort anyway, and I liked to learn as much as possible about any ballpark I was playing in, especially in the importance of the World Series.

I got Bill Dickey to hit balls off that wall all during our batting practice. I wanted to know every angle, what the ball did when it hit a certain spot and how it bounced off the concrete along the bottom. And, as I always did, I checked the shadows, the glare of the sun, the resiliency of the outfield turf, and the haze caused by cigarette smoke. By the time the game started, I was satisfied that I knew my part of Ebbets Field.

It was another one-run game. We won again, this time 2–1, with a native of Brooklyn, Marius Russo, pitching a four-hitter against the Dodgers. Russo pitched a superb game, holding Brooklyn to four hits, striking out five, walking only two, and going the full nine innings. To make his contribution complete, he was the key figure in the weird play.

Russo was one of the league's best-hitting pitchers. He got 18 hits for us that season, so the Dodgers knew he was no automatic out when he came to bat in the seventh inning with Joe Gordon on second base, two outs, and the game still scoreless.

Russo lined a DiMaggio-like shot off the left leg of Fitzsimmons on the mound. The ball was hit so hard it bounced thirty feet into the air after hitting Freddie, and Pee Wee Reese caught it at short for the third out of the inning.

When we came up to bat in the eighth, with the score still 0–0, we saw that the Dodgers had a new pitcher, their relief ace, Hugh Casey. Fitzsimmons had turned forty that July, and they were calling him "Fat Freddie" by then, but he didn't leave the game because he was tired. He just couldn't continue after taking that smash by Russo.

Casey was considered the National League's best relief pitcher in 1941, but we got to him right away. We roughed him up for four straight singles—Rolfe, me, DiMaggio, and Keller in that order—and came away with the victory. Yankee singles, instead of Yankee homers, got us our runs that day.

The speculation set in right away. Suppose Russo's blast had not hit Fitzsimmons—would he have shut the Yankees out? The Dodgers scored a run off Russo in the eighth, so they might have won a 1–0 game without the injury to Freddie. They would have been leading in the Series, two wins to one, with the next two games in their home park.

But that's not what happened, so we, not the Dodgers, were leading, two games to one. The fans could have been forgiven if they went home thinking that now, in the thirty-eight years since the start of the World Series, every possible way to win a Series game had occurred. But as one of my favorite entertainers, Al Jolson, might have told them, "Folks, you ain't seen nothin' yet."

What happened the next day has been forever known as "the Mickey Owen game." That was the game when I came to bat with two out and nobody on in the ninth inning and the Dodgers leading, 4–3, and struck out. Only I didn't strike out. The Dodgers tied the Series at two wins each. Only they didn't tie it.

Both managers were getting their money's worth out of their bullpens. Atley Donald started for us, and McCarthy brought in Marv Breuer and Johnny Murphy. Higbe was Brooklyn's starter, and Durocher went to Larry French and Johnny Allen in the first half of the game.

With two outs in our fifth inning, Durocher called to the bullpen and summoned Casey, for the third time in the four games. He hadn't pitched that much in either of his other two appearances, so it looked like the thing to do. And when we got a look at him, we knew Durocher had made the right call.

Casey got the side out, and then Reiser came up with a two-run homer to bring Brooklyn from a 3–2 deficit to a 4–3 lead. That was all Casey needed. Hugh slammed the door on us and shut us out the rest of the way, until I found myself up there in the ninth with a full count, only one strike away from a Brooklyn victory.

Casey, a right-hander, took his windup and cut loose with the craziest curveball I ever saw. Only Tommy Bridges of the Tigers, the acknowledged curveball king of the American League, ever threw one as good, and none better.

I had to get on base somehow. My team needed a base runner so we could keep the game alive, manufacture a run one way or another, and then get the win after that. Even with two outs, none on, and the count three balls and two strikes on me, I knew I had to do my damnedest to make something happen.

The one thing I was hoping for was a fastball. I was a dead fastball hitter, but the curve was my sworn enemy. I reminded myself that this was a fastball situation. Pitchers in that spot will throw the pitch that is easiest to control, their fastball. But—and this is where the mental part of baseball that makes it such a fascinating sport comes into play—I also had to remember that Casey had enough confidence in his ability to control his curve that he might throw it even in this situation.

I reminded myself about one of the most important factors in hitting: Be ready for the fastball, but also be ready to adjust if it's a curve. The reason is simple. If you're ready for the fastball and it's a curve, you still have time to hold up on your swing a split second and then hit the curve. But if you're ready for a curve and the pitcher surprises you with a fastball that you're not ready for, you'll never catch up with it.

The baseball heads toward the plate, and it looks like a pitch that is going to be close enough to swing at, given the situation of the moment. I begin my swing. When I'm halfway through it, I think to myself, "You must be crazy to be swinging at something like this." I miss, and it's not even close.

Strike three, end of game. The Dodgers win and tie the World Series. Or do they?

As I completed my swing, realizing that Casey just conned me with one of the great curveballs of all time, another thought occurred to me in that split second: "If I'm having this much trouble with this pitch, maybe Mickey is, too." In the famous picture of that play, as I'm finishing my swing, you can see that I'm turning my head to see where the ball is, even while the home-plate umpire, Larry Goetz, has his right fist in the arm signaling "strike three."

The pitch bounced off Owen's mitt and rolled toward the Brooklyn dugout on the third-base side. I dropped my bat, put my head down, and bolted toward first base. I made it easily. When I got there, Dolph Camilli never said a word.

The crowd burst into a roar when I missed Casey's pitch, in that split second before the ball got past Mickey, too. Police officers ran onto the field to keep the fans off, thinking I had struck out and the game was over.

Durocher dashed onto the field because he was afraid the policemen were interfering with the action, especially with Owen's attempt to retrieve the ball. Tom Meany wrote in later years that it was "the only time I ever saw a citizen chasing the cops."

Owen has said since that at this critical point, he should have gone to the mound and tried to calm Casey down. "I should have gone out and told Casey that I blew it and to settle him down. But all of us were in shock from what happened."

DiMag was the next hitter, and he went right to work. He jumped on the first pitch he saw from Casey and lined a single to left field over Pee Wee Reese's head. He said later, "I didn't want Casey throwing me any of that garbage." The picture had changed dramatically. Now it was the Dodgers who were under pressure. I was at second with the potential tying run, and Joe was on first with the run that would put us ahead. But we still had to avoid that last out.

Keller did. He doubled against the right-field wall, the one I experimented with so thoroughly during batting practice the day before. I scored standing up. The score was tied. It's a good thing I paid attention to Art Fletcher in the third-base coach's box and kept running hard, because Joe was running up my back. With his speed and grace, he slid in right behind me with the go-ahead run. We were winning, 5–4.

Keller's double won the game and the Series. We still had to play the Brooklyn ninth inning and another game the next day, but there was an unmistakable air everywhere in Ebbets Field at that point. The Yankees had all but won the 1941 World Series, and everyone knew it. Forget what the rule book said about the need to let Brooklyn come to bat in the bottom of the inning. And forget what the schedule said about another game tomorrow.

This World Series was over.

Bill Dickey kept our inning going with a walk, and Joe Gordon, the outstanding hitter in the Series, hit another double to score Charlie and Bill. The final score was 7–4.

In our dressing room after the game, Joe D. said, ''They'll never come back from this.'' Joe DiMaggio *never* talked like that. But that's how crushing that turn of events was. Joe knew that *no* team could come back from something like that.

Everyone knew it, including the fans. One Dodger supporter walking out of Ebbets Field after the stunning turn of events called the outcome ''an American tragedy.'' A banner hung over the center-field wall when the Series moved to Brooklyn before the third game was still draped there. It said:

WE WAITED 21 YEARS—DON'T FAIL US NOW

In the years since, Mickey Owen and I have been asked a million times—maybe more—if Casey crossed him up and threw a spitball. In the interviews we've given separately and when we've been together, Mickey and I have always agreed on this. It was definitely not a spitter. Spitballs drop down. This was a big, breaking curveball—what we called ''a roundhouse curve,'' the doggonedest one you ever saw.

Casey was so good with the curveball that he had two kinds, a sharp breaking one and the big roundhouse. He had been getting us out since the fifth inning with the sharp one, and Mickey, who used only one signal for any kind of curve because of his confidence that he could handle whichever Casey felt like throwing, was not expecting the roundhouse. He was looking for the other, and when he was fooled, he wasn't able to react in time to catch it.

Some ''experts'' who weren't wearing either a New York or a Brooklyn uniform that day have said that Owen is ''protecting'' Casey with this explanation. That may be or may not be. If so, give him credit for being a loyal teammate. But I don't agree with them. If Mickey says it was a curve, you can be sure of it. And here's something else you can be sure about: I don't have any reason to protect Casey, and I'm telling you it was a curve.

The fifth game of the World Series was not exactly a foregone conclusion, but there was no doubt in the minds of the Yankees that we were going to win it and the Series. Still, it was no runaway. There was a total of only ten hits in the game, six for the Yankees. Ernie "Tiny" Bonham and Whitlow Wyatt were both in top form, and Bonham was tougher. He allowed only one hit after the third inning. This was his first World Series game, and he wasn't going to let it get away.

Tiny was ready. He used to hold a heavy ball made out of lead in his pitching hand, even between innings on the days when he was pitching. He said it made the baseball feel lighter and so he was able to throw it harder, the same principal that hitters apply in swinging a leaded bat before taking the wooden one to the plate with them.

What impressed me was that Bonham had excellent control. It seemed to me that if the baseball felt that light, it would be harder for Bonham to control his pitches, but control was never a problem with him. When Dickey was going over the Dodger hitters before the start of the game, he asked Bonham, "Ernie, are you comfortable with the way we want to pitch to their hitters?"

Tiny said, "Bill, I'll never remember any of this stuff. Just put your glove where you want me to throw it and I'll throw it there." With all the pressure of that game, he walked only two batters.

Gordon singled home Dickey in the second inning with what proved to be the winning run, and I hit a home run in the fifth to stretch our lead to 3–1. That meant the Dodgers couldn't play for one run. If they got a man on base, it wouldn't do them any good to try to bunt him into scoring position and then get him in with a base hit. They needed two runs now.

Bonham never gave them the chance for any. By the eighth inning, the banner that had been draped over the center-field wall of Ebbets Field since the start of the third game was gone.

There was a flurry of extracurricular activity right after my home run. Wyatt came in with a couple of pitches uncomfortably close to DiMaggio's head. Then he popped out to Reiser in center field.

As he was trotting back across the infield toward our dugout, he let Wyatt know that there wasn't any reason to be low-bridging him with his pitches—and reminded him that "this Series isn't over yet." Wyatt quickly told him that if he couldn't take it, he shouldn't be playing the game.

Joe DiMaggio is about the last player in the history of our sport who would deserve that kind of a comment. Before we knew it, the two were headed for each other. At that point, as usual, players from both teams flocked onto the field. And, again as usual, nothing happened. After the game, Wyatt said he liked Joe and tried to downplay the incident.

Joe was a little more blunt. James P. Dawson of the New York Times quoted Joe the next morning as saying in our dressing room, "I was just waiting for him to throw the first punch."

Mickey Owen kept drawing attention to himself, whether he wanted or not. When he came to bat for the first time, a nice thing happened. The Brooklyn fans gave him a warm round of applause. When I drew a walk early in the game, believe it or not, the ball got away from Mickey. Unlike the day before, no harm was done.

"The Mickey Owen play" is the story of that World Series, and it has become one of the most famous plays in Series history. I get my picture in the paper every year—striking out. But the real factor in our victory that year was our pitching, just as it was in other years. Our pitchers held the Dodgers to an average of only six hits a game. Their team batting average was only .182, sixty-five points below ours.

We didn't care what the reasons were. We knew only that we had beaten Durocher's team and its aggressive, hell-bent style of play.

In our dressing room, we whooped it up again, starting with our now-traditional rendition of "Roll Out the Barrel" under the direction of Maestro Art Fletcher. Earle Combs let out a blood-curdling scream of "Y-i-i-p-p-p-e-e-e!" Selkirk and Crosetti were hooting and hollering, and Bill Dickey was joining in the festivities with all of his catching gear still on—chest protector, shin guards, even his mask. There were towels flying through the air and punches and slaps all around, including a few for my home run.

Bonham was jubilant in his triumph. McCarthy gave him two more World Series starts, one in 1942 and his third in '43, but he lost them both.

Hugh Casey was anything but jubilant. He threatened to quit the game to operate a chain of gas stations in Atlanta. He said in the Brooklyn dressing room that Larry MacPhail promised him a raise if he pitched well in '41. "I think I had a pretty good season," he told reporters, "and what I want to talk about now is more cash for 1941, not for next year. If I don't get it, I'm going to take the job that's been offered me and quit baseball."

Maybe he got more money or maybe he just recovered from his disappointment and frustration, or both, but Hugh pitched in the major leagues until 1949.

Ed Barrow came into the clubhouse and congratulated all of us, and told McCarthy it was his first visit of the year "to your clubhouse." McCarthy was already well aware of that. Durocher, still wearing his sweatshirt, was nice enough to come over and congratulate us. Later, in the Dodger dressing room, he told reporters, "They played five games without making a mistake." I thought that said it all.

One reason for our mistake-free baseball was that we were bearing down so hard in our determination to beat Durocher. Of all the World Series championships that I was part of with the Yankees, 1941 was by far the sweetest. Every one of us felt that way.

The *Brooklyn Eagle* expressed another opinion. In a column that stretched across all eight columns of its front page, the *Eagle* published a headline that became the annual slogan of Dodger fans everywhere for years to come:

WAIT TILL NEXT YEAR!

The Changing of the Guard

The start of the war changed a lot of things as 1941 turned into 1942, but it didn't change management's treatment of players.

I felt sorry for Joe DiMaggio. After all he did for the Yankees, all the people he attracted to Yankee Stadium and every other park in the league and all the money he made for the organization, Ed Barrow asked him to take a pay cut. Worse than that, he stooped to a new low when he did it. He told Joe, "You ought to be happy you're not in the army making $21 a month."

What made me feel even worse was that Joe wasn't the only Yankee being treated that way. Ruffing, Dickey, Gordon, and Keller were getting that same statement, and they all rebelled. Barrow wanted all of them to sign for '42 without a raise, and Dickey and Ruffing were even asked to take cuts. Eventually, Keller and Gordon received small raises, and Dickey and Ruffing were able to avoid cuts.

Joe signed a contract for $43,750 for the 1942 season, but he wasn't happy about it. Looking back over his career years later, the bitterness was still there. He said, "I don't think anything ever burned me up as much as that did."

Barrow was a real tyrant. He pulled that same stuff on a lot of the players, telling them how grateful they should feel about not being in the army on $21 a month, but I never read in the papers that he cut his own salary.

We opened the 1942 season in Washington on April 14, and the atmosphere of wartime Washington was already noticeable. President Roosevelt didn't throw out the traditional first ball. He was too busy in the Oval Office running the war, so his vice-president, Henry Wallace, performed the honors.

On the front page of the *Washington Post* there was a story about a "blackout test" scheduled for that night sometime between 9:00 and 11:30. Communities all over America were conducting these tests as a rehearsal for blacking out our cities in the event of an enemy attack by air. People were told that when the sirens sounded, pedestrians should head for the nearest shelter and "DON'T try to cross the street."

The reason was simple: The streets would be dark, and drivers of emergency vehicles, with their headlights dimmed by black paint over the top half, might not see you. Motorists were told to "pull over to the curb and park . . . Leave the ignition keys in your car; it can't be stolen, as only emergency vehicles are allowed to move." There was no explanation as to why you should leave the keys in your car in the first place.

On the sports page, Shirley Povich, one of the most respected baseball writers in America that year and every year, captured the significance of this particular Opening Day:

Blessed by a nod from the White House in a war-torn world, Major League baseball moves in again on the Nation's proceedings at 3 o'clock this afternoon.

That "nod from the White House" was the historic "green light letter" from Roosevelt to Landis encouraging the major leagues to play ball in 1942 even in the face of all the difficulties, such as the loss of players to military service and travel complications caused when teams would have to defer to the wartime priorities of others.

Roosevelt said he felt the American people would need baseball as one of their main sources of entertainment. In his letter to Landis in January, FDR wrote, "I honestly feel that it would be best for the country to keep baseball going."

Next to Povich's article about the game coming up that afternoon was a story saying Pete Reiser of the Dodgers had been classified 1-A by his draft board in St. Louis, event though he had just been married and was also supporting his mother, father, four sisters, and one brother.

Out at Griffith Stadium, the fans lined up for seven-thousand bleacher seats at fifty-five cents each. After they sat down on the long wooden benches of the bleachers along the Fifth Street side of the ball park, they saw Vice-President Wallace uncork one of the longest throws in the history of Washington's Presidential Openers, dating back to when William Howard Taft did it for the first time in 1910. One of our first basemen, Buddy Hassett, caught it and got Wallace's autograph on it.

History was repeating itself. In 1918, the president, Woodrow Wilson, another avid baseball fan, was too busy in the Oval Office running the war, so he sent a District of Columbia commissioner.

In the vice-presidential party on the first-base side next to the Senators' dugout were Senator Alben Barkley of Kentucky, the senate majority leader; Senator Charles McNary of Oregon; Senator Tom Connally of Texas, the chairman of the Foreign Affairs Committee, and Representative Joe Martin of Massachusetts, chairman of the Republican National Committee.

Americans proved FDR right that day as 190,775 of them flocked to the eight major-league ballparks, ready for the start of another baseball season and equally eager to forget the horrors of war for as long as they were inside the insulation of their stadium.

The Army Band marched to Griffith Stadium's flagpole in center field, along with Wallace and the president of the American League, Will Harridge, to raise the American flag and play the National Anthem. Below the Stars and Stripes was another. It said:

BUY DEFENSE BONDS

We started the 1942 season the way we ended '41, with a win.

The Senators started it the way they had started every season since 1937, with a loss. Charley Ruffing defeated Sid Hudson of the Senators, and he did it the sure way. He didn't allow a run. Red pitched a three-hitter, at the age of thirty-seven, and we began our defense of the American League pennant and our World Series championship with a 7–0 victory. I was able to contribute with a single and double. Joe D. got a single.

Not every Yankee was as lucky as we were. On the day we defeated the Senators in the season's opening game, Johnny Sturm, our first baseman in 1941, was involved in a tractor accident at Jefferson Barracks, Missouri, where the army sent him after he was drafted over the winter. He lost the first two joints of his right index finger. That was the bad news. The good news was that Johnny was left-handed.

We swept the three-game series from Washington and headed back to New York to open our home season on April 17. At Yankee Stadium, the wartime patriotism was showing itself as prominently as in Washington. James P. Dawson described it the next morning in the *Times*:

> Banners floated from on high. Flags draped the field boxes. The dugouts of the Yankees and the Boston Red Sox were covered in red, white and blue.

There were 1,243 servicemen in the crowd of 30,308 fans, along with two ladies who enjoyed special places in the New York baseball community: Mrs. Lou Gehrig and Mrs. John McGraw. The Seventh Regiment Band marched to the flag pole in the outfield with Mayor La Guardia and the managers of the two teams, Joe McCarthy and Joe Cronin. Together they raised the American flag and then our 1941 American League pennant. Judge Landis awarded us our World Series rings, the mayor threw out the first ball to Bill Dickey, and we were ready to begin our 1942 home season.

Tiny Bonham was pitching for us against one Thomas William Oscar Judd, a left-hander from Canada who was trying to make the grade as a thirty-four-year-old rookie, prompting some of us to wonder if the wartime manpower shortage was already that bad. Judd showed he belonged. We beat him, but the score was 1–0. I scored the only run after getting a single.

You couldn't completely forget that there was a war on, and the public was always quick to remind you about it. One of the umpires, Bill Summers, picked up a foul ball and instinctively put it in his pocket for use later. The fans, remembering that they were being asked to throw all foul balls back onto the field so they could be sent to our military camps, let Summers have it with a Bronx cheer. Summers, thus reminded, gave the ball to the home team to be included in the next shipment to our GIs.

In the paper the next day, there was an announcement from the government's Food Requirements Committee: Meat would be rationed, beginning in four months. Every American would be limited to two and a half pounds per week.

We were a solid team again, just as in '41. With the exception of Sturm, we had been undamaged so far by the military draft. That changed during the season and kept on changing throughout every season and every winter. The teams that were going to be winning pennants and the World Series during the war were not necessarily going to be those with the best organizations; they were going to be those with the most 4-Fs, those men who were too young, too old, or physically unfit for military duty.

This wasn't the case yet, even though the first stars had already marched off to war. Bob Feller, the biggest and highest-paid pitching name in baseball, voluntarily signed up two days after Pearl Harbor and joined the navy, even though he was exempt as the sole support of his mother, his dying father, and his teenage sister.

Feller was asked later why he didn't enjoy his life as a major-league star for as long as he could, especially with his 3-C draft deferment. In the feeling of national support that typified those times, Bob said, "Because we needed heroes—fast."

We still had the core of our team, and with it we were able to beat out the Red Sox again, this year by nine games. We led both leagues in runs and the American League in home runs, fielding, and making double plays. Our pitchers maintained their excellence, leading the league in complete games, shutouts, saves, and earned run average. Tiny Bonham led the league in shutouts and complete games and was second to Boston's Tex Hughson in wins with 21.

Joe Gordon was one of the biggest stars in baseball that year. The one we called "Flash" won the American League Most Valuable Player Award by hitting .322, fourth highest in the league.

DiMag had another banner year. He hit .305 and was fifth in the league in homers, second in runs batted in, and second in runs scored, with his brother Dom right behind him. Rizzuto and Gordon led their positions in making double plays.

The first signs of the wartime "manpower shortage" flared up when our catcher, Buddy Rosar, left the team to go home to Buffalo so he could take the examination to become a policeman. We needed a starting catcher, so Ed Barrow scrambled around and came up with Rollie Hemsley, one of the best in the business in his prime, who was between teams at the moment.

Barrow found Rollie in St. Louis, and Hemsley traveled on an all-night train and arrived at Yankee Stadium barely in time for the first game. He caught both ends of a Sunday doubleheader on a hot summer day at the age of thirty-five. Near the end of the second game, McCarthy, full of admiration and gratitude for the way Rollie stepped right in, told him on his last at bat of the day to take it easy—and not to worry about running hard down the first-base line.

It must be the only time Joe McCarthy said that to any player, but he could see that Rollie was out of gas from catching two games in New York's blistering, sticky summer weather at his age. So what does Rollie do? He lays a bunt down the third-base line. He was still playing his hardest.

Rollie stayed with the Yankees for two more seasons. But not Rosar. Barrow traded him to Cleveland that December.

For me it was an eventful year, much more than my .267 batting average would indicate. My knee behaved itself again, so I was able to play in 127 games and get 30 doubles, 5 triples, and 13 home runs. I made the American League All-Star team—and before the season was over I was wearing a different uniform.

By the time of the All-Star Game at the Polo Grounds on July 6, we were leading the Red Sox by four games. The American League went right to work in that game, with three runs in the first inning off Mort Cooper of the Cardinals.

Lou Boudreau of the Indians hit a home run. I doubled, and Rudy York scored us both with another homer. We won it, 3–1, with the only National League run coming on a home run by Mickey Owen, who was having more fun than when I saw him the previous October.

I caught a fly ball in right field from Ernie Lombardi for the last out of the game—and not a moment too soon. The minute the game ended, the Polo Grounds went pitch black. New York was conducting a blackout drill.

There was a special arrangement that year because of the war. We played two All-Star Games, something that had never been done before. We took an overnight train to Cleveland right after the game in the Polo Grounds and played a game the next night under the Indians' new lights against a team of service All-Stars, mostly major-leaguers, managed by Mickey Cochrane.

The game was the idea of the Baseball Writers' Association of America, to raise funds for the war effort. There was a parade, and it was declared a holiday in Cleveland so the fans could enjoy the day and the opportunity to see their hometown hero, Bob Feller, back on the pitcher's mound at Municipal Stadium.

In addition to "Rapid Robert," Cochrane's team had Green-berg, Johnny Berardino, Cecil Travis, Buddy Lewis, and others, but we won it anyhow, 5–0. The two games raised a total of $100,000 for baseballs and bats for the GIs, plus $60,000 to help the early widows and orphans of America's fighting men. That's a lot of money, and it was a lot more almost fifty years ago.

Two more events associated with the war occurred the next month. Babe Ruth faced Walter Johnson, the man many consider the greatest pitcher of all time, in an exhibition before a game between the Senators and us at Yankee Stadium on August 23.

It was supposed to be a duel between these two all-time greats. There were 69,136 fans in the stands, and they saw the Babe hit a "home run" off Johnson. Part of the proceeds went to the Army and Navy Relief Fund again.

Eight days later, I was ordered to report immediately for duty in the Coast Guard. When they said "immediately" in that war, they weren't kidding. I was on my way the next day.

I did allow myself the luxury of playing one final day with the Yankees, on Sunday, August 30. There were 49,221 fans in Yan-kee Stadium for a doubleheader with the Tigers. We won both games 7–1 and 4–3, as the team continued on its way to another World Series.

I singled in the first game, and in the second game I had a single and a double by the time I came to bat in the eighth inning for the last time. Paul "Dizzy" Trout was pitching for the Tigers.

As I stepped into the batter's box and prepared to hit, the public address announcer told the crowd:

> Ladies and Gentlemen, Tommy Henrich has been ordered to report for active duty with the Coast Guard. This is his last appearance in a Yankee uniform until the war is over.

With that, the crowd "rose as one to accord Tommy Henrich a thunderous ovation," in the words of the next day's newspaper article. I stepped in and waited for Trout's first pitch, as the ovation continued. It was one of the most touching salutes I've ever received. I wasn't sure I deserved all of it. I was just going into the service like everyone else. That made it even more touching. The start of the war made us appreciate each other.

I called out to Dizzy to go ahead and pitch, but he shook his head and just stood on the mound while the noise went on. He called in to me, "Not yet, Tommy. This kind of moment happens only once in a lifetime. Take time to enjoy it."

Dizzy was giving me good advice. Besides, if those people wanted to say thank you for that long, who was I to tell them when to stop? It was nice of Dizzy to say that. When the crowd stopped its cheering, I got another hit off him, because he was nice enough to give me a fastball.

I found out quickly that I was not essential to the success of the New York Yankees. With me in the service, they kept on winning and found themselves in the 1942 World Series against the St. Louis Cardinals, who beat out the Dodgers by two games. The Cards were as good as we were that year. They won 106 games to Brooklyn's 104 and our 103.

To many Yankees, including me, the Cardinals were the second team in the league we'd like to beat in the World Series, next to the Dodgers. Disliking the Cardinals in the 1930s and early '40s was easy to do because of the way Branch Rickey and Sam Breadon treated their players.

On top of that, the Cards were an aggressive team like Brooklyn. They told you they were going to run you out of the stadium, and they usually did. They had classy guys like Terry Moore, who made no secret that he wanted to beat us. He was an outstanding center fielder, and that attitude just made me respect him more.

He was willing to say hello to us when both teams started spring training each year in St. Petersburg, and he was willing to say goodbye in the fall. In between times, he'd rather just go out onto the field and try to beat you. I liked that.

But we wanted to defeat them for the same reason that Cardinals like Moore wanted to beat us. If you were to ask me which team I'd rather lose to in the World Series in those years, I'd have to say it was a tossup.

Enos Slaughter was their leader. He had the National League's second highest average, with .318 behind Lombardi's .330. Stan Musial, playing his first full season, showed immediately that he was going to be a star for many years by hitting .315, the league's third best average. Mort Cooper and Johnny Beazley finished one-two as the league's best pitchers. Mort won the ERA championship and won the most games—22, one more than Beazley.

The World Series got off to the kind of start people now expected of the Yankees. As I went through basic training with the Coast Guard, my old teammates went to Sportsman's Park in St. Louis and won the first game, 7–4, behind good ol' Charley Ruffing, who didn't allow a hit until there were two outs in the eighth inning. He became the first pitcher in history to win seven World Series games.

But something happened that was a tipoff that things may not have been the way they appeared on the surface. New York had a comfortable lead, 7–0, by the ninth inning, but by the end of the game my team was hanging on. The Cardinals scored four runs in the bottom of the ninth. It was the only game the Yankees won.

Charlie Keller hit a two-run homer in the eighth inning of the second game to tie the score, but the Cards won it when Slaughter doubled and Musial singled him home. Then Slaughter, the one from Roxboro, North Carolina, who was called "Country," saved the victory by throwing out a pinch-runner, Tuck Stainback, when he tried to go from first to third on a single in the ninth.

When the Series shifted to Yankee Stadium, the Cardinals were not intimidated. Ernie White handed New York its first World Series shutout defeat since 1926, a five-hitter. They came right back in the fourth game and won again in a battle of big innings. The Cardinals scored six runs in the fourth, and the Yanks got five in the sixth. It was a 6–6 game going into the seventh, when the Cardinals scored two more runs on a single by Walker Cooper, the other half of the Cardinals' brother battery, to score Slaughter, and a long fly ball by their shortstop, Marty Marion, to score Musial.

By the time the fifth game started, with the Series still being played in New York, the country was alert that an upset victory by the Cardinals was more than just a possibility—it was now likely. The two teams battled even into the ninth inning, 2–2. But the St. Louis third baseman, Whitey Kurowski, hit a two-run homer to win everything for the Cardinals. It was the first World Series defeat for the Yankees in their last nine appearances, and it came at the hands of the same team; the Cardinals had beat them in 1926, when Lou Gehrig was in his second full season and Calvin Coolidge was president.

In the dressing room after their defeat, Lefty Gomez pierced the disappointment by telling his teammates that the victory party that year would be held at the Horn & Hardart automat.

Who was leaving for the armed forces was as big a part of our conversations as who was winning the pennant or the World Series. In the offseason, Feller, Greenberg, Travis, Berardino, Lewis, the first major leaguer drafted—Hugh Mulcahy—and I were joined in the service by Joe DiMaggio, Cookie Lavagetto, Billy Cox, Fred Hutchinson, and others. The Red Sox were among the teams hardest hit. Ted Williams, Dom DiMaggio, and Johnny Pesky all enlisted in the service after the '42 season.

That was just the first full year of the war. By its end in 1945, more than five-hundred major-league players and four-thousand minor leaguers had joined the armed forces. DiMag told a writer after it was all over, "I thought it would never end. Those years never seemed to move at all."

The war cost some more dearly than others. All of us were young men in our twenties working in a profession that almost always lasts only into your thirties. The war was a disaster to our hopes for long careers. Besides, there were two things no one knew, not even President Roosevelt: how long the war would last, and who was going to be killed.

We didn't sit around and mope. Everyone in every profession was being dealt a serious blow, not just baseball players. The mood of Americans wasn't to feel sorry for you if you had to go into the military, regardless of your circumstances. Every young man was expected to be in the service. Those who weren't were followed by whispers asking, "Why isn't he in uniform?"

So we did what all Americans were doing—we adjusted. We lived our lives as normally as possible while preparing for our departures. We sang the hit songs like "I've Got a Gal in Kalamazoo," and we saw Jimmy Cagney in the 1942 performance that won him the Academy Award, *Yankee Doodle Dandy*.

When our time came, some of us paid a different price than others. Dom DiMaggio, for example, didn't make it into Baseball's Hall of Fame, and his enlistment in the navy to serve during the war probably is the reason. The justification given is that he "didn't play long enough." He played ten years, and it would have been thirteen without the war, and that's plenty long enough—longer than several men whose plaques line Cooperstown's walls.

Dom was another man—and that's the right word—like Bob Feller, one who didn't have to go into the service at all. His eyesight gave him a draft exemption after he flunked the army eye test. But Dom wanted to go, so he talked his way into the navy.

If he hadn't done that, he might be in the Hall of Fame today—and he should be. The Hall of Fame Committee on Baseball Veterans, the ones who choose older players who haven't been elected in their earlier years of eligibility, should think about that. What could be more appropriate at Cooperstown than to pick the golden anniversary of World War II as the time to enshrine those stars like Dom who missed two, three, or even four prime seasons to serve their country?

In effect, Dom, Charlie Keller, Phil Rizzuto, and a few others who volunteered for military duty during World War II were penalized for it by being told their careers weren't long enough.

Surely some exceptions or special considerations can be given, especially during this anniversary period, for men like Dom, Charlie, and Phil, all of whom would have played three years longer. I don't say that about myself, because I didn't have some of the numbers that others did. I'm perfectly content that I got the most out of my ability and was a devoted team player who achieved as much as possible for my team first and myself second. Hall of Fame? I don't think so; not in my case.

Mickey Owen, my old pal from my 1941 World Series strikeout, disagrees. He has developed and analyzed some intriguing data on the subject, and in his public appearances he very charitably pushes for my election, and that of others, into the Hall of Fame, based on his own formula for determining the most productive offensive players of all time.

Mickey must be the world's foremost authority on the Baseball Encyclopedia. That reference work is now the size of the Manhattan telephone directory, but Mickey lifts it into his lap every night and pores through it to develop statistical analyses on all sorts of subjects to illustrate key points about baseball's players and teams over the generations.

By allocating one point each for a player's total bases, runs scored, runs batted in, bases on balls and stolen bases, adding bonus points for extra base hits, and dividing that total by the number of lifetime at-bats, Mickey has determined the most productive hitters, a relevant list since membership in the Hall of Fame, except for pitchers of course, is based so heavily on a player's hitting.

Under the Owen formula, the most productive hitter in history is Babe Ruth, with a grade of 1.468. Ted Williams is second with 1.38, just ahead of Lou Gehrig's 1.318.

Mickey's formula reveals that of the thirty-three most productive players, from Ruth to Chuck Klein, twenty-eight are in the Hall of Fame. The five who are not are Charlie Keller, who holds ninth place on Mickey's list; Dick Allen, who finished at the top of various offensive departments 12 times in 15 years in the 1960s and '70s; Ken Williams, with a .319 average from 1915 through 1929 and American League championships in home runs, runs batted in and slugging average; Bob Johnson, with a .296 average for 13 seasons in the '30s and '40s, plus more than 20 home runs in each of his first nine years and a career average of almost 100 RBIs a year, and myself in the 26th spot.

Conversely, fourteen players in the Hall of Fame do not finish in the top thirty names on the Owen honor roll, including such acknowledged greats as Charlie Gehringer, Al Kaline, Joe Cronin, Ernie Banks and even Honus Wagner.

But Dom DiMaggio, a man who played ten years in the majors and was voted to the American League All-Star team eight times? Charlie Keller, one of the most feared hitters of his time? Phil Rizzuto, the American League's Most Valuable Player one year and runnerup another, who has the seventh most career hits in the World Series, the fourth most walks, and the tenth most runs? Yes. Acknowledge that they answered the call to duty when this nation was at war, and then give them what they deserve: induction into the Baseball Hall of Fame.

Some of us were lucky. We were assigned to stateside duties and spared the dangers and ordeals of combat. Others, like Bob Feller, were legitimate heroes. Bob was assigned to the Navy's physical fitness program under former heavyweight boxing champion Gene Tunney, but the same man who could have kept on pitching because of his father's illness and his family's dependence on him requested a transfer to gunnery school.

After his training, Bob became chief of a gun crew aboard a battleship, the *U.S.S. Alabama*, in the North Atlantic and later in the South Pacific. In command of twenty-four men, he participated in eight invasions including Iwo Jima and Okinawa and was gone from his family and his career for almost four years, not returning until midsummer of 1945.

Even today Bob won't let you describe him in hero terms. "The only heroes," he says, "were the ones who didn't come back."

When Tommy Comes Marching Home

When the war ended and we were able to report to spring training for the start of the 1946 season, we returned to our old routine, but the war made it new again. All those things we took for granted before Pearl Harbor were returning, and we knew to be grateful for them.

You could buy a new car again, if you didn't mind spending almost two thousand dollars for one. Detroit hadn't turned out a new car since 1942 because its plants were producing planes, ships, and tanks. Now you could replace your prewar car with a new model from the same lineup of makes that we had before the war — Ford, Chevy, Chrysler, Buick, and some that aren't around any more, like Packard, Nash, and Hudson — or with one of the "cars of the future," the Tucker, Kaiser, and Frazier. Fortunately for us, our futures were longer than theirs.

Detroit was doing its best to make automobiles for the car-hungry public. At the beginning of the year it was announced that the industry would produce between 2.4 million and 3.3 million new cars, depending on the availability of materials.

Another form of transportation was also enjoying a comeback. Civilian airlines were ready to attract the public with advances in air travel—at reasonable fares. American Airlines was proudly advertising its "new four-engine flagship flights" on DC-4 airliners that could hold as many as fifty passengers on its New York–Washington route. The air fare was $10.05.

Rationing was a thing of the past. You could buy all the meat, sugar, butter, and shoes for yourself and gasoline for your car that you wanted. Best of all, people were back at their old jobs, doing what they wanted for a living. These were, as the title of that year's Oscar-winning movie said, *The Best Years of Our Lives.*

For those of us who played baseball for a living, Opening Day showed just how glad some of our returning players were to be back, and just how good they were at being able to pick up where they left off.

Bob Feller, who was discharged from the navy late in the 1945 season after three years and eight months of military duty, pitched a three-hitter against the Chicago White Sox and shut them out, 1–0. Ted Williams hit the longest home run in Washington in fifteen years as the Red Sox beat the Senators, 6–3. Hank Greenberg, who came home after four years of army duty in time to hit a grand-slam home run that won the 1945 pennant for the Tigers, hit a home run that beat the St. Louis Browns, 2–1. Billy Herman of the Brooklyn Dodgers, thirty-six years old, went 4-for-5 in his first game since 1943. Ken Heintzelman of the Pittsburgh Pirates, in relief, helped his team beat the St. Louis Cardinals and picked up the win.

The service veterans who came home to the Yankees did all right on Opening Day, too. Spud Chandler, now thirty-eight, shut out the A's, 5–0, in front of 37,472 fans at Philadelphia's Shibe Park. Joe D. hit a two-run homer, Bill Dickey hit a single and a double, and I was able to get a double. Three of our other returning veterans, Phil Rizzuto, Charlie Keller, and Joe Gordon, were out of the lineup recovering from nagging injuries, one of the risks of returning to spring training after being in the armed forces for so long.

In Washington, the Presidential Opener was reinstituted. Harry

Truman, in his first full year as president after the death of FDR, surprised everyone by throwing out the first ball left-handed, just to fool the White house press corps. In Philadelphia, they didn't have the president, the governor, or the mayor. They had an army private, Roy Heikiner of Waskish, Michigan, a surgery patient at Valley Forge Army Hospital. He was there with a nurse at his side as he tossed out the first ball to our former teammate, Buddy Rosar.

We weren't able to maintain our Opening Day success over the course of the season, and 1946 became the kind of year you don't associate with the New York Yankees. We didn't win the pennant, and we didn't even come in second. We were behind the Red Sox, who got off to a phenomenal start and continued their pace, and Detroit. To make matters even more un-Yankee, we had dissension both on the field and in the front office.

Larry MacPhail had joined the Yankees after serving as a major in the army. He eased Ed Barrow out of his job, and the friction hurt us. MacPhail and McCarthy simply never got along. Joe was gone as our manager after only thirty-five games. MacPhail said he fired him. Joe said he quit.

Regardless, Joe was gone, and I was crushed. All of us were in a state of shock. McCarthy was the only manager many of us had ever played for in the big leagues. I may have been more disappointed than any other player on our team because of my unlimited respect for him and confidence in him as our leader and strategist.

Besides, it was exactly the wrong time to lose Joe McCarthy. No manager ever handled a team or its individual players better in troubled times than McCarthy did, and these were definitely troubled times. We needed his mother-hen understanding and patience as we struggled to fight our way through this thing, and now he wasn't there.

Bill Dickey took over as our manager, and that didn't solve a thing. Dickey didn't want the job, and he was one of the boys for so many years it was impossible for him to transform himself overnight into an authoritarian figure over the same men who were his buddies only the day before.

It showed in one particular incident, when he gave DiMaggio the bunt sign. Joe bunted, but he didn't like it. He felt, and understandably, that his value to our team wasn't in laying down a bunt. He was one of the most productive hitters in the history of baseball, so the prevailing thinking was that you don't take the bat out of the hands of Joe DiMaggio, of all people, by making him bunt. But he laid down that bunt, even though it had to hurt his pride, because he was a loyal team man, and because he didn't want to do anything to get in the way of Bill's chances to succeed as our manager.

Joe's dedication didn't help. After only 105 games as our skipper, Bill was gone, too, replaced by Johnny Neun as interim manager for our final 14 games.

Too many of us didn't really get on track in 1946. It took us longer to chip off the rust from the war than it did the Red Sox. The first three hitters in Boston's batting order—Dom DiMaggio, Johnny Pesky, and Ted Williams—were among the top five hitters in the league. Williams finally won the Most Valuable Player Award, for hitting .342 with 38 home runs and 123 runs batted in. DiMaggio hit .316 and Pesky's average was .335.

Contrast that to our performances. I hit .251, and so did our third baseman, Snuffy Stirnweiss. Rizzuto hit .257. Our first baseman, Nick Etten, had a .232 average, and Joe Gordon's dropped almost out of sight to .210. Keller hit .275, but much of that was accomplished early in the year. His performance slipped in the second half because, as he put it, "I still had my sea legs" from his duty aboard ship in the war.

We didn't have a .300 hitter on the ball club. A new name, Aaron Robinson, came closest with .297 while doing most of our catching. Joe D. had our second highest average, .290. When a team has three of the top five hitters in the league, and a second team—Detroit—has Hank Greenberg leading the major leagues with 44 home runs and George Kell hitting .327 and Roy Cullenbine at .335, and a third team doesn't have one .300 hitter, you can figure out which team will finish in third place.

Some of us—although obviously not Dom DiMaggio, Pesky, Williams, Greenberg, Kell, or the other leading hitters in the American League that year—were having trouble with something Bob Feller brought back from the war. It was as about as welcome as another notice from the draft board. It was the slider.

I found out later that Feller practiced it onboard ship in the

Pacific when he wasn't ducking bullets or bombs or firing rounds on the *U.S.S. Alabama*.

When he was rotated back to the States in early 1945 after more than two years of overseas duty, he was stationed at Great Lakes Naval Training Center near Chicago, where he managed the base team and was its top pitcher. Against other navy teams with other big-league players, Bob was able to keep refining his slider, a pitch that was almost nonexistent at that time.

When we returned to baseball in 1946, there was Feller, throwing this thing that looks like a fastball—until it's right on top of you. It has almost the same speed, but it doesn't break until the last minute, when it's only a few feet in front of the plate. It doesn't have the big trajectory that a curveball does. Instead, at the last second it darts six or eight inches away from a right-handed hitter when thrown by a right-handed pitcher. When you commit yourself to swing, you swear you're swinging at a fastball. Then it takes that little darting action and you're all messed up.

To this day I can't tell anybody how to hit the slider, because I don't know myself. I can give you this much of a tip, though: Don't try to pull it. Go with the pitch wherever it is just before you make contact. It's hard enough to hit as it is. Trying to pull the ball by getting your arms and body around early will only reduce your chances from slim to none.

You have to make adjustments in every phase of hitting, and hitting the slider where it's pitched instead of trying to pull it is the adjustment you have to make on that particular pitch. However, I have to confess that we didn't make that adjustment. Joe D. never changed anything in his swing, and he never hit the slider well. I was just as dumb. The same pitch gave me trouble, and for the same reason. I just didn't adjust as well as I should have.

I spent my whole career making a living off the fastball. If Feller and anybody else wanted to start throwing sliders, it was just one more pitch I'd let go while waiting for the fastball. Sooner or later, I knew they had to throw their high, hard one. But other hitters weren't that patient, and patience is another essential ingredient in successful hitting. They kept going after that slider, and it kept darting away from them—and the batting averages of many pre-war players began to drop in the postwar years.

I was talking hitting with Paul Waner after my retirement as a player, and I couldn't have found a better authority on the subject. Paul, "Big Poison," is in the Hall of Fame with a .333 average for twenty seasons, the ninth most doubles, the tenth most triples and three National League batting championships with the Pirates in the 1920s and '30s.

When I asked him the secret of such success over twenty years, he said, "You have to hit the ball with a seven-degree downward swing. That gives you a better chance to hit a line drive. Pick out the top half of the ball."

A seven-degree downward swing? I said, "Wait a minute. What did the ball look like to you when you were hitting?"

He told me, "I had funny eyes. I didn't see well in the outfield, but at home plate, the closer the ball got to me, the bigger it got. By the time it reached the plate, it looked as big as a grapefruit."

I laughed and told him, "Now I know why I couldn't pick out the top half of that *aspirin tablet* I saw coming toward me."

As if all of this didn't add up to enough trouble for the Yankees, there was that upheaval in the front office. Barrow was eased out of his position. One of the first tipoffs to the reporters was when they began to see MacPhail occupying Barrow's box seat in the mezzanine. Later events proved that MacPhail, even though he was one of the owners, was just as vulnerable as Barrow. A year later, MacPhail was also gone.

While the power struggle was going on upstairs, we were adding some players who were going to prove instrumental in the success that would come our way again beginning the next season: Bobby Brown, Vic Raschi, and Tommy Byrne.

Of the three, Brown was by far the most widely publicized. The writers called him "the Golden Boy" because he had blond hair and baseball people said he had all the makings of a future star. As the saying goes, he was his father's son, the product of dad's influence, help, and guidance.

His father, Billy Brown, had been a semi-pro player around New Jersey. His ambition, like every other amateur baseball player's, was to make it to the big leagues. He didn't, but he was determined that his son would have every chance. For starters, he gave Bobby a baseball bat when the boy was five years old. Then he moved the family to California so his son could play baseball every day all year long in the warm temperatures. In the meantime, Billy became a successful San Francisco businessman.

Playing baseball every day is exactly what Bobby did. He developed so well both physically and as a player that by the time he was thirteen he was able to participate in a week-long tryout camp held by the Newark Bears for 150 professional prospects. The Bears cut the number to 40 for the final few days. Bobby made the cut.

When he was fifteen he was good enough for his father to take a bold step. He escorted his son around the major leagues and showed off Bobby's talents, including his textbook batting stroke, to every one of the sixteen teams.

The elder Brown was no shrinking violet when it came to assessing his son's talents or what he was worth. The owner of the Giants, Horace Stoneham, was impressed enough to ask Mr. Brown what he thought Bobby was worth, and Billy Brown didn't hesitate. He told him $60,000, far higher than the going rate for fifteen-year-olds in 1946.

Stoneham said, "That's ridiculous. The kid has never played a game of professional baseball."

Fifteen of the sixteen teams made offers for Bobby. When the father-son team arrived at Yankee Stadium for its exhibition of Bobby's abilities, especially as a hitter, Joe McCarthy told him, "Son, you're a great hitter. Don't ever let anyone change you."

Bobby, who was always polite and refined and still is today as president of the American League, said to the legendary McCarthy, "Thank you, sir. My dad will be glad to hear that."

"Did he teach you to hit that way?"

"Yes, sir."

McCarthy said, "We sure could use a man like your father around here, son."

He hit .425 for Galileo High School in San Francisco, the school that produced the DiMaggio brothers. Every major-league scout gave him the highest ratings, but the offers were for amounts in the $1,500–$3,500 range, figures that his businessman father found easy to reject. "If my boy isn't worth more than that," he said, "he'll never play major-league ball. He'll go to medical school and stay there."

He did both.

As a rookie in 1937 with two Hall of Fame immortals, first baseman Lou Gehrig (right) and manager Joe McCarthy.

We begin practice after arriving at Wrigley Field in Chicago to play the Cubs in the 1938 World Series. From left, Red Ruffing, Joe Gordon, George Selkirk, Bill Dickey, Lou Gehrig, Joe DiMaggio, myself, Red Rolfe, and Frank Crosetti. We won the Series in four straight, outscoring the Cubs 22-9. (UPI/Bettmann News photo)

Celebrating in Philadelphia's Shibe Park in 1939 after hitting twelve home runs in a doubleheader against the A's. From left, George Selkirk, myself, Babe Dahlgren, Joe Gordon, Joe DiMaggio, and Bill Dickey. (AP/Wide World Photo)

Johnny Sturm and I hoist Joe DiMaggio to our shoulders after he broke Wee Willie Keeler's record by hitting in his forty-fifth straight game. It happened at Yankee Stadium on July 2, 1941. Joe hit in eleven more before being stopped after fifty-six games on two sensational plays by Cleveland third baseman Ken Keltner. (UPI/Bettmann News Photos)

The most famous strikeout in World Series history—the fourth game of the 1941 World Series. Catcher Mickey Owen and I both look at the ball as he races for it. I dash for first base and umpire Larry Goetz has his right hand in the air signalling strike three, apparently ending the game. Only it wasn't over. The Dodgers were leading with two out and nobody on base when it happened. I reached base safely and we scored four runs. We won the game and crushed the spirits of everyone in Brooklyn. The next day we won the Series in five games. (UPI/Bettmann News Photo)

The Yankees whoop it up in the dressing room at Brooklyn's Ebbets Field after defeating the Dodgers in the '41 World Series the day after my "strikeout." Coach Art Fletcher (left) performs his traditional role of leading us in "Roll Out the Barrel." From Art's left are Gerry Priddy, Earle Combs, Phil Rizzuto, Red Rolfe, myself, and Johnny Sturm. (AP/Wide World Photo)

Our outfield for part of the dramatic 1949 pennant race against the Boston Red Sox—Charley Keller, Joe DiMaggio, and me. (UPI/Bettmann News Photo)

The historic "summer of '49" pennant race in the American League ends as I pull in a foul popup by Birdie Tebbetts, the Red Sox catcher, while second baseman Gerry Coleman stands by. Right field umpire Ed Hurley watches behind me and first base umpire Eddie Rommel straddles the foul line. One fan is already on the field and another is jumping the fence. I still have the ball among my souvenirs. (AP/Wide World News Photo)

I ran all the way home after hitting a home run off Don Newcombe in the bottom of the ninth to win the first game of the 1949 World Series against Brooklyn. Yogi Berra (8) and Bill Dickey, by then our first base coach, gave me a hero's welcome. (National Baseball Library, Cooperstown, N.Y.)

Casey Stengel leads the cheering after we won the '49 World Series in his first year as our manager. The Yankees went on to win a record five straight World Series under Casey. (National Baseball Library, Cooperstown, N.Y.)

Lefty Gomez was still making us laugh, even in retirement, when DiMag and I
appeared with him on a game show.

Being introduced to the
crowd before an Old
Timers Game at Yankee
Stadium.

We got him thanks to the work of Joe Devine, who, believe it or not, scouted Bobby's father years earlier. Devine watched Bobby's development as a seventeen-year-old pre-med student playing college ball for Stanford University. Joe told Bobby's dad that the boy was the greatest prospect he'd ever seen. The father told Devine his son wouldn't sign with any team without talking to Devine again.

Connie Mack started the bidding with an offer of a bonus of $10,000 for signing, but Bobby's father was confident that better offers were coming, so the two said no thanks to Mr. Mack. Then the war came and Bobby, who was already in the navy's accelerated V-12 college program, was reassigned from Stanford to the University of California at Los Angeles to continue his studies. At UCLA he raised his batting average twenty-five points to .450.

When the war was over, the Yankees continued their pursuit. Our new owners, Dan Topping, Del Webb, and Larry MacPhail, entertained Billy Brown at the 1945 World Series, and Topping later visited the family at its home in San Mateo.

It was no surprise, then, that Bobby showed up at our spring training camp in St. Petersburg, Florida, before the start of the 1946 season. He was twenty-one years old and still a medical student, attending Tulane University in New Orleans every off-season. The Yankees signed him for $35,000. Dan Daniel, writing in *The Sporting News,* called Brown "the most expensive college acquisition since 1941, when the Tigers paid $52,000 to get Dick Wakefield, then a sophomore at the University of Michigan."

There is even more evidence that Bobby was destined all along to be a baseball player. When he was thirteen years old and attending Maplewood Junior High School back in New Jersey, he won an essay contest. His subject was—what else?—baseball. One of the judges was Ford Frick, a New York sportswriter who later became president of the National League and commissioner of baseball.

In his judge's comments, Frick, one future league president writing about another, said, "I regard this as a remarkable piece of work for a boy of his age. He covered every position like an expert."

There was something else that Bobby covered like an expert: home plate with his baseball bat. After our careers were over, a reporter asked me who the best third baseman on our team was during my years with the Yankees. My answer was Gil McDougald. Then I told my questioner about Bobby Brown.

"Bobby couldn't run well," I said, "and he wasn't the best fielder we ever had over there, and he didn't have as good an arm as some of our other third basemen. But there was one thing Bobby Brown could do better than any other third baseman during my years as a Yankee: With a million dollars on the line, he wouldn't choke up at the plate."

In every pressure situation where I saw him as the hitter, Bobby was always the one in charge at the plate. The pitcher was the one in trouble, not Bobby. You can't teach that attitude, and you can't practice it. Either you have the attitude of a champion up there with men on base and the pennant or World Series hanging in the balance, or you don't. Bobby did.

Vic Raschi's story bore a remarkable resemblance to Bobby Brown's. Vic had three things in common with Bobby: He was a baseball prodigy, a pitcher who pursued a college education every offseason, and one of the promising newcomers of 1946.

The Yankees were scouting Vic when he was only fourteen years old. When he signed a contract with them later, it contained a provision for him to complete his college education. He graduated from the College of William and Mary in 1950 after eleven years of part-time studies.

The writers nicknamed him "the Springfield Rifle," a reference to the gun factory in his neighborhood in West Springfield, Massachusetts, when he came up to the Yankees after a high-school career as a star in baseball, basketball, football, and track. Beginning in 1947, Vic won respect from all of us as a "money player," one who could go out and get the win for his team when the chips were on the line. He did it in '47, in our historic race with the Red Sox in '49, and in other seasons as well.

Vic was up with us only long enough to win two games in '46. He spent most of the season in the Yankee farm system and was called up late in the year. "We were out of the race," he remembered, "and they told me I was starting when I got to the locker room. My hands were sweaty. I couldn't believe it when I went on the runway to the dugout and saw the stadium."

Vic won the game, and along the way he got some unofficial

help from one of the capable and reasonable umpires, Bill Summers. This was in the days when we played with only three umpires. With the bases empty, the two base umpires stood behind
first and third, but with runners on base, one of them stood between the pitcher and second base.

The game was in the late innings and there were two on. The
next thing Raschi knows, he hears a voice whispering to him that
the guy at bat couldn't hit a high fastball. Vic looks around and
it's Summers, who happened to be from Boston. He said it again,
and then he added, "We Massachusetts boys have to stick
together."

Vic went back to the minors for the first part of the '47 season,
then came to our rescue and helped to lead us to the pennant and
the World Series, but that's a story for the next chapter.

He won exactly twice as many games as he lost—132 wins
against 66 defeats—in a ten-year career. He could have been as
good a hitter as he was a pitcher. He got 112 hits in his career
and drove in 50 runs, setting the American League record for
pitchers by driving in 7 runs in a game against the Tigers. He
came up three times with the bases loaded and delivered like a
cleanup hitter each time with a two-run single, a three-run, double
and another two-run single—and he played only six innings because the Yankees won in a romp, 15–0.

Raschi pitched all but two years of his career with our team,
but he left the Yankee organization in an atmosphere of bitterness
and disappointment, something that happened in too many cases
including Stengel's and Rizzuto's.

George Weiss and Vic were rookies in the same year, Vic as a
pitcher and George as a general manager. Raschi later committed
what Weiss considered an unpardonable sin. The man who won
21 games for us in each of the first three seasons during the Yankees' feat of winning the pennant and the World Series for five
straight years from 1949 through 1953 refused to take a pay cut
after winning 13 games in '53.

While pitchers and catchers were reporting to their teams for
the start of spring training in 1954, Weiss sold Vic to the St. Louis
Cardinals for $85,000. Vic learned about it from a reporter. He
said Weiss "didn't even have the guts to call me himself. That
they didn't have the respect for me to tell me is what hurts."

Vic's biggest fan was his brother, Gene, who was an occasional visitor to our clubhouse at Yankee Stadium and went to some of our games in Boston. He could tell you everything you wanted to know about his brother's career from listening to the games and going to them in person. He was at his happiest when Vic would bring him into the clubhouse to meet all of us. It was a happy closeness between brothers, one that was nice to see, especially because Gene was blind.

Then there was Tommy Byrne. He was a left-handed pitcher. To people in baseball, that's sometimes a tipoff that he might be on the flaky side. He was.

Management gave us an attractive clubhouse after the war, and Tommy was a welcome addition to it. There were deep green leather chairs in one wing with ashtrays, thick carpeting, framed prints of hunting scenes hanging on walls painted a soft green, even a library, plus telephones and a writing desk stocked with stationery bearing the Yankee letterhead.

It couldn't be called a locker room, because there weren't any lockers. We dressed in cubicles that lined the walls in another wing. Tommy kept us loose there, and on the field too.

He was the classic eccentric left-hander, a returning GI from Baltimore who was up with the team in 1943 long enough to win two games before the war got in his career path. By '46 he was twenty-six years old. He was 0–1 in '46, but he made it big enough later to win 85 games in all with a curveball that kept him in the big leagues for thirteen seasons including 16 victories in 1955 and two 15–win years.

He also had the most walks of any pitcher in the American League for three straight seasons. He had his control problems, like many other left-handers, and they led to a conversation I had with him right in the middle of the game one day that almost made me envious of his frame of mind.

I was playing first base. Tommy kept digging himself into a hole with his walks, so the bench told me to go over and talk to him and stall so the bullpen could have time to get somebody warmed up. I went over and started a conversation that would not only buy some time for the bullpen but might also convince Byrne to bear down and pitch his way out of the jam.

I said, "Tommy, don't you think it's about time we got some-body out?"

To which he cheerfully responded, "That's a good idea, Tom. What do you suggest?"

In 1946, life in the United States was again something to be enjoyed. Eileen and I had married on July 7, 1941, and now we were living in a house I bought in Massillon as soon as I was discharged from the Coast Guard in October 1945. A couple of years later, we moved to Ridgewood, New Jersey, a New York suburb, as our year-round home to get away from the gypsy life of moving every six months at the start and finish of the baseball season. The interest rate on our mortgage was 2 percent.

We had "August's children" with us: Patricia, born on August 10, 1942; Ann, born on August 17, 1943; and Thomas David, Jr.— we call him "T.D."—born on August 3, 1945. After the war we broke the August spell. Mary Louise was born on our eleventh wedding anniversary in 1952, and Paul joined us on April 22, 1959.

While we were settling in after the war, Joe D. was getting back to normal, too. He and his pal George Solataire, a New York ticket broker, took an apartment in the Hotel Elysée on New York's East Side. Joe used to tell us that it was an eventful place, with tenants like Tallulah Bankhead the actress, Robert Ruark the columnist, and Frank Conniff, another writer.

Joe said Tallulah liked his record player and the collection of records he had with it, so she dropped in unannounced at almost any time to borrow one or the other, or both. Tallulah was one of the movie industry's biggest baseball fans, so the two became friends even though she rooted for the Giants. Joe, never a name-dropper, told us that when he had a good game, he could always count on a refreshing telegram or note from her.

There were some great shows on Broadway as the lights along the Great White Way seemed to shine brighter than ever. Betty Garrett was appearing at the National Theater on West 41st Street in *Call Me Mister*, and George Bernard Shaw's *Pygmalion* was being presented at the Barrymore on West 47th, starring Gertrude Lawrence and Raymond Massey. *Song of Norway* was at the Broadway Theater, and the circus was back at Madison Square Garden.

For moviegoers—and all baseball players are moviegoers, with so much time on our hands, especially on road trips—one of the great films of the year was *Kitty*, with Paulette Goddard and Ray Milland, at the Rivoli on Broadway at 49th. Cornell Wilde was starring in *The Bandit of Sherwood Forest* at Loew's Criterion, four blocks down from the Rivoli on Broadway at 45th.

I found some fun of my own. After the season ended and the Cardinals defeated the Red Sox in the World Series when Enos Slaughter dashed all the way home from first on Harry Walker's hit, Eileen and I returned to Massillon. I became active in the local chapter of the Society for the Preservation and Encouragement of Barber Shop Quartet Singing in America, Inc.

I was the tenor in the Massillon Tomcats quartet. We practiced twice a week at the American Legion Hall. We won the 1946 state championship with our versions of "Down by the Old Mill Stream" and "Carolina in the Morning." It made 1946 a winning year for me after all.

Eleven

"It Seems Like Old Times"

Our organization underwent so many changes in 1947 that some-one should have hung a sign on Yankee Stadium saying UNDER NEW MANAGEMENT.

That's exactly what we were. We had a new field manager, Bucky Harris, a respected baseball man who had been in our sport as player and manager since 1919. Our owners—Dan Topping, Del Webb, and Larry MacPhail—were still relatively new on the job, and by the end of the World Series MacPhail had resigned his general manager's job only one year after getting it.

We welcomed Bucky warmly. After all we had been through the year before in playing for three managers in one season, we weren't going to find anything wrong with him. And we were hoping he wouldn't find anything wrong with us.

Besides, all of us knew that Bucky was a solid baseball man, the onetime "Boy Wonder" player-manager of the Washington Senators who led them to their only World Series championship, in 1924. After Washington he managed Detroit, the Red Sox, the Senators again, and the Phillies. He was expected to bring leadership, stability, and wisdom to our managerial position, and he did. Of the three managers I played for in the big leagues—Joe McCarthy, Bucky Harris, and Casey Stengel—Bucky was the easiest to play for. That helped in 1947, but in 1948 it led to his downfall.

Bucky was the typical scrappy, hard-nosed competitor who made things happen. He was willing to do whatever it took to win as a player, and as our manager he expected us to do the same thing, just as McCarthy did. He never flinched, not as a player in the heat of combat and not as a manager making crucial decisions.

He had a story he used to tell about his first and only showdown with Ty Cobb. "I had only one brush with Cobb," he said. "He tore into second on a force play with his spikes waving in my face and yelled at me, 'Get out of my way or I'll cut you to ribbons.'

"I wasn't a big hero, but I knew I'd be a clay pigeon for every bully in the league if Cobb got me on the hip. I told him, 'Try it and I'll throw the ball down your throat.'

"Mr. Cobb gave me no further trouble."

One story especially tells you about Bucky. He was hit by a pitch in a game—always willing to "take one for the team," as the players say. It was a pivotal development, and the Senators went on to win. At dinner that evening with his wife and father-in-law, Bucky, whose real name was Stanley, was being kidded by his wife for getting hit on purpose. Her father was shocked at her reflection against Bucky's integrity and said to her, "Why, Stanley would never do such a dishonest thing."

He was a manager in the big leagues for twenty-nine years, has the third most wins, and was elected to the Hall of Fame in 1975. In 1947, he was just what the management ordered, someone who could provide us not only with baseball experience and leadership but with the stability that we needed in view of all the tensions and changes in the organization.

There were changes on the team itself, too. Aaron Robinson and a rookie, Yogi Berra, shared the duties behind the plate to replace Bill Dickey, who retired the year before. George McQuinn was acquired from the Philadelphia A's to strengthen us at first base, and on the mound we improved enormously with the acquisitions of Allie Reynolds and Frank Shea, the return from our farm system of Vic Raschi, and the explosive development of Joe Page.

Berra was the most prominent of them all, although his looks gave no hint of the greatness that awaited him. He was built like a fireplug—five-feet-seven-and-a-half, 185 pounds. Jimmy Cannon, one of the New York writers, said Yogi looked like a penguin, and Larry MacPhail said Berra reminded him of "the bottom man on an unemployed acrobatic team."

Because of his outstanding ability, and also because success in baseball is not decided on the basis of good looks, Yogi won the Most Valuable Player Award three times and was inducted into the Hall of Fame in 1972.

Yogi was the boyhood pal of Joe Garagiola in "the Hill" section of St. Louis, and the two of them yearned to become major-league baseball players. Garagiola signed with the Cardinals after Branch Rickey offered him a bonus of $500—but he offered Berra only $250. Yogi remembers something else about his conversation with Rickey: "He told me I'd never by anything more than a minor-league player."

Eventually he signed with the Yankees, after George Weiss, who was then the director of our farm system, agreed to his demand for a bonus of $500 to match Garagiola's. Yogi reflected the special Yankee pride that the rest of us always showed, but in 1947 he received a lesson on the subject from the master himself, Joe DiMaggio.

He was a "bad-ball hitter," one who swung at pitches outside the strike zone but still managed to get hits on them. He may have been influenced by his boyhood hero in St. Louis, Ducky Medwick of the Cardinals, another notorious bad-ball hitter. Phil Rizzuto said Berra hit pitches that were not just outside the strike zone but were almost outside Berra's reach: "I've seen him hit pitches that came in on the bounce. I've seen him leave his feet to hit them."

Yogi divided his time between the outfield and behind the plate in 1947. Harris thought he had too many deficiencies as a catcher to stick him back there every day, but Bucky wanted that bat in the lineup whenever he could work the rookie into our batting order, so he had Berra play the outfield in twenty-four games and catch in fifty-one.

He was in a mild slump early in '47. After popping up in one of our early games, he walked out toward the outfield for the start of the next inning, and DiMaggio saw it. Following our next turn at bat, Joe was one of the last of us to head out of the dugout and run to his position, which was rare. He was always one of the first. He went over to Berra and said, "Get moving, Yogi—start running."

Yogi started to trot onto the field. Joe trotted with him stride for stride toward the outfield. As they were running, DiMag told the rookie, "Always run out to your position. It doesn't look good when you walk. The other team may have gotten you down, but don't let them know it."

The man has a heart of gold. My very favorite story about Yogi concerns a church father-son banquet in St. Louis. The audience included a group of orphans from an orphanage supported by the church. Each son received a ball and a bat, and the kids were invited to come up and get their souvenirs autographed by Yogi.

Robert L. Burnes, the sports editor of the St. Louis Globe-Democrat, was there. He noticed that the orphans didn't get anything. Yogi noticed it, too.

He asked one of the adults running the program, "Ain't they getting anything?" The man told Berra that some bats were being sent to the home for the kids to use, and then added, "We think it's enough of a thrill for them just to be here."

Burnes wrote later that Yogi got up from the head table, walked to the corner where the table for the orphans was, and sat down and autographed their programs for them.

One of the officials at the head table called over, "Yogi, we'd like you to come back up here and say a few words."

Yogi told the whole room, "Go on with the program. I'm busy. I'm talking to some friends."

Berra and Burnes left together at the end of the evening. Yogi told him, "I'll never get over that as long as I live."

Burnes wrote, "For what he did . . . I'll always love him."

Yogi played for Casey Stengel beginning in 1949 and until the Yankee management fired Casey after the 1960 World Series, and he had Stengel's respect as an intelligent baseball man. Casey used to refer to him as "my assistant manager." Yogi deserved it. All of us knew he was smarter than the folklore that the writers built up about him. Ted Williams knew it, too. He said Berra noticed the smallest changes in the position of an opposing hitter's feet in the batter's box that escaped the attention of other catchers.

He showed his smarts right away in 1947, in a game in his hometown against the Browns. St. Louis had men on first and third when Johnny Berardino bunted toward the right of the plate on a squeeze play, but the ball went only three or four feet. Berra leaped out, scooped the ball off the ground, even before Berardino had a chance to break away from the plate, and slapped it on him in a split second. He immediately dived back toward the plate and tagged out the runner sliding in from third.

When people tell that story, they end it by quoting Yogi as saying, "I just tagged everybody in sight, including the umpire."

That's funny, but that wasn't all that happened. As soon as he got the runner coming from third, Yogi cocked his right arm and was ready to throw out Walt Judnich, the runner on first, if he hesitated before breaking for second base on the play. It was an unassisted double play, and it would have been a triple play if Judnich hadn't broken for second immediately or if he had slipped on his way.

As I was trotting in from right field at the end of the inning, I told myself that only an athlete with great skill and alertness could have made such a quick and difficult play.

My second favorite Yogi story shows how quick he was in putting people on. It happened in a radio interview with the host of a sports call-in show who wanted to play a word association game with him. The host explained it all to Yogi before air time: "I'm going to throw out a few names, and you just say the first thing that pops into your mind."

Yogi agreed.

When the broadcast began, the host said, "I'm here tonight with Yogi Berra, and we're going to play word association. I'm going to mention a name, and Yogi's just going to say the first thing that comes to mind. Okay, Yogi?"

"Okay."

"All right then, here we go. Mickey Mantle."

Yogi says, "What about him?"

Frank "Spec" Shea was another addition who knew how to win. He won 14 games for us in 1947 and lost only 5, plus winning two World Series games for us over the Dodgers, the kind of rookie year that would make any player proud.

He picked up "Spec" as a nickname because his father, a freckle-faced Irishman who played minor league baseball, was called "Speck" for his freckles. As Frank emerged as a player, they called him "Little Speck," later dropping both the "little" and the "k".

Mel Allen gave him a second nickname, "the Naugatuck Nugget," after Shea's hometown in Connecticut, and no small town was ever prouder of a native son. When he made his first start for us, so many school kids in Naugatuck played hookey they had to call off exams.

Paul Krichell, one of our most respected scouts, discovered Frank in high school, but he never got to see enough of him as a pitcher because he played the outfield much more than he pitched. After high school, Krichell got Frank a job on a semi-pro team in Watertown, New York, so he could evaluate the kid's talents as a pitcher.

Spec's first start was against the Mohawk Giants. The Giants were two and a half hours late arriving, and when they did, according to Krichell, "a dilapidated car rolled into the park and out fell six ballplayers in various stages of the condition in which you feel no pain."

Frank's performance that night was one Krichell never forgot. "With his blinding speed, the poor lighting system and the temporary blindness of the Giants," he said, "Shea struck out 22 hitters."

That and other performances were enough to convince Krichell to make another trip to Connecticut to sign Shea before the scouts from any of the other big-league teams beat him to the punch. But a funny thing happened on his way to Connecticut. A police officer pulled him over for speeding. Kirchell alertly told the officer, "I'm a scout for the New York Yankees, and I'm on my way to Naugatuck to sign a pitcher named Shea."

The cop said, "If it's Frank Shea, what are you waiting for? Let's get going. You've got a police escort."

Our 1947 season was only two months old—June 22—when the folks from Naugatuck and Waterbury put on a Frank Shea Day at Yankee Stadium and gave Frank a new Hudson, a watch, and luggage. Mayor Harry Carter led the festivities, and when Frank propped his right foot up on the front bumper to pose for photographers, he drew attention to the Connecticut license plate with no numbers, only letters that spelled out SPEC.

Frank was a fun-loving Irishman who livened up our clubhouse from the day he joined us. He was such a comical character, like Lefty Gomez, that Shirley Povich of the *Washington Post* wrote in his column, ''Shea is that rarity—a right-hander with a south-paw psychosis.'' Bucky Harris said, ''I don't see how he missed being a left-hander.''

His personality was exactly what you need in a clubhouse to give a team's players a good feeling about the team and each other, the kind of camaraderie that extends onto the playing field and makes any team a better team.

Frank used to delight us with impromptu routines, and he wasn't above telling us about his own greatness. He'd stick an empty cup on top of a bat, pound the bat on the floor for attention and then take on the delivery of a radio broadcaster while telling us:

> . . . and now it's Frank Shea—what a pitcher!—who is on the mound for the Yankees, the great Frank Shea from Nau-gatuck, Connecticut, folks. With his blinding speed and scrumptious curve . . . Ladies and gentlemen, the major leagues have never seen the equal of Frank Shea, from Nau-gatuck, Connecticut . . . and now we give you Frank Shea, himself!

About the only member of the Yankee organization who had any problem at all with Frank was our traveling secretary, Frank Scott, who chewed Spec out on one of our trips to St. Louis in 1947 for signing five meal checks in one day. When Scott asked how come Shea was spending so much of the Yankees' money on meals, Spec told him, ''Take a look at that 7–1 pitching record and don't ask silly questions.''

Shea was the perfect match for Larry MacPhail, and he wasn't intimidated by MacPhail's position, even when Spec was still in the minor leagues. The year before he broke in with us, he suffered an appendicitis attack during our spring training trip to Panama and underwent an emergency appendectomy. After the Yankees farmed him out to their Oakland team in the Pacific Coast League, they also farmed out his hospital bill. The tab was $300, and when they received it from the hospital in Panama, they forwarded it to Shea.

At the end of the '46 season, Spec sent the most original dunning letter of them all to MacPhail at Yankee Stadium:

Dear Mr. MacPhail:

I know you want to win the pennant with the Yankees next year. Here's the way to do it. Besides bringing me up to pitch for the team, you can also hire me as the new manager. That way you can't miss. You know my record was 15–5 at Oakland. I'll handle both jobs for $25,000 and we'll forget about the bill the team sent me after I had my appendix removed in Panama.

He didn't get the managerial job, but he did get his $300 back— plus an invitation to report to our spring training camp again for the 1947 season.

Allie Reynolds came to us in one of the biggest deals the Yankees made during my years with them. George Weiss has been given the credit in some articles about that trade, but he didn't make it. Larry MacPhail did. He traded Joe Gordon to the Indians to get Allie, and Joe DiMaggio deserves a huge assist on that one.

Reynolds had been with the Indians since pitching in two games for them in 1942. He was a consistent winner, with three 11-win seasons for them and an 18–12 record in '45. He was a hard-throwing Oklahoma native of Scotch-Irish and Creek Indian descent. We called him "Superchief."

In his last start against us for the Indians in 1946, Reynolds was awful. We played against him at Yankee Stadium and knocked him out early. MacPhail traded for him anyhow, giving up one of the biggest names in the American League and a favorite with Yankee fans and us players.

Gordon was on the down side of his bright career. He had only two more respectable seasons, hitting .272 for the Indians in '47 and .280 for them in '48 while playing a key role in their pennant and their victory over the Boston Braves in the World Series. But

Flash hit only .251 for the Indians in 1949 and left the big leagues after slipping to .236 in 1950. He played the last three seasons of his career in the minors.

MacPhail didn't make the deal entirely on his own confidence. He sought out Joe D. and told him, "We have a chance to get one of three of the Indians' starting pitchers in a trade—Red Embree, Steve Gromek, or Allie Reynolds. Which one would you take?"

Joe needed only two words to give MacPhail his answer: "Take Reynolds."

Reynolds pitched for the Yankees for eight years. During that time, the team won six pennants and six World Series.

His baseball excellence became even more impressive when we found out he never played our sport as a kid. His father was a minister who did not like baseball, especially on Sunday, so Allie played tennis and ran track. He didn't play baseball until after he graduated from high school.

At Oklahoma A&M, he went out for his college team, became a pitcher and went 25–2, and signed with the Indians.

Fate plays a fascinating role in the development of sports stars. In some cases your fortunes are decided as much by who your managers, coaches, and teammates are as by what you do with your opportunity. In Allie's case, he was lucky enough to pitch early in his career on a team where one of the other pitchers was Bob Feller.

"Bob worked a lot with me on a curveball," he said later in his career. "He was always eager to discuss batters, ready to do what he could to help me." Another helpful teammate was Eddie Lopat, who came over to us from the Chicago White Sox the following season. Lopat told Reynolds, "Take four pitches—the fastball, the curve, the slider, and the screwball. Now throw each of these at three different speeds and you have twelve pitches. Next throw each of these twelve pitches with a long-armed or short-armed motion, and you have twenty-four pitches."

Allie is a highly intelligent man. He was one of the first player representatives after Johnny Murphy and Dixie Walker began organizing the players, and after his career he became a minor-league president and a successful business executive. When Lopat spoke,

Allie listened. As a result of their combined talents and Lopat's theories on pitching, the blazing right-handed fastballer and the left-handed "junk" pitcher won 244 games for the Yankees.

Joe Page was, well, different. He was never going to be a star with the Yankees as long as Joe McCarthy was our manager, especially after a blowup they had on our airplane on the runway at Willow Run Airport in Detroit early in '46. McCarthy suffered one of his occasional gall bladder attacks, and Page didn't make him feel any better with one of his tours of the local nightlife.

On the plane, McCarthy did something I never expected to see. He chewed out one of his players, Page, in front of the rest of us. Page never offered any excuses for his nightlife, but he never forgave McCarthy for humiliating him. Two days later, McCarthy resigned.

Page was in his fourth season with the Yankees when 1947 and Bucky Harris arrived. Bucky developed the same skepticism about Page that McCarthy had. As a starting pitcher, Page had seasons of 5, 6, and 9 wins, something less than a Hall of Fame pace.

Like McCarthy, Harris felt Page didn't take care of himself or push himself enough to get the most out of his ability. Leo Trachtenberg wrote in *Yankee* magazine, "There were candles to be burned at both ends, and in his roistering existence Page burned plenty of them."

Larry MacPhail exercised his authority to control Page to a certain extent in 1947. He had an arrangement under which he would go to Bucky Harris on the first and fifteenth of the month—payday—and ask if Joe was behaving himself. If Bucky said yes, MacPhail would hand Page ten $100 bills to hold him until the next payday. MacPhail remembered later that he had to turn Joe down only once, "and then I had to fork the money over anyway, when Page asked me, 'Isn't a man entitled to one mistake?' "

Joe's enthusiasm for living may have been the result of an early life that was both hard and tragic. He grew up one of seven children in the Pennsylvania coal town of Springdale, where he worked in the mines as a boy. That was hard enough, but life soon became much harder.

In 1943, when Joe was pitching in the minor leagues, his mother died. Eight months later, his oldest sister, who was trying to take the place of their mother, was hit by a car and died five days later. Only a few months after that, his father died of a heart attack, the third death in the immediate family in less than a year. Joe helped to keep his brothers and sisters together as a family. Any young man who can endure that kind of a test is well prepared for coming in from the bullpen in the World Series with his team's chances resting on his shoulders.

By the time Bucky took over the club, Page was a man on the spot. Management was getting tired of waiting for him to deliver, and all of us knew from the first days of the '47 season that if you couldn't play for Bucky, you couldn't play for anybody.

On the night of May 26, Joe Page stood on the mound and on the brink. We were playing the Red Sox in front of 75,000 fans at Yankee Stadium, and it was common knowledge that Page was about to be farmed out to Newark, another humiliation for a player who had three years in the big leagues already.

By this point, Page had lost his job as a starting pitcher. Bucky was trying to find a role for him in the bullpen, something that Page found to his dislike. That didn't help his situation with Bucky either, and by the night in question the front office was about to hand Joe a one-way ticket to Newark.

Then fate stepped in. Frank Shea was slapped around for three runs in two innings. Harris motioned for Page to come in from the bullpen to relieve Shea. The bases were loaded, and Rudy York, one of the best power hitters in baseball, was the hitter.

Page said later that when he reached the mound, he took one look at York, a strong-as-an-ox Cherokee Indian, and said to himself, "Well, Page, it's goodbye Broadway, hello Market Street" — Newark's main drag.

Joe's first three pitches missed the strike zone. With three balls and no strikes and the bases loaded, the reality of it all hit Page: One more ball and he'd be on his way out of the big leagues. Harris later verified that.

Joe threw a fastball down the middle for the automatic strike. Then he threw another. His next pitch was a curveball, which fooled York. He swung and missed for the strikeout. Then Joe struck out a future Hall of Famer, Bobby Doerr, and got the Boston shortstop, Eddie Pellagrini, on a fly ball to me.

The paperwork on Page's return to Newark was actually being

processed in our front office while this drama was unfolding on the field. After the inning, Bucky sent word to MacPhail to delay the action.

We tied the score in the fourth inning, scored three more times in the fifth, and added three runs in the seventh. While we were exploding with our own fireworks, Joe was mowing the Red Sox down inning after inning. Boston got only two hits against him in his long relief appearance.

Harris, with the wisdom of his managerial years, knew he had come up with something. Page's confidence and enthusiasm were restored. He went on to appear in 56 games that season and averaged almost three innings per appearance. He won 14 games, lost only 8, and saved 17. At the end of the season, Bucky said Page was responsible more than any of the rest of us for out 1947 American League pennant—and that's not counting his heroic performance in the World Series, which comes in the next chapter.

On the day after his do-or-Newark appearance against the Red Sox, Joe sat by himself in our bullpen, ten feet from the rest of our crew out there. That was the spot he had occupied the night before, and baseball players being as superstitious as they are, he wasn't taking any chances. He sat in that same spot, away from his bullpen mates, for the rest of his career.

As his career took off and so did our team, we started calling him "Fireman Joe," and not just for his excellence as a relief pitcher. He lived with a retired New York City firefighter, Dan Malkin, in a four-room apartment in the Bronx. New York was still suffering from the same postwar housing shortage that every other city was experiencing, so we baseball players had to take our living quarters where we could find them.

Joe and his wife, Kay, lived with the Malkins in the late '40s. They got along so well that the old firefighter gave Joe a red shirt that Joe used to wear to Yankee Stadium just to get a laugh out of the rest of us.

Page's best friend on our ball club was DiMaggio. Joe worshipped DiMag to such an extreme that he tried to carry Joe D.'s luggage on our road trips, something that DiMaggio stopped in a hurry. But he ran errands for the Yankee Clipper and did everything he could to be of service to him, and the fact that the rest of us climbed all over him with our sharp-needled ribbings didn't discourage Page one bit. He was awed by DiMaggio, and if the rest of us thought it was funny, that didn't make any difference to him.

On our road trips, the two Joes ate together, went to the movies together, and seemed to be together every minute of the time, except on those evenings when Page went looking for the bright lights. DiMag got on Page's neck from time to time about breaking training, telling him that Page, who came to be called "the Gay Reliever" in the times when "gay" meant "happy-go-lucky," was only hurting himself and his team with his nightlife.

When the Clipper told Page those things, they always found their mark, even if their effect wasn't permanent. No amount of chastisings or warnings from management ever had the effect on Joe Page that only a few words from Joe DiMaggio did. Harris gave Page his one last chance, and after that, DiMaggio did more for Page's career than anyone else.

Buck Newsom also joined our team in 1947, and joining a new team wasn't anything new for him. Buck had a new pitch and a new name by '47. He developed a "blooper pitch," one of those rainbow jobs that goes up into the sky instead of on a straight line to the hitter and seems to need a parachute for its descent. And he was going by his new, self-conceived nickname of "Bobo." It was all part of his scheme to prolong his career by making himself into a personality, which he always was anyhow. But he was more than that, because in '47 he could still pitch, even though he started his big-league career eighteen years earlier in 1929.

The first generation of great Yankee teams, the era that included the 1927 Yankees, was still in its prime when Newsom began his major-league career with the Brooklyn Dodgers, going 0–3. He lasted until 1953 and pitched for nine teams in twenty years, which sounds like a lot and becomes even more when you realize that he pitched for the Senators five times, the Browns three times, and the Dodgers and A's twice. In seven seasons he pitched for two teams, and one year—1943—he pitched for three.

Through his career as baseball's gypsy, Buck topped the magic career level of 200 wins with 211. He was a key factor in the

Tigers' pennant year of 1940, when he was a 21-game winner against only 5 losses. And he helped us in '47, even though he turned forty. Then he was gone again, this time to the Giants.

He and DiMaggio were no strangers to each other. During one of Newsom's terms in Washington he was facing the Clipper after telling reporters he knew DiMaggio's weakness. The next time they crossed paths, Joe D. clobbered him with three doubles. In the clubhouse after the game, the reporters reminded Newsom of his claim. Newsom, never to be topped, told them, "Yeah, I know what his weakness is—doubles."

Newsom had a blustering personality, and he could talk his way out of anything, even when he was wrong. One example was the time in Washington that he got into an argument with the *Post*'s Shirley Povich over Shirley's statement to him that Sonny Dixon, one of the Senators' pitchers, beat the Yankees the year before.

Bobo argued that it never happened, Povich said he was there, and they bet ten dollars. They agreed that the first one to see Dixon, who was traded to the A's over the winter, would ask him the question so the bet could be settled.

Povich was in Philadelphia a few weeks later and obtained verification from Dixon that he did, in fact, beat the Yankees the year before, 3–2, at Griffith Stadium. When Povich told Newsom, Bobo said, "He's lying."

Newsom displayed the same kind of logic when he got into an argument with another writer, who went to the record book and then quoted it to Bobo to prove that Newsom was wrong. Bobo's response: "Who are you going to believe, me or the record book?"

One player who is almost never mentioned in the talk about our great season in 1947 but was a key factor in our success is George McQuinn. George was an outstanding first baseman and a good hitter, too, who began his years in the majors with the Cincinnati Reds in 1936 and joined the St. Louis Browns in '38 for an All-Star career.

He reminded me of Mickey Vernon of the Senators, a graceful left-hander around the bag and a consistent left-handed hitter. He used the "claw mitt" for first basemen, a three-section glove that was especially useful in scooping up throws in the dirt from the other infielders. A few miles up the road in New Haven, Connecticut, another first baseman was using the same kind of mitt: the captain of the Yale team, George Bush.

McQuinn was traded by the Browns to the A's in exchange for Dick Siebert for the 1946 season, but he hit only .225 for them at the age of thirty-six and was given his unconditional release, enabling him to make his own deal.

At that time, we still needed a first baseman. No one had really worked out there since Lou Gehrig. We tried Dahlgren, Joe Gordon, Nick Etten, Buddy Hassett, Johnny Sturm, and even me. In later years Joe Collins and Dick Kryhoski joined the parade as the search continued until the arrival of Bill Skowron in 1954, fifteen years after Gehrig retired.

I was an outfielder, but as early as 1939 the Yankees started playing me at first base from time to time. I played one game there in '39, two in 1940, and seven in '42. After the war, the number increased to forty-one games in 1946.

I wasn't looking forward to playing that many games there in '47. It was difficult to keep making the adjustment from the outfield to the infield. One of the differences was in the throws. You use different muscles for different kinds of throws, and I wanted to be sure the ones I used for throws from the outfield to the bases and into home plate were strong enough and coordinated enough to ensure continued accuracy.

You want your strongest throwing arm in right field to keep opposing base runners from going from first to third on base hits to right. You don't have to worry about that on balls hit to center and left, because those fielders are much closer to third than the right fielder. The strength required for that throw from right is hard to maintain when you're playing first base and making much shorter throws, many of them sidearm, more than forty games a year.

The environment is different, too. In the outfield, you're all alone. At first base, you can almost conduct a church social if you want to. You can chat with the first-base umpire, the other team's first-base coach, or any runner who reaches first. The second baseman and the pitcher are close enough for conversation if you want to include them.

Even though I was always considered an outgoing person, I never talked to the runners at first base. I wasn't going to be buddy-buddy with anybody there. I wanted to be alert to what was going on so I could anticipate what I should do if the ball came my way on the next play.

Even with that, I found that the outfield required much more concentration. There are more things to think about: What's the hitter going to try to do? Am I likely to be involved? If so, where's the ball likely to be hit, and what am I going to do with it if I get it? How fast is the hitter? How fast are the other runners already on base? Will the hitter try to stretch a single into a double?

You also have to concentrate more on ground balls in the outfield. If one gets past you in the infield, it's one base and the outfielder gets the ball into second base. If you're playing the outfield and the ball gets past you, it might bounce and roll all the way to the wall and the hitter might make the rounds and score.

At first base, either the ball is hit to you or not. If not, you break for the bag to take the throw. The biggest challenge I found playing first base was simply how far to go to my right for a ground ball before yielding to the second baseman and dashing back to the bag for his throw.

I was always willing to play wherever my manager wanted me, but I didn't like switching back and forth between right field and first base. It was harder for me to return to the outfield after a week or so at first base.

A week of not making that major-league overhand throw from right field to keep the runner from going from first to third on a single to right or to cut down the runner trying to score from second on a hit to the outfield makes a difference. Your outfield throwing arm goes downhill fast if you've been temporarily shifted to first base. I wanted to stay in one place or another, preferably in right field.

McQuinn solved everyone's problems. Larry MacPhail went after him when he learned the A's had released him. "We were desperate for a first baseman," he said in later years, "and I decided I might take a gamble on McQuinn."

MacPhail called McQuinn and asked if he thought he could help the Yankees. George told him, "If you take me to training camp, you will win the 1947 pennant. If you give me the chance, I'll hit .300 for you and give you the best first-basing in the league."

McQuinn, a quiet guy who was definitely not the bragging type, made good on his predictions. The Yankees were smart enough to give him a chance. We won the pennant, and George, still the smoothie around the bag, hit .304. He played in 142 games at first base, and I had to play there in only half a dozen while spending the rest of my time in right field next to Joe D., where everyone felt I could help the team the most.

We began to win with the help of "Fireman Joe" Page coming out of our bullpen, and we picked up even more steam two months later when Vic Raschi was recalled from Portland, Oregon, after being farmed out there at the start of the season. He arrived just in time, because Spud Chandler and Frank Shea came down with sore arms at the same time. We needed a starting pitcher who could go out there and win consistently, along with Reynolds and any other patchwork combination Bucky could come up with while Chandler and Shea recovered from their miseries. We were a hot ball club, and we didn't want to lose our momentum in the middle of the season.

Raschi reported to us in Chicago on the morning of July 13, and his trip to join us is a story by itself. He pitched for Portland in the second game of a twilight doubleheader in San Diego and won his fourth straight game on a Thursday night. When he reached the clubhouse ready for a relaxing shower, the manager, Jim Turner, came over to his locker and said, "Vic, you've been recalled by the Yankees. Harris wants you to work in Chicago on Sunday. That means you have twenty minutes to shower and dress and catch the plane for Portland."

Raschi made the plane, then flew on to Chicago. He dashed into Comiskey Park, and when he did he hadn't slept for forty-eight hours. He pitched the second game of a doubleheader against the White Sox. It was our fourteenth straight win. He won again four days later in Cleveland, our nineteenth straight and our last win in that streak, again in the second game of a doubleheader. We tied the record set by the White Sox in 1906 when they were "the hitless wonders."

Even after our winning streak was stopped, Vic kept his own going. A week after pitching us to our nineteenth straight, he won his third in a row, beating the Browns, with a little help from his friends. We got Vic fourteen runs on twenty hits. In his next start he beat Detroit, 5–1, at Yankee Stadium and then made it five in a row with a three-hit shutout over the Indians.

It may have been only a coincidence, or it may have been the baseball gods smiling down upon us, but the starting pitcher who won the first game in both of those doubleheaders at the beginning of Vic's streak was Bobo Newsom. Raschi, Newsom, Reynolds, Page, McQuinn, Berra—our new faces were coming through for us. We were on our way to another American League pennant. For those of us from the prewar Yankees, the words of one of the popular songs summed it up: "Seems like old times."

Joe Cronin was still managing the Red Sox in '47, fresh from their pennant in '46. They didn't do as well, finishing fourteen games behind us and two behind the Tigers. After that, Joe retired from managing and moved into the Red Sox front office, succeeded on the field by our old leader, Joe McCarthy.

It shouldn't have surprised anyone when Cronin tapped McCarthy as his successor. Cronin worshipped him. He thought he was the best manager in baseball, and I agreed. For his part, McCarthy relished the prospect of managing for Cronin.

Before turning over the managerial job to McCarthy, Cronin decided to try to stop Raschi's streak of immediate successes in 1947 by rattling him, a tactic that often works on a rookie. Cronin argued with Charlie Berry, the home-plate umpire, that Raschi's foot was breaking contact with the pitching rubber. Every pitcher does it, and Cronin and Berry both knew it. Technically it's a violation of the pitching rules, but it's almost never enforced.

It was that day, though, thanks to Berry, who was never one of my favorite umpires, but that's a subject we can cover later. On this day, Cronin convinced Berry to warn our rookie pitcher. He did, so Vic started to pay more attention to his footwork than to his pitching, just what Cronin wanted.

I was playing first base that day. I asked for time out and then went to the mound and told Raschi, "I know what Cronin is trying to do, Vic. He just wants to upset you. Make sure you keep contact with the rubber for the next few pitches, and then go back to your usual way of pitching."

He did, and that satisfied Berry. So then we started to get on the Red Sox pitcher, Jim Bagby, about the same thing. I led the hollering, yelling out to Berry from the dugout when Bagby was pitching, "Keep his foot on the rubber! Keep his foot on!"

Bagby, of course, took exception to our position on the issue and to my involvement in it. On my next trip to the plate, he knocked me down with a high, inside fastball that was too close for comfort and intentional beyond any reasonable doubt. I turned to Berry and protested, but Berry, who knew better, copped out and said, "Oh, I don't think he was throwing at you, Tom."

Berry didn't want anything to do with an incident that he was afraid might be building. When I saw he was not going to take a stand, which I thought was what umpires got paid for, I resorted to the hitter's time-honored way of protecting himself for the future.

I laid a bunt down the first-base line, trying to draw Bagby into the baseline or get him to cover first so I could plow right into him and send him a message not to throw at my head any more. Bagby knew what was coming, so he let his first baseman, Rudy York, handle my bunt and cover the bag, too. Bagby was ducking the play.

I still had to send him a message, so I knocked York down. I was going to get somebody, so I got Rudy. After the play was over, I said to him, "I'm not mad at you, Rudy."

York was such a classy guy that he just knocked the dirt off his shirt and said, "I know, Tom, I know."

To this day, that incident bothers me because of what it represents. Pitchers always tell you that they have to knock a hitter down so he won't take advantage of them. But what about the hitter? What can he do for *his* safety?

And there's a difference between pitching inside to move a hitter away from the plate and throwing at the man. Sal Maglie pitched inside. That's why we called him "the Barber," because of all the close shaves he gave us. He was an artist. He did it to keep you from leaning into his curveball to get a better swing at it.

But knocking a hitter down and taking a chance of hitting him in the head is one of the cheapest shots in any sport. There should be no place for it in baseball.

We were the kind of blend that year that you find on championship teams. While our newcomers were delivering for us in grand style, so were those who had been Yankees over the years. We performed successfully as a team, but Ted Williams dominated the individual hitting statistics. He won the triple crown with the highest average, the most home runs, and the most runs batted in, and he was first in slugging average, total bases, bases on balls, and runs scored.

I beat him out in one department, though. I led the league in triples with 13. Because the triple is considered by many to be baseball's most exciting offensive play with its combination of speed and power, it was flattering to find myself at the top of that category in a league with so many exceptional hitters like Williams, Joe D., Boudreau, Jeff Heath, and George Kell.

We didn't have Williams-level numbers, but we were a solid lineup from top to bottom. DiMag hit .315 and was our only other .300 hitter besides McQuinn, but we got averages in the .280s from Yogi, Bill Johnson, our third baseman, and me, plus seasons in the .270s from Rizzuto, Johnny Lindell—while he filled in for Charlie Keller, who was suffering from disk problems in his back—and Aaron Robinson, who divided the catching with Berra while Yogi also played twenty-four games in the outfield.

Joe D. and I led the team in home runs. Joe hit 20 and I hit 16, and I was able to lead the team in runs batted in with 98, second best in the American League behind only Ted Williams. Besides leading the league in triples and finishing second in runs scored, I was tops on the team in doubles and third in the league with 35. Ted, Joe, our old teammate Joe Gordon, and I were the top four hitters in the league in slugging average and also in total bases.

DiMag also had the highest fielding average of any center fielder in either league. He made one error all season, a phenomenal achievement for any center fielder, especially one who reached as many balls as Joe did. For all that, he won his third Most Valuable Player Award.

The '47 season was a happier experience for Joe than he might have expected at the beginning. He missed spring training because of surgery on his heel, and then management fined him $100 for refusing to pose for the team photographer.

The photographer was late getting to the stadium for the usual spring picture of the team, so Joe took the opportunity to get in a few more swings in the batting cage to help make up for his lost spring training. When the cameraman finally arrived, Joe refused to pose for him and kept taking his cuts.

A few nights later, Ted Williams hit the most "home runs" of any left-handed hitter in a pregame contest at Yankee Stadium. He was awarded $100. No right-hander cleared the fence, but in the game Joe hit a three-run homer.

After the game, our traveling secretary, Red Patterson, handed Joe a check for $100 in our clubhouse with the explanation that it was for being the first right-handed hitter to hit a home run that night.

Joe refused the check and told Red, "Give it to the Damon Runyon Cancer Fund."

We didn't have a 20-game winner on our pitching staff, an unusual situation for a team that wins the pennant. Reynolds had 19 wins, and Shea and Page were second with 14. Chandler won only 9, but he had the league's best earned run average.

Those numbers prove how well we played as a team. Individually we didn't have that many statistical leaders, but together we led the league in runs scored, triples, home runs, team batting average, and team slugging average. Our pitchers combined to achieve the best team earned run average.

Even though our statistics weren't enough to give us individual leaders, they were enough to do what your numbers are supposed to accomplish—they won the pennant for us.

Twelve

"Give Me Page"

The Brooklyn Dodgers won the National League pennant, and they deserved as much credit for it as we did for finishing first in the American League. The Dodgers beat out the St. Louis Cardinals by five games while playing under even more upheaval than we did.

The commissioner of baseball, Happy Chandler, who succeeded Judge Landis following his death in 1944, suspended Leo Durocher for the entire season because of "conduct detrimental to baseball." It caused a furor, but Chandler, a man who was comfortable with difficult decisions after serving as governor of Kentucky and in the United States Senate, stuck by this one. He later wrote in the *New York Times*, "The cause was numerous things, too numerous to mention. He broke a fellow's jaw in Brooklyn . . . He was fighting everyone, just a troublemaker, and gambling. It was an accumulation of things."

Chandler also wrote, "If I made any error, it was on the side of being too lenient. Just suspending him for a year was no great thing . . . I signed thirty-six death warrants as governor, so it wasn't anything for me to get excited about."

176

Chandler handed down the suspension on the eve of the opening of the season, and Clyde Sukeforth, one of the Dodgers' coaches, was pressed into service as their manager for their first two games, which the Dodgers were able to win. Then Burt Shotton, a veteran baseball man who managed in street clothes like Connie Mack, took over and guided them to the pennant.

In the same season that the Dodgers lost Durocher as their leader, they gained a new one, Jackie Robinson. Branch Rickey, the subject of so many complaints about paying slave wages and blocking the careers of his minor leaguers when he ran "the St. Louis chain gang," did just the opposite in Robinson's case. He boldly and courageously brought the opportunity for a career in major-league baseball to black players everywhere by signing Jackie to a contract with the Dodgers' Montreal farm team in 1946 and bringing him up to the Dodgers in '47.

What Jackie accomplished in 1947 has been well documented, and so has the abuse he endured from other teams and their fans as officially the first black man to play our sport in the Major Leagues in the twentieth century—"officially" because there is some evidence that others did it before him under names that made them sound Cuban or Native American.

Jackie put up with staying in separate hotels, eating in separate restaurants, dodging spikes around the bag at first base, getting knocked down by high, inside fast balls, and all sorts of verbal abuse, hate mail, and threats against his life. Through all of that, he still had the ability, the maturity, and the sense of purpose to hit .297, lead the league in stolen bases with 29, score the second most runs with 125, and win the National League's first Rookie of the Year Award.

There was no particular reaction among us one way or the other when the Dodgers signed Jackie. Every player knew blacks would get their chance in the big leagues sooner or later. Our attitude was, if they can play, let them.

The Dodgers were a team like us. They led the league in only a few individual or team statistics, but they won the pennant. Offensively, their only league-leading category was stolen bases, with Robinson's help. Defensively, they made the second most double plays with Pee Wee Reese and Eddie Stanky as their second-base combination, and Stanky led the league's second basemen in fielding. In pitching, they tied the Boston Braves in shut-outs and topped the league in saves by their relief pitchers, thanks to my old friend from the 1941 World Series, Hugh Casey.

What was significant with the Dodgers was the departments where they did not lead the league, and yet they still won. They didn't have the batting champion—that was Harry Walker. They didn't have the runs batted in leader—that was Johnny Mize. They didn't have the co-champions in home runs—they were Mize and Ralph Kiner. They didn't have the pitcher with the most wins—that was Ewell Blackwell. And they didn't have the pitcher with the best earned run average—that was Warren Spahn.

As a team, the Cardinals had the highest fielding average, but the best they could do was finish second behind the Dodgers. The Braves scored the most runs and had the highest batting average. They finished third. The Giants scored the most runs and hit the most home runs. They finished fourth.

That tells you something about the way the Dodgers played. They were a *team*, a single unit committed to helping each other to win. The players from that team like Pee Wee Reese, their captain, and Duke Snider, who was a rookie that year, will tell you that the credit for that starts with Rickey, who shaped the team to his liking and then insisted that his players work as one team instead of as twenty-five individuals.

The result was that the Dodgers tied the Cardinals for the pennant, the first tie in history, and lost a one-game playoff in 1946, won the pennant in '47 and '49, lost it on the last day of the season in 1950, lost the historic playoff in '51 on Bobby Thomson's home run, won the pennant again in '52 and '53, won everything—including the World Series—in '55, and won the pennant again in '56 before leaving Brooklyn after the 1957 season for Los Angeles.

That adds up to six pennants, plus a World Series champion-ship, from 1947 through 1956. People remember that the Yankees won five pennants in a row from 1949 through 1953, but what they don't remember is that the Dodgers missed doing the same thing over the same period by only two games—the last game of 1950 and the playoff with the Giants in '51.

That's what dedication to team play can do for you. Branch Rickey had his critics, and for good reason, but he also had his defenders, also for good reason. An executive who instills such a strong team attitude in his organization, whether it's the Brooklyn Dodgers or General Motors, will produce success, and Rickey deserves all the credit in the world for doing that with the Dodgers.

Brooklyn got another good year out of its Flatbush favorite, Dixie Walker, "the Peepul's Cherce," who played right field and hit .306. The only other hitter in their lineup that year was Pete Reiser, who made a habit of banging into outfield fences all his life but still had one good season left. He hit .309, the last time he hit .300 in what should have been a long and brilliant career.

Instead, his out-of-the-way-wall-here-I-come style of play and the repeated injuries to his head and body limited his time in the major leagues to ten years and a lifetime batting average of .295, that from one who was so good he won the batting championship in 1941 at the age of twenty-two with a .343 average over the likes of Johnny Mize, Enos Slaughter, Mel Ott, Stan Hack, and Dolph Camilli.

By the time we took the field for the '47 World Series, "Pistol Pete's" flame was flickering, although it was not noticeable on the surface. He wasn't playing center field any more. Now he was Brooklyn's left fielder, replaced in center by another emerging favorite, Carl Furillo. Reiser hit only .236 the next season. Then Ricky, a superb judge of talent and how long a player could perform at an acceptable level, got rid of Reiser. He played two seasons with the Braves and one each with the Pirates and Indians, and then he was gone.

Carl Furillo was enjoying life without Leo Durocher and hit .295 as the Dodgers' young center fielder that year, eleven points higher than his rookie year under Durocher. Leo had a preference for platooning Furillo, playing him against only certain pitchers, and Carl hated it. He felt he was good enough to hit all kinds of pitching, which he proved with a lifetime batting average of .299 over fifteen years and the National League batting championship with .344 in 1953. With Durocher gone for the season for allegedly associating with known gambling figures like actor George Raft and others, Furillo was enjoying life under Burt Shotton.

Bruce Edwards didn't know it, but he was in his last full season as the Dodgers' full-time catcher. With Jackie Robinson blazing the trails for black players in the National League and Larry Doby of the Indians doing the same thing in the American League, some players lost their starting jobs, and Edwards was one of them. He caught in 128 games for Brooklyn in 1947, but with Roy Campanella on the scene in 1948, Edwards caught in only 48 games and filled in at other times by playing in the outfield and at first and third base.

Edwards helped Brooklyn with a .295 average in '47. Pee Wee Reese had the only other respectable batting average on the Dodgers, .284, and he was providing them with all the leadership you want out of the shortstop position. That's one of the key positions on the field because of all the action that takes place in the middle of the diamond and all the split-second decisions that have to be made by the shortstop and second baseman, so a baseball team must have more than just talent there if it is to be a winner. It must also have leadership there, and the Dodgers had plenty of it in Pee Wee.

Reese was the player I feared the most on the Dodgers in those years. It was always my feeling that Pee Wee, more than any other Dodger, had the ability to "make things happen," as people in athletics say. He was capable of stepping into a pressure situation with the game, the season, or the World Series hanging in the balance and get the key hit, steal the key base, or make the key play in the field that his team needed at that crucial moment. In fact, he was more than just capable of doing it—he was eager to do it.

Other Yankees over the years felt the same way. I asked Don Larsen at an Old Timers Game which player in the Dodgers' batting order he feared the most on the day of his perfect no-hit game in the 1956 World Series. By then, Pee Wee, who was destined to be elected to the Hall of Fame in 1984 and is called "Captain" to this day by his respectful former teammates, was thirty-eight years old and playing on bad legs.

Larsen didn't hesitate before giving me his answer: "Pee Wee Reese."

Brooklyn had another star that year, and he was just a kid: a twenty-one-year-old right-handed pitcher who stood six-foot-three and came from one of the New York suburbs in Westchester

County, Mount Vernon. His name was Ralph Branca. It's a shame that too many people remember him for being the pitcher when Bobby Thomson hit his "shot heard 'round the world" to win the pennant over the Dodgers in their famous playoff game in 1951. Ralph should be remembered instead for many of the other great things he accomplished for his team, starting with what he achieved in 1947.

Ralph came up to the Dodgers during the war, as an eighteen-year-old kid who didn't win a game and lost two in 1944. In '47, he hit his stride, and it is no accident that the Dodgers hit theirs, too.

Ralph won 21 games that year, the second most in the league, and was third in earned run average. On a staff that included an ace relief pitcher, Hugh Casey, Branca was a workhorse, leading the league in games started and finishing second in innings pitched.

When it came time to perform in the pressure cooker of the World Series, with all American listening on the radio to the Gillette Cavalcade of Sports, the kid got off to a sensational start.

Women's dresses came down to their ankles in the New Look in 1947. Perry Como was crooning "Prisoner of Love," and we were singing and whistling "Heartaches" along with Elmo Tanner and the Ted Weems orchestra.

That new invention called "television" that we saw at the New York World's Fair in 1939 was beginning to show up in people's living rooms and in the windows of neighborhood taverns all over America. People turned out all the lights at home or gathered around those store windows to watch the Friday Night Fights, and the fights on almost every other night of the week, too.

Onstage at the Roxy, Milton Berle was breaking up the joint. At the Victoria, two men who weren't even actors were the stars of a movie called *Spirit of West Point*. They were Doc Blanchard and Glenn Davis, the Military Academy's All-American football players. On the legitimate stage, *Oklahoma!* was still packing them into the St. James Theater on 44th Street.

When the talk turned to politics, almost everyone agreed that the governor of New York, Thomas Dewey, would defeat President Truman the next year, probably in a landslide.

It was an exciting period in America, and the 1947 World Series seemed to be a reflection of those eventful times.

Burt Shotton chose his kid, Branca, to start the first game of the World Series. It was asking a lot of a twenty-one-year-old to pitch the first game, with all the buildup that you have to cope with, plus the added pressure of doing it in Yankee Stadium, the most famous stadium in all of sports then and now.

It was a celebrity crowd, as usual, for the first game. Herbert Hoover, not the favorite ex-president in our history in 1947 because too many Americans remembered the Great Depression and blamed him for it, was at the game, and so was our secretary of state, George Marshall. There were governors from all over the Eastern seaboard there—from Pennsylvania, Rhode Island, Connecticut, and New Jersey as well as Governor Dewey. Among the baseball greats there were Babe Ruth, Ty Cobb, and Tris Speaker.

The baseball commissioner, Happy Chandler, was there. Only a few boxes away sat the man suspended by Chandler for that entire season, Leo Durocher, with his wife, Laraine Day. The papers said the two never spoke. Helen Jepson, a soprano with the Metropolitan Opera, sang the National Anthem before a packed house of 73,365 fans on a chilly, breezy afternoon when the temperature climbed only to 61 degrees.

Branca started like a house on fire. Wearing uniform number 13 because he was one of thirteen kids back home in nearby Mount Vernon, New York, he mowed us down in order through four innings, facing the minimum of twelve batters and striking out five of us, including me.

In the fifth, though, he never got a man out. We were trailing 1–0, when DiMag singled on a ground ball between third and short to lead off the inning. McQuinn walked, and Billy Johnson was hit on the arm by one of Branca's pitches. Branca, after breezing untouched through those first four innings, now faced the worst kind of problem for a pitcher: bases loaded and nobody out.

Johnny Lindell, one of the few players to break in during World War II who was good enough to stick after the war, doubled down the left-field line to drive in Joe D. and McQuinn. Suddenly we had broken Branca's serve and were winning the game, 2–1. Then Rizzuto walked. The bases were loaded again.

Here Bucky Harris made a move that turned out to be as smart as it was gutsy. He lifted Shea, even though Brooklyn had only one run against him in five innings, and inserted his rookie, Bobby Brown, as a pinch-hitter. Bucky was going for the big inning. He was a wise old veteran who had learned long before that there are certain points in a game where that game can be won, and it isn't always the ninth inning. In fact, it's usually some other inning. Bucky was alert and experienced enough to recognize that opportunity in this situation.

Harris was also showing his confidence in Brown, our "Golden Boy." That's not an easy spot for a rookie, but Bucky knew that Bobby had all the ingredients of a great hitter, including the ability to hit in pressure situations and the eagerness to get up there and try. He also knew that Bobby led the American League in pinch-hits that year with nine in twenty-seven trips, a .333 average.

After Branca missed with his first two pitches to Brown, Shotton lifted Branca and brought in Hank Behrman, a right-handed relief pitcher who was born in Brooklyn, started the season with the Dodgers, was traded to the Pirates with four others for Al Gionfriddo and $100,000 on May 3, and was sold back to the Dodgers on June 14.

With the count 2–0 on Brown already, Behrman walked him, forcing in Johnson with our third run. Stirnweiss hit a ground ball to Jackie Robinson, who threw home for the forceout on Lindell. Then I got my chance. I singled to left, scoring Rizzuto and Brown and giving us a 5–1 lead. It turned out to be a timely piece of hitting, because Brooklyn scored single runs in the sixth and seventh innings.

That five-run fifth inning made a winning pitch out of our starter, Frank Shea, 5–3. Joe Page—who else?—saved the game for us by pitching the last four innings. Our fifth inning was also proof that managers know what they're talking about when they warn you to stay away from the big inning on defense. Without that inning, Brooklyn would have won the game, 3–0.

In that spacious new dressing room of ours after the game, Bucky Harris explained how important it is for a team to get its first win in the World Series. His logic was beyond argument: "You have to win one before you can win four."

MacPhail, Webb, and Topping all poured into our clubhouse,

something that never would have happened under McCarthy, even in the excitement of winning the first game of the World Series. Some show business celebrities were in there, too, something else that never would have been allowed by McCarthy, but there were two favorites of mine: comic actor Bill Frawley and Bill "Bojangles" Robinson, who celebrated our victory by strutting into our clubhouse in his famous "cakewalk."

The longest ball of this game wasn't even hit. Joe DiMaggio hit a fly ball to Carl Furillo in the ninth inning that traveled 415 feet, another example of balls hit by DiMag in Yankee Stadium that would have been home runs in any other park in the majors.

Over in the Brooklyn dressing room, Branca's confidence and poise were unshaken. When a reporter asked him if he thought he could beat us if he got another opportunity in the Series, he said, "I don't see why not. I didn't see any infielders getting killed out there today."

When they went over to Burt Shotton in the dressing room and asked who his pitcher would be for the second game, he refused to say.

Allie Reynolds and our bats put us in a commanding position in the second game, or that's what everyone thought at the time. Superchief went the distance and beat the Dodgers on a nine-hitter, striking out six. Shotton's decision turned out to be his five-foot-seven left-hander, Vic Lombardi. We chipped away at him and his successor, Hal Gregg, a six-foot-three right-hander, for fifteen hits and won the game, 10–3. We scored in six of the first seven innings, starting with one run in the first and ending with four in the seventh. I had the pleasure of hitting a home run off Lombardi, my third World Series home run, on a shot over the 367-foot sign in right-center field. We also got triples from Stirnweiss, Lindell, and Johnson to tie a World Series record.

It was another cold day. Before the game, photographers took pictures of our battery for that day, Reynolds and Berra, snuggling under a blanket on our bench looking like two football fans at a game in late November.

The Dodgers simply played a terrible game, the kind of thing that can happen to any team, even the good ones. Pee Wee Reese tied a Series record of sorts by not getting any chances at shortstop, for which he could be grateful. The rest of the Dodgers were acting as if the ball were radioactive. Pete Reiser committed a two-base error in center field. Eddie Stanky dropped a throw at second. Jackie Robinson overran a bunt. On another play Jackie fielded a ground ball but had nobody to throw to at first. Reiser jammed his ankle on a slide into second base.

I had the pleasure of being involved in the first run of the game. Snuffy Stirnweiss led off our first inning with a single to right field. I followed him with a single to center on an 0–1 pitch, sending Snuffy to third base. Lindell then hit into a double play, but Stirnweiss was able to score while I was getting forced at second and Lindell was being thrown out at first.

When I hit my home run, Eileen paid a heavy price for it. Eddie Condon's Dixieland band was a favorite of mine in those years, and I heard them at the nightspot owned by Pete Pesky in Greenwich Village at every opportunity. Joe Sullivan, the in-between piano player when the Condon band was on its breaks, broke into one of my favorite songs of the day, "Sweet Lorraine," every time he saw me walk into the place. I got tickets for Pete to this game. During practice he yelled out to me from his seat, only instead of calling "Hey, Tom!" he hollered, "Sweet Lorraine." I knew immediately who it was.

When I hit my homer, he dashed over to Eileen, who was sitting nearby, and planted a big kiss on her. She told me about it after the game and then said, "Don't hit any more home runs."

By the time we came to bat in the seventh inning, we had nibbled our way to a 6–2 lead. We put the game away with four more in the seventh. With the way Allie Reynolds was pitching, nobody was going to score ten runs against us that day. The score was 10–3.

Bucky was a gracious winner. He said in our dressing room, "They just can't be as bad as they played. They really had a tough day, didn't they?"

The Dodgers were becoming testy. Hank Behrman, one of our victims the day before, was the first Brooklyn player out of the dressing room. A reporter asked him about the team's outlook for the rest of the Series, and Hank said, "I ain't got no comment."

Shotton was being as secretive as usual about his plans for the next game. He said in the dressing room, "You can quote me that we'll be on the field and we'll have a pitcher. I haven't announced my pitcher so far, and I see no reason why I should change that policy now. We'll have a pitcher out there, don't worry about that.''

Meanwhile, back in Brooklyn, Nat Kopel, a forty-three-year-old unemployed hotel worker, remained optimistic about his Dodgers. He became the first person in line at Ebbets Field for tickets to the third game. He waited at the bleacher entrance. For the first twelve hours of his wait, he was the only one there. He brought a blanket and pillow with him, plus cigars, cigarettes, and sandwiches.

He brought a positive attitude with him, too. He predicted that the Dodgers would win the third game. He even picked the score: 5–0.

With the Series moving to Brooklyn, at least for the third and fourth games, the Dodger fans got to go to their home ballpark, and the Yankee fans were the ones who had to spend a nickel to get to the game in the first Subway Series since 1941. The fifth game, if necessary, would also be played there, but a lot of people were saying—and writing—that the fifth game might not be necessary.

Brooklyn's optimistic first-in-line fan was half right. The Dodgers came back and won their first game, and they didn't waste any time doing it. The Flatbush Faithful were barely in their seats when their beloved Dodgers thrilled them with six runs in the second inning off Bobo Newsom and Vic Raschi. Newsom had turned forty two months before and was the second oldest pitcher ever to start a World Series game. We narrowed the gap slightly to 6–2 by coming right back with two runs of our own in the third, but the Dodgers got one back in their own third.

Obviously, this was going to be one of those days—a lot of runs and hits, and a lot of pitchers. We got two more in the fourth, but so did the Dodgers. We got another two in the fifth, one in the sixth when I doubled Brown home, and another in the seventh. The Dodgers didn't score after the fourth inning, but we could never catch up. We lost, 9–8, in a game that included 26 hits, 13 by each team, and eight pitchers. Hugh Casey's luck in World Series games showed signs of getting better. He was the winning pitcher.

No one had a right to expect a game that exciting when we took the field the next day, October 3, for the fourth game. But Bill Bevens was waiting in the wings. So was Cookie Lavagetto, ready to make Bevens his victim—and me, too.

Bevens, with the first name of Floyd but nicknamed "Bill" after a hometown friend, was a big right-handed pitcher from Hubbard, Oregon, and he had certain similarities to Branca. He was tall like Ralph, six-foot-three-and-a-half, and strong, 210 pounds to Branca's 220. He broke into the major leagues the same year Branca did, 1944, but he was ten years older. And like Ralph, when Bill took the mound in the only World Series he ever played in, he got the opposition's respect immediately. Before the game was over, he had the whole nation's attention.

There had never been a no-hit game in the history of the World Series, dating back to its start in 1903, but Bill had one going into the ninth inning. He wasn't perfect, because he was walking too many men, but he was making excellent pitches when he had to and getting the Dodgers out while we scored a run in the first inning and another in the fourth. His walks got him into trouble in the fifth and led to a run by Brooklyn, but he still had his no-hitter.

Burt Shotton started Harry Taylor, a rookie right-hander who won 10 games for the Dodgers that year but only 9 more over the four more seasons before leaving the majors. With his 10 wins in '47 against 5 losses, he had a much better record than Bevens, who was 7–13 that year.

On this day, however, their 1947 fortunes were reversed. Taylor gave up two hits and a walk in our first inning and was quickly replaced by Gregg, who pitched seven excellent innings and held us to one run—a triple by Billy Johnson and a double by Johnny Lindell. We got a run from Taylor's troubles in the first, but Pee Wee Reese stepped into the crisis, as he did so often, and got the Dodgers out of any further difficulty by starting a double play.

Bevens gave us an indication of what kind of a day it might be by walking two Brooklyn hitters in the first inning, Eddie Stanky and Dixie Walker, but he got out of the inning without the Yankees scoring a run. Our disappointment in that first inning was nothing compared to our letdown in the last.

In the fifth inning, Bill's wildness continued, but his luck didn't. Spider Jorgensen, Brooklyn's rookie third baseman, walked and was sacrificed into scoring position on a bunt by Stanky. Reese—there he was again—drove in Jorgensen later on a fielder's choice. The Dodgers had a run, but they still didn't have a hit.

When he was in the strike zone, Bevens obviously was making what we now call "quality pitches." He struck out only five batters in this game, so he obviously wasn't overpowering the Dodgers. He had enough stuff on his pitches to get them out if he could just get the ball in the strike zone. And we were giving him help. Lindell went deep to make an outstanding catch of a long fly ball by Robinson in the third inning. Joe D. hauled in a long drive by Hermanski in the fourth, and I went back to the fence to catch Hermanski's fly ball in the eighth.

Bruce Edwards led off the ninth inning for Brooklyn with a long fly ball to Lindell. Johnny made another excellent catch. Bevens was only two outs away from World Series history, and we were only that far from taking a prohibitive lead in the Series, three wins to one.

But Bevens continued to flirt with trouble. He walked Furillo for his ninth walk of the game. Jorgensen got us only one out from our goals by popping out to McQuinn, MacPhail's prized offseason acquisition, in foul territory on the first-base side.

Now Shotton, in his white dress shirt and bow tie in the Brooklyn dugout, made his moves, two of them. He sent in Al Gionfriddo, a substitute outfielder who came to the Dodgers that year from the Pittsburgh Pirates, to run for Furillo at first base. Then he sent in Reiser, who didn't start the game after injuring his ankle the day before in a slide into second base, to hit for Casey.

With the count two balls and one strike, Gionfriddo stole second. It was Brooklyn's seventh stolen base of the Series so far. The Dodgers were running Yogi ragged. The pitch to Reiser on Gionfriddo's steal was ball three. Now Bucky Harris waved to Berra to put Reiser on, setting up a force play at any base and avoiding the danger of having to come in with a 3–1 pitch to a good hitter like Reiser.

But Bucky, while avoiding that risk, was taking another, one that conventional baseball wisdom says you should never take. He was putting the potential winning run on base. A long hit could score both Gionfriddo and Reiser and win the game for the Dodgers, and they would tie the Series. Bucky never had trouble making decisions. Nobody had to tell him the gamble he was taking. But he did it anyhow.

Shotton made two more moves. He sent in Eddie Miksis, a substitute infielder, to run for Reiser. Shotton wanted two healthy legs to reach the plate with the winning run if the opportunity developed. And to develop that opportunity, he sent Cookie Lavagetto to pinch hit for Stanky.

Lavagetto was another favorite of the Flatbush Faithful, one whose trips to the plate used to produce cries of "Lookie, lookie, lookie! Here comes Cookie!" He had broken in with the Pirates thirteen seasons before. He was less than two months away from his thirty-fifth birthday, and 1947 was to be his last season in the big leagues.

When Cookie came up to the plate, DiMaggio and I looked at each other in the outfield. We weren't sure where to play him. We looked into the dugout for help from Chuck Dressen, who had managed against Lavagetto as Cincinnati's skipper, but Dressen wasn't giving us any.

Lavagetto took a swing at the first pitch. Then Bevens came in with his 137th pitch of the game, and Cookie hit it. Right away I know it's a low line drive to my left—but in the white shirts of the lower deck of the grandstand, when the style was still for men to wear white shirts, the white ball becomes lost for just a split second.

As soon as it comes out of those shirts, I know that if I catch it, the game is over and Bill Bevens has history's first World Series no-hit game. I also know that if I don't catch it, the game will be over with the Dodgers winning it, because Gionfriddo and Miksis don't have to wait to see if I can make the play. There are two outs, so they're running as soon as Cookie makes contact.

As soon as I see the ball again, I'm afraid I can't catch up with it. I tell myself, "Get away from that wall!" I don't want it to fly back past me toward the infield. As I'm backpedaling away from the wall, the ball hits it and bounces back to me, striking the heel of my glove.

I put my breaks on as well as I can, pick up the ball in a hurry, and throw it back to the infield, but I can't get anything on the throw because I don't have the leverage necessary. Gionfriddo and Miksis score, and Lavagetto's hit breaks up the Bevens no-hitter. The Dodgers win the game, 3–2, and tie the Series.

If I had seen the ball throughout its flight, I could have headed straight to the right-field foul line, parallel with the wall, and adjusted enough to catch it or field it on one bounce and get some steam on my throw, preventing Miksis from scoring Brooklyn's winning run.

That fly ball created one of the most difficult predicaments I've ever been in, and the outcome was one of the most bitter disappointments any of us ever experienced on a baseball diamond. The whole team was downcast in our locker room, but there was no sense of doom. Bevens was not an emotional man, and he showed no particular distress that afternoon.

I've always regretted that I wasn't able to make the play, but I've never second-guessed myself. I played it the only way you can, especially when you lose the ball in white shirts on its way to the outfield.

I never worried about it. I just went out the next day and did everything I could to get us another win. In baseball, unlike some sports, you don't have a week to lick your wounds or look at films or plan new strategy. You have to pick yourself up and be ready less than twenty-four hours later. That's what the Yankees did. It was the Yankee way.

Frank Shea gave us the big lift we needed the next day. The rookie with one win in the Series came back with a four-hitter and defeated the Dodgers when we got only five ourselves. It was a 2–1 game, and Joe D. won it on a home run in the fifth inning, but Shea wasn't entirely dependent on the rest of us. He got two hits and drove in our first run.

This was a tense game from start to finish, and Spec was at his best when the tension was at its worst. In the seventh inning, after the Dodgers got a run in the sixth to make it 2–1, he struck out Reese with the bases loaded. In the bottom of the ninth, Spider Jorgensen came up with the potential tying run on second base and a chance to tie or win the game.

And who was in the on-deck circle as the next hitter? Cookie

Lavagetto. To lose two days in a row in such similar circumstances would be almost too much to bear.

Shea got Jorgensen out on a fly ball to me in the right center. While DiMag and I were still near each other after I made the catch, he said, "Say a prayer." Spec struck out Lavagetto on a slider, his best pitch of the year.

In the clubhouse later, I told Frank Crosetti that DiMag asked me to say a prayer when Lavagetto came to bat. The Crow said, "Why didn't you tell *him* to pray?"

I put the matter to Joe D., and he said, "I *was* praying, but I wasn't sure I was getting through."

It's hard to imagine Joe DiMaggio feeling the need to look to anyone for help on a baseball field, but at least he was looking in the right place.

We went back to Yankee Stadium for the sixth game, ahead three wins to two and hoping to win the championship behind Allie Reynolds. Those vendors who yell "You can't tell the players without a scorecard" must have loved this one. The two managers used thirty-eight players in an 8–6 slugout that included twenty-seven hits—but no home runs.

The play that is remembered from this game wasn't one of those hits. It was a catch, the one by Al Gionfriddo against DiMaggio. It happened in the sixth inning, when we were behind, 8–5. Against Joe Hatten, with two on and two out, Joe hit a long fly ball to left center, and Gionfriddo, just inserted into the game that inning, took off and hauled it in near the bullpen in what has gone down in history as one of the greatest catches ever made in the World Series.

As good as it was, it didn't have to be that good. Gionfriddo could have gotten there sooner, and should have. He overran the ball slightly while running toward the bullpen and had to pivot slightly and come back a bit, making a longer run than necessary to get to the ball. Once he did, he made an excellent stab and held the ball for his famous play.

Joe was dashing toward second base at the moment of Gion-friddo's catch. He pulled up, and slapped at the infield dirt with his foot and kicked up a little cloud of dust. It was the only time in all the years we played together that I ever saw Joe show any kind of emotion, positive or negative, about anything on a ball field. I don't think anybody else ever saw it either, except at that one moment in his thirteen-year career.

Nor did he ever talk about anything like that. When he came back to the dugout after the Gionfriddo catch, and when we trotted out to the outfield for the next inning, he never said a word about it.

Once again, Joe had hit the ball a mile in Yankee Stadium and missed a home run. He didn't even get a base hit, out of a drive that was caught right in front of the 415-foot sign.

Branca picked up the victory in relief after his disappointing loss in the first game, and Joe Page was charged with the defeat. Ten pitchers appeared in this game, and we used six of them. But one, Joe Page, wasn't finished.

Fireman Joe and I teamed up to win the seventh game and the World Series. Shea tried to come back on only two days of rest for his third start of the Series, but he didn't have it. Bucky lifted him in only the second inning, with one out and the score 2–0 in favor of the Dodgers.

Trouble comes as no great surprise when a pitcher tries to pitch his third game in only seven days under the constant tension of the World Series, but what did surprise us was that Bevens couldn't help us either. He couldn't get his arm loose after his Superman performance of three days before. We got two and two-thirds innings from him, but he couldn't go past the fourth.

Page came in from the bullpen to start the fifth inning; we were ahead by one run, 3–2, on a run in the second and two runs in the fourth. Now all we had to do was shut out the Dodgers for five innings and we would be the world champions again.

That was unusually early to bring Page in, but Bucky knew he needed somebody who could shut the Dodgers out in what obviously was not going to be the same kind of free-swinging game we played the day before.

Harris could have brought in others who were more rested. This was Page's fourth appearance of the Series, and we didn't have a day off for travel, so it was four games in six days. It was asking a lot of your ace relief pitcher to bring him into the game in the fifth inning, especially in those years when we didn't have such specialization. There were no middle relievers and setup relievers and closers. There were just relief pitchers.

In the seventh game of the World Series, every pitcher on your staff is a relief pitcher. There's no reason to save a pitcher for the next game, because that won't be until spring training, so you're ready to throw in everybody if necessary.

As our fourth inning rally came to a close, Frank Crosetti got on the telephone and talked to Art Schulte, our coach in the bullpen. Then he turned to Bucky in the dugout and shouted, "Schulte says Page doesn't have a thing and that the Indian is knocking the glove off his hand."

Larry MacPhail was hiding on the steps leading to the dugout; he couldn't stand the excitement in his mezzanine seat. He said later he knew what Bucky was thinking: that Page was the man he wanted. Now they were telling him that Page had nothing.

MacPhail said Harris turned to him and said, "Well, it means as much to you as it does to me." Larry said he shrugged his shoulders, telling Harris it was his decision.

Then Bucky turned to Crosetti and said, "Give me Page."

MacPhail was awed by Bucky's firmness, courage, and instinct. "That was one of the gamest and greatest moves I ever saw by a manager," Larry said. "He was standing by his guy, and he had everything to lose in view of what he had been told—if Page hadn't won it."

Bucky knew what he wanted. He wanted his best. That was Joe Page. That's exactly what Page gave him. He pitched expert baseball for the five innings, shut out the Dodgers the rest of the way, and saved the game and our World Series championship in a 5–2 victory. He threw a total of one curveball, to Gil Hodges, and one slider, to Harry Walker. Everything else was a fastball.

I was privileged to drive in the go-ahead run. Shotton lifted Gregg with two outs in the fourth inning and brought in Behrman to face Stirnweiss. He walked Snuffy. Then I came up. I hit his first pitch for a single to right field to score Rizzuto with what turned out to be the winning run. It gave us the lead for the first time in the game, 3–2. It was the third time in our four victories that I was able to drive in the clutch run.

After our victory, Burt Shotton congratulated us as the better ball club, but he made a prediction about what the future held for both teams. "A better ball club beat us this time," he said to reporters. "I'll tell you this: We'll beat the Yankees during the next ten years a whale of a lot more times than they'll beat us."

The Yankees met the Dodgers in the World Series again in 1949, 1952, 1953, 1955, and 1956. Brooklyn won only in 1955.

For two of our youngest teammates, that World Series held different fortunes. Bobby Brown, the golden boy with the sweet, sweet swing, was called on by Bucky to pinch-hit four times. That's an unusual number of times to put so much pressure on a rookie, but Bobby responded successfully in each at-bat. He hit two doubles and a single and drew a walk that forced home a run. He scored twice and drove in three other runs. Any rookie in the game would give his bonus for that kind of a World Series.

The gods were not so kind to Yogi Berra. He hit only .158, and the Dodgers stole him blind with those five steals against him in only three and one-third games behind the plate. His new claim to fame as the first man to hit a pinch-hit home run in the World Series wouldn't be much consolation. What most people didn't know about Yogi, however, was that he had a strep throat infection all through the Series. He received penicillin shots every day so he could take the field.

For many of the men who played in that World Series, it was a fateful time. Three who were key figures in dramatic plays— Lavagetto, Gionfriddo, and Bevens—never played another big-league game. Harris, having managed in his third World Series, never managed in one again.

Fate was kinder where Joe Page and Jackie Robinson were concerned. Page repeated his heroics the next time he played in a World Series. Robinson continued to make baseball history.

As for me, I felt good about my contributions to the team's success during the year and in the Series, where I drove in the key run in three of our four wins and hit .323, the highest average on either team for those who played in every game. I also felt flattered that my teammates elected me to a new responsibility on every team—player representative. Major-league players were getting organized, the inevitable result of the harsh attitude owners had shown toward players for so many decades.

Johnny Murphy on our team, Dixie Walker of the Dodgers, and several other leaders around both leagues began to speak with a unified voice on issues of concern to us as players. It was the start of the movement that led to the establishment of the Major League Baseball Players Association, the players' union. Dom DiMaggio was active in the cause for the Red Sox, and so was Bob Feller for the Indians.

I didn't look forward to being busy on nonplaying matters during the season, but I knew we had a lot of things to get corrected. The salaries were not the main issue, but some of our working conditions were—not to mention baseball's own form of modern slavery, the reserve clause, which bound each of us to our teams and prevented us from changing employers like any other American worker.

Joe D., Bob Feller and Ted Williams broke through the $100,000 barrier in the years just after the end of World War II, the first baseball players to earn that much in salary for one season. That dazzling amount was as rich in meaning as it was in money for all three of them. It was a new peak at the top of their profession. Not even Babe Ruth had earned that much.

The financial significance was not lost on any of them either. After all, they started their professional careers with modest salaries. Joe began by making $350 a month with the San Francisco Seals in the mid-1930s and earned $8,500 when he and Feller were rookies in '36. In 1938 the payroll for the whole Yankee team was $350,000.

As a bonus to such an action-packed and productive season, I picked up a nickname, one that stuck with me through the rest of my playing career and even to today.

Mel Allen and Russ Hodges were our announcers that year. In an extra-inning game in Philadelphia, when we were in danger of missing our train back to New York, I doubled to drive in the winning run just in time. In the broadcast booth that day, Mel and Russ said my habit of getting important hits late in the game reminded them of the name of a train that used to run through Mel's home town back in Alabama.

Mel's townfolks knew you could set your watch by the time that train came through town every day. They called it ''Old Reliable.''

More Changes at the Top

The weirdest thing happened at the end of the '47 Series. After succeeding Ed Barrow early in the season, Larry MacPhail, the most impulsive of human beings, suddenly resigned right after Joe Page finished pitching us to victory, on the same day.

He spent the ninth inning of the seventh game in the press snack bar at Yankee Stadium, listening on the radio. He told the people around him, "If they win it, I'm through." When Bruce Edwards hit into a double play to end the World Series, he said, "That's it. That does it. That's my retirement."

In our dressing room, holding a bottle of beer, he said, "I've got what I wanted, and I'm through. I can't take any more of this. My health won't stand it . . . From now on, I'm out of the picture."

Then, at our victory party that night, he impulsively assumed his authority again and decided to fire George Weiss as our farm director. Weiss went outside with Russ Hodges and sat in his car and cried. The whole explosion was finally resolved in MacPhail's resignation and Weiss's appointment as his successor in the general manager's position. It was as big a story as our victory.

Then something else happened. Russ Hodges was fired by Weiss, and the players always suspected it was because Russ saw Weiss crying. George's reputation was that he could do something like that against Hodges or anyone else.

The principal owners, Dan Topping and Del Webb, remained above the battles as much as possible. They were wealthy and successful executives who knew that they didn't have to become involved in such warfare, and that it was better for the organization if they didn't, at least not publicly.

Topping was a handsome, tall man, always tanned and well groomed. One of his grandfathers was president of Republic Steel. The other owned a fortune in tin. Topping was married six times, once to ice skater Sonja Henie, owned two football teams named the Brooklyn Dodgers and the New York Yankees—yes, football—and kept busy serving on several corporate boards including National Airlines and Madison Square Garden. During World War II he was a major in the Marine Corps and spent twenty-six months in the Pacific.

Webb was an eminently successful construction executive, the head of Del E. Webb Construction Company in Phoenix, partner in thirty-one other companies, and a member of the board of forty-three corporations. He didn't splash his wealth around on his appearance. He wore horn-rimmed glasses that one newspaper man said made him look like the president of the local civic association. Another said he looked like a junior college chemistry professor.

Although he did not look like a clothes horse, he made sure he had enough to wear. He admitted to owning between a hundred and fifty and two-hundred suits and fifty-two pairs of golf shoes. Webb had a legitimate baseball background as a player, having been a semi-pro pitcher in California.

With Webb's interest in baseball and Topping's background as an owner of sports teams, they were a natural combination to team up with MacPhail to buy the Yankees, which they did late in 1945. The papers said they paid Colonel Ruppert's estate $2.8 million for the team, about what you would pay as one year's salary to a utility infielder today.

The combination of ingredients within the ownership, however, was a fatal one. All three men were successful, confident, and decisive executives. But MacPhail was also erratic, impulsive, and explosive. In contrast, Webb and Topping were reserved and stable, always the picture of professionalism and businesslike behavior. With such fundamental differences in personality and conduct, the partnership was doomed from the start.

How it came unstuck after only two full seasons is the rest of the story. We were enjoying our 1947 victory party at the Biltmore Hotel when MacPhail got into an argument about Branch Rickey and allegedly slugged John MacDonald, who had been a member of MacPhail's staff in Brooklyn. Then he fired Weiss. Then he almost got into a fight with Topping.

The story we players got later was that Webb and Topping visited Weiss in his room and calmed him down. Then they went looking for MacPhail but couldn't find him. As their next step, they called their lawyers and told them to draw up the papers to buy out MacPhail.

The next day they offered him $2 million, almost as much as their combined purchase price only two years before, and made it clear that accepting their offer would be the wisest course of action for MacPhail. They gave him a deadline of six o'clock that evening.

MacPhail signed the papers but visited Webb's office that afternoon and asked to see him. When Webb came out of his private office, MacPhail offered his hand and said, "Del, you've been a good partner to me."

Webb said, "I don't want to shake your hand." He made a few choice comments and walked away as MacPhail stood there.

That whole weird episode was a prelude to a disappointing season for the team in 1948, and maybe the most bizarre part of it all was that it happened on the very night that we won the Series. It made us wonder what the season ahead might hold for us, but as players we had to put the front-office uproar out of our minds and concentrate on our own performances.

Several of our key players had off years in 1948. Coupled with Bucky's leave-them-alone style of managing, the effect in a close race was enough to cost us the pennant. The Indians, behind a strong pitching staff of Bob Feller, Bob Lemon, and a knuckleball rookie named Gene Bearden, plus the leadership of Lou Boudreau, their shortstop and manager, finished in first place. They did it the hard way, beating the Red Sox in the American League's first playoff after they finished the season in a tie.

Only three wins separated our three teams, and some of us Yankees felt that we were still the best team in the American League and should have won the pennant again. We didn't have anybody to blame but ourselves as a team.

Joe D. had another banner year, winning the league's home-run and RBI titles and hitting .320. One of the reasons that he didn't win the Most Valuable Player Award for a third time is that Lou Boudreau won it by managing the Indians skillfully while hitting .355 and leading the league's shortstops in fielding. Nobody else is going to be voted MVP when someone is doing all those things, and doing them so well on a team that wins the pennant.

DiMaggio played in our opening game of the season, and some of us were hoping that it was the sign of a good year ahead for the team. Joe had played in only four of our openers since coming up in 1936. He was hitting in the cleanup spot when we opened in Washington. He hit a single and a double as we romped over the Senators, 12–4, on the strength of seven runs in the first inning of the season.

I hit .308 and finished among the league leaders in doubles and triples again. I was second in doubles with 42, seven more than the year before and second only to Williams, and I was first in triples again with 14, one more than the year before. After finishing second to Williams in '47 in runs scored with 109, I led the league in '48 with 138, eleven more than Dom DiMaggio.

My fun didn't stop there. I tied the American League record for the most home runs with the bases loaded in one season with four—and how I missed breaking it is as good a story as the home runs themselves.

With four grand slams already to my credit, I came to bat against the Philadelphia A's at Yankee Stadium late in the season with the bases loaded. I was facing Dick Fowler, a good right-handed pitcher. The count went to three balls and one strike. That count, or two balls and no strikes, is a hitter's delight. You know the pitcher must throw a strike to avoid walking you, and the chances are he'll throw a fastball, which is usually the easiest pitch to control.

Fortunately for the hitter, it is also usually the easiest pitch to hit. This was especially true of me, because I was always a tough fastball hitter. Curveballs were a different story, but fastballs were my meat.

When I looked down to the third-base coach's box for the signal to hit or take, I was surprised. Chuck Dressen was giving me the "take" sign. With the kind of year I was having, I thought I might get the green light. On 3–0 it would have been understandable, but there are few times when I would give a hot hitter the take sign on a 3–1 pitch.

In fact, I've often wondered if Bucky really flashed "take" to Dressen for him to relay to me. I just can't imagine Bucky doing that at that stage of things. But that's what the signal said.

I had to let the pitch go—a fastball, right down Broadway.

Now the count was full. I swung at the next pitch and sent a long fly ball into the third deck—foul. In my frustration and disappointment, I rounded first and second anyhow, pretending not to know the ball was going foul.

On the next pitch, I hit another long fly ball to right. The A's right fielder, Elmer Valo, caught it within five feet of the wall. I had to settle for a tie in the record books with Lou Gehrig, Rudy York, Fred Schulte, and Vince DiMaggio, and I'll be proud to be put in that company any time.

However, I'm one of those who believe that every record is meant to be broken. In the case of four grand slams in one season, Jim Gentile of the Baltimore Orioles broke it with five in 1961. Then Don Mattingly of the Yankees hit six in 1987.

McQuinn's batting average dropped fifty-six points and Rizzuto's twenty-one. With George's dropoff in hitting, Harris was back to the Yankees' old post-Gehrig problem of finding somebody who could hit and play first base. He penciled me onto the lineup card as his first baseman 46 times, the most games I had played at first base up to that season, plus 102 games in right field.

If you had to single out one difference in our team in '48 over '47, it would have to be in the effectiveness of Joe Page. He was second in the league in saves with 16 and tops in games pitched with 55, only one less in each department than the year before, but the difference was more than the numbers involved. He just didn't have that overpowering effectiveness of '47. In that season, when he strutted in from the bullpen with all the confidence in the world, every one of us felt that our lead in that game was money in the bank. In '48 we didn't get that feeling from Joe.

Page led all American League pitchers in the balloting for the 1947 Most Valuable Player Award, including the dominating Bob Feller, who won 20 games. As a reward, George Weiss, in one of his first major decisions after replacing MacPhail as general manager, changed Page's contract from one with a bonus arrangement to one recognizing Joe's outstanding '47 season with a straight salary of $20,000 for 1948.

Page was bothered by a throat infection for part of the season. He pitched in one game when he had a temperature of 103 degrees, but he didn't tell Harris. He answered Bucky's every call, so another possibility is that after pitching in the most games in the league in '48 and the second most in '47, he was becoming overworked.

Then there was always Joe's fondness for the bright lights. Among the players, the only ones who knew Joe was breaking training were the ones who were doing it with him. The rest of us were not aware of it. But Weiss was.

In late July, Weiss ran out of patience with what he considered Page's failure to keep in shape. He hired a private detective, who reported later that Fireman Joe was a frequent visitor to the nightclubs in Westchester County.

The day after one of those alleged nights on the town, or on the county, Page was knocked out of the game. The front office fined him and raised that standard Yankee threat to ship him back to Newark.

By this point, Bucky's relaxed manner of managing was catching up with us as a team. But Bucky was the most loyal man on earth. He stuck by his boy Page, even though he ended the season as a below-.500 pitcher. He dropped from 14 wins and 8 losses in 1947 to only 7 wins against 8 losses, and his ERA, only 2.48 in '47, jumped to 4.26.

When Weiss put a gumshoe on Page's tail, it was only one of two times he did something like that in 1948. The other time came on one of our western road trips. We were in Chicago for a series against the White Sox when the word began to spread among us that Weiss had a detective following us when we weren't at the ballpark. But something happened that Weiss hadn't counted on: The detective seemed to find out that she—yes, she—enjoyed certain newly discovered fringe benefits in her job.

The favorite hangout for most teams when we were in Chicago was a place called Neal's Bar, across the street from our hotel, the Del Prado. The story flashed through the Yankee players that somewhere between the bar and a park along Lake Michigan only about four blocks away, the detective propositioned one of our players.

Maybe she wanted some firsthand information to include in her report to Weiss at the end of our road trip about our carryings-on. Whatever her reason was, she and her favorite player apparently staged a rendezvous on the rocks along the lake. All of us heard about it.

At the end of our road trip, the detective submitted her report to Weiss. Whether she included information about her unique meeting by the shores of Lake Michigan we didn't know. But two things we did know: One, Weiss made Bucky read the report. Two, the mere fact that management had a detective following us, regardless of what she put in her report or didn't put in, did us no good at all as a team.

In the close finish that followed, Weiss might have wished he hadn't stirred up so much resentment among his players. We finished only two and a half games out of first place. A happier team might have won the pennant for him.

In the final weeks of the season, we made a run at the Red Sox and Indians but were eliminated in the last week, before they finished in their tie. A few days after the Indians beat the Boston Braves in the World Series, Bucky was fired and Weiss began shopping Page around to the other teams looking for a trade.

In contrast to Page's performance in '48 versus '47, Vic Raschi, after his sensational string of wins that helped us to the pennant, was even better in '48, but we never would have guessed it from his start.

He was knocked out of the box in his first start, in two and a third innings, against the Senators. Vic was anxious to increase his velocity, so over the winter he had intentionally put on some weight. He had a ready explanation for his poor first showing:

"My body had yet to coordinate with the additional weight." For that and his cuffing-around in his first start, Bucky sent him to the bullpen.

Harris brought Raschi into our game on May 1 against the Red Sox in Boston, and he worked an inning and a third. Then Bucky started him again a week later against the Tigers in New York. Vic was pitching a four-hitter in the eighth inning when he had to leave the game because of a cramped muscle in his pitching arm. We beat the Tigers, 9–1, and Vic was off on another one of his winning streaks.

He beat the A's, 3–0, on a three-hitter, then the White Sox on a seven-hitter, 13–2. Then he beat the Tigers again, 16–5, and the A's again, 2–1, in a game stopped after five innings because of rain. Then he knocked off the Tigers for the third time, 1–0, on a five-hitter, and added the St. Louis Browns to his list of victims, 3–0, on another three-hitter.

It added up to a personal string of seven straight victories for Vic, and at one point he pitched twenty-two straight shutout innings. Another highlight for him came when Bucky picked him for the All-Star team. Harris pitched him in the middle three innings, and Vic responded by pitching shutout ball and driving in two runs with a single as we beat the National League, 5–2, in the years when we beat them regularly.

Vic finished the season with 19 wins—the fourth highest number in the league—the fifth most strikeouts, third most complete games, second most shutouts, and the third most strikeouts for every nine innings pitched.

He was doing everything right, even when it came to chewing tobacco. "Nobody can chew or hold as much chewing tobacco as I can," he said. "When I'm pitching I like to eat a whole dime's worth. They tell me that over television it looks good."

Despite the contributions by Vic and others, our ball club just did not seem to have that feeling and atmosphere in 1948 that we expected to find on our Yankee teams. The environment never was the same after McCarthy left, even with Bucky's championship in '47. McCarthy ran a tight ship, but Harris just wasn't that kind of a fiery manager at that stage in his career.

One example that I still remember occurred not in 1948 when

we sputtered at times, even though we won 94 games and finished 34 games over .500, but in '47, when we won it all. It happened in a game in New York against the Washington Senators.

We were in the ninth inning. We were losing, but we had men on first and second when I came to bat. Mickey Vernon was playing first base for the Senators. Before stepping into the batter's box, I looked down to the third-base coach's box for a sign. Nothing. I asked for time out, went back to our bench on the first-base side, and asked Harris if he wanted me to bunt the runners to second and third or swing away trying for an extra-base hit that might drive in both runners and tie up the game.

Bucky said simply, "Do what you want, Tom."

It was a compliment to me, and I appreciated Bucky's respect for my ability to get a big hit and win a game from time to time— but now I had to dictate the strategy, too. I noticed that Vernon was playing back, expecting me to swing away instead of bunting. I decided to try to get him to take some bait from me. On the first pitch, I faked a drag bunt to draw Mickey in for the next pitch.

Mickey took the bait. He crept in a little closer than he had been. The pitch was ball one. I did the same thing on the next pitch, and Mickey crept in a little more. As it turned out, I wasn't able to get a hit, but I was able to avoid hitting into a rally-killing double play—all because the strategy was dictated not by the team's manager but by his hitter.

Nothing like that would ever have happened under Joe McCarthy. He was firmly in charge at every moment, and he, not the player, ordered the strategy to be followed. The player's job was to obey McCarthy's orders and carry out his strategy. McCarthy led us firmly and confidently, and we, as his players, responded well to his leadership.

Under Bucky we were a very relaxed ball club—too relaxed in my opinion. We didn't have that fire in our bellies that McCarthy kept stoking all season long, and we didn't have as many clubhouse leaders as we did under McCarthy. This, plus only average years by Page and a few others, was enough to keep us from winning the pennant in 1948. Some others outside the team also thought we should have won it. Unfortunately for Bucky, that group included the Yankee management.

Weiss fired Bucky after the 1948 season. He never did like the

Harris style of managing. He thought Bucky was too soft. He wanted someone he respected more, and when he announced Casey Stengel as his choice to be our manager beginning in 1949, I was shocked. And I wasn't the only one.

Weiss, blessed with the same great ability that Ed Barrow had to come up with important additions to the team at critical points, produced a couple of new faces for us in 1948 who would help us to begin a string of successes the next year that would break our own record. They were Hank Bauer and Ed Lopat.

Bauer was one tough, determined leader, and he looked the part. Jan Murray, the comedian, said Hank's face looked like a clenched fist. No less than Joe DiMaggio said, "The only guy I ever saw who hustled more than Bauer was Enos Slaughter."

After what he went through during World War II, playing baseball and getting paid for it must have been a piece of cake. He was a marine in the South Pacific. He came down with malaria almost as soon as he got there and lost thirty pounds, dropping to 160. Over the next four years he had twenty-four malaria attacks.

Hank was wounded on Guam, and Joe Page used to clown around in our dressing room by picking pieces of shrapnel out of Hank's back. After Guam he survived the invasion of Okinawa, when his platoon hit the beach with sixty-four men and only six got out alive. Sergeant Bauer was wounded again, this time with a piece of shrapnel that tore a hole in his left thigh.

His fighting was finished for the duration. His line in the box score read: thirty-two months of combat, eleven campaign ribbons, two Purple Hearts, and two Bronze Stars.

Bauer was a Yankee for twelve seasons, and during that time they won nine pennants and seven World Series. He was a leader in baseball just as he was in the marines. *Time* magazine once wrote, "He never led the league in anything—except hustle. And that made him a Yankee great."

To say he never led the league in anything is almost true—he led the league in triples in 1957—but it doesn't give a full picture of Hank's abilities. He was an aggressive, hustling outfielder, and at the plate he was a big help to the Yankee offense with two .300-plus seasons and three others in the .290s. He was a respected power hitter with 164 career home runs, including ten straight years in double figures and two seasons when he hit 20 and 26 homers.

In World Series competition, the old marine's competitive fires burned brighter than ever. He still has the fifth most hits, fourth most triples, tenth most home runs, tenth most runs scored, and eighth most runs batted in. If you can get that kind of superb performance from a guy who "never led the league in anything," I'll take a whole team of them—and beat any team you want to send against us in the World Series.

Hank played the only way he knew how—hard. Johnny Pesky of the Red Sox remembers seeing him roaring into second base many times. "When Hank came down that base path," Johnny said, "the whole earth trembled."

Whitey Ford remembers his first game for the Yankees. "I came flying into the locker room at one o'clock," he said. "I had overslept. Nobody said anything, but Bauer gave me that look of his. I dressed and ran. As it turned out, I won the game."

Whitey remembers what happened after the game, too. Bauer went over to Ford's locker and said, "Whitey, if you'd lost that game, you'd be dead."

I was overjoyed when I heard we had gotten Ed Lopat from the White Sox in a trade for Aaron Robinson, Fred Bradley, and Bill Wight. There were two reasons for my happiness:

  1. I was sure Lopat would be a big winner for us.
  2. Now I wouldn't have to hit against him.

Billy Evans, an umpire in the American League for twenty-two seasons, called him "the most exasperating pitcher in baseball" because of his mixture of breaking pitches, different speeds, and masterful control. Evans said, "Opposing batters accuse him of throwing phantom balls. Every pitch looks different to the confused hitters." Evans also said umpires didn't like Lopat any more than we hitters did because "frequently he fools both."

Ted Williams came up to me in Boston during the '48 season in the runway leading to the playing field in Fenway Park and asked me, "Do you ever walk up to the plate and feel as if your coordination is all shot?"

I laughed at him and said, "Sure, too many times. Why?"

Just then the playing field came into view, and Ted nodded in

Lopat's direction and said, "Well that's how I feel every time I have to hit against this guy."

Lopat had won fifty games in four years with Chicago, but when he came to New York, he was coming home. He was born Edmund Lopatynski on East 5th Street along new York's Lower East Side, the son of a shoemaker. When he was four, his family moved uptown to East 98th Street and Madison Avenue, where Ed attended St. Cecilia's School, P.S. 72, P.S. 171, and DeWitt Clinton High School in the Bronx, not far from Yankee Stadium.

He didn't own a baseball glove until he was fifteen, and then it was a used first-baseman's mitt because that was his position. He jumped at the chance to make $50 a month playing for Greensburg in the Penn State League, beginning a seven-year tour in the minor leagues with other stops at towns named Jeanerette, Louisiana, in the Evangeline League; Kilgore, Texas, in the East Texas League; Shreveport, Louisiana, in the Texas League; Longview, Texas, back in the East Texas League; Shreveport again; Marshall, Texas, in the East Texas League; Salina, Kansas, in the Western Association; Oklahoma City, in the Texas League for his third term; and finally Little Rock, Arkansas, in the Southern Association.

Lopat was not an imposing figure on the mound. He was on the stocky side, five-feet-ten and 185 pounds. He had a couple of bouts with ulcers, probably caused by a combination of anxiety to make good and the lousy food we used to eat in the minor leagues. His lowest point must have been the time in 1941 when he was hospitalized for six weeks with them.

Ed was out of action for nine weeks—and had to pay the hospital bill himself. It came to $240. He scraped up some cash for part of the bill and paid off the balance at two dollars a week over the next year and a half.

Someone asked him once if he thought about quitting. Ed told them, "Of course I thought of quitting. Who wouldn't?"

He worked his way through those trying times, and in the process he decided to see if his luck would change as a pitcher because his hitting ability might not get him to the big leagues.

When he became a pitcher, Lopat also became a serious student of the art. He studied hitters from the bench or the bullpen on the days when he wasn't pitching. He learned their tendencies and then took advantage of them. He combined this with such consistent control of his pitches that he earned the nickname of "Steady Eddie." One of our coaches, Red Corriden, said, "He walks sixty men a season—fifty-nine of them on purpose."

He explained his philosophy and strategy of pitching by using Rudy York as an example: "If York had two balls and no strikes against me," he said, "he'd look for breaking stuff. If the count was two strikes and no balls, he'd look for fastballs. I'd do the opposite, and he'd give me the damndest look you ever saw."

Bobby Doerr of the Red Sox had some success against Lopat when Ed came into the league. Lopat threw slow stuff to whoever was hitting in front of Doerr that day, setting Doerr up for the fastball on the first pitch. Eventually Doerr got wise and started hitting him. Then Lopat got wise too, went to slow stuff, and got Doerr out.

"You have to find out a hitter's way of thinking as well as his way of hitting," Ed said. "The way a batter shows you his way of thinking is by his reflexes in relation to the ball. If I throw a batter a fastball and he just ticks it, he wasn't looking for a fastball.

"Then I may throw him another fastball, but that depends on where the first one was. Now, if you get a smart hitter out with a pitch and you give it to him again his next time up with less than two strikes on him, you're crazy. After two strikes your chances are better because he has to protect the plate and can't take the full swing."

Williams got rid of that uncoordinated feeling against Lopat to hit the longest home run that Ed ever gave up—thirty rows into the seats in Fenway. Later he told Lopat, "You've been getting me out for two years with that slider on the first pitch. How stupid could I get?"

When Lopat came to us, he thought of himself as mainly a hot-weather pitcher, but Bucky Harris, the old pro that he was, convinced Ed that the business about hot and cold and spring and fall was all in the head.

Bucky told him, "A good pitcher will win in the cold and in

the heat. A bad one won't win at any time. A great horse will win on any track. I think *you* can win on any track.''

It was interesting that Billy Evans said what he did about Ed Lopat's pitches fooling umpires as much as they fooled hitters. I never had serious problems with umpires in person, just the usual disagreements that all players and managers have with them from time to time. I was never thrown out of a game in either the majors or the minors. But as a group of people, they were not on my list of the professional groups I admired the most.

I felt when I played, and still feel today, that too many members of the umpiring profession approach their jobs with precisely the wrong mentality. Those are the ones who seem to be impressed with their own power. When they were wrong, I didn't expect them to admit it, because they never do. But I didn't think it was unreasonable to expect them to be willing to discuss the question or at least to hear what my point was. Too often they don't let you do that. Instead they hide behind their authority by telling you, before you've had a chance to tell them your point, "One more word and you're gone."

What kind of attitude is that? Yet I had umpires tell me that more times than I want to remember. Today, with the all-powerful influence of television, the problem is even worse—and so is the umpiring. Too many of them know they're on camera, so they make theatrical gestures and give the arguing player or manager a flamboyant arm wave out of the game as part of their own private little performance.

The truth is that's the sign of a poor umpiring performance. The best umpires are the ones you never notice: those who keep the game under control, work hard to be where they are supposed to be to make the right call on the play, and listen with respect to a player or manager before telling him that he's ending the discussion.

After we retired, I asked Joe DiMaggio, "As a breed of man, did you like umpires?"

Joe said, "Oh, I got along with them all right, Tom."

I said, "Joe, that's not what I asked you. I got along with them all right, too. But my question was did you *like* umpires?"

He never answered.

Umpires have always made a major point of saying they want the players to show them respect as they perform their jobs. That's entirely reasonable. But if that's reasonable, isn't the reverse also reasonable? Shouldn't the umpires treat the players and managers with respect? Too many of them don't. Instead, they light their short fuse and then go into their TV show.

There are refreshing exceptions, and in those years the best of them all, in my opinion, was Cal Hubbard. There was a reason for that: He was a former professional athlete.

Hubbard was a big man, the only man to be elected to a hall of fame in two sports, the Baseball Hall of Fame as an umpire and the Pro Football Hall of Fame as a great football lineman with the New York Giants. He's in a third one, too—the College Football Hall of Fame—after starring at Centenary College in Shreveport, Louisiana, and Geneva College in Beaver Falls, Pennsylvania.

At six-feet-two-and-a-half and 265 pounds, Hubbard earned our respect for more than just his size. He played football until he was thirty-six. He umpired in the American League for fifteen seasons and was the league's supervisor of umpires for another sixteen years. All of that experience as an athlete made Cal a better umpire. As a result, he was a favorite among almost all American League players.

He was always in control of the game. Mike Tresh of the White Sox was catching in a game during the 1940s and complaining about Cal's calls on balls and strikes, and he continued for what Hubbard thought was too long. Cal leaned over to Tresh, who was five inches shorter, and said, "Mike, if you don't shut up, I'm going to hit you so hard on the top of the head that it will take a derrick to pull you back up to level ground."

Mike shut up.

You couldn't fool Cal, and that goes back to his own experience as an athlete. He was umpiring a game between the St. Louis Browns and us when Luke Sewell, the manager of the Browns, tried to get cute with him.

Our pitcher, Hank Borowy, put the fingers of his pitching hand to his lips, which is illegal, and Hubbard warned him about it. Hank didn't usually do that—but Nelson Potter, the Browns' pitcher, did it all the time, so Hubbard warned both managers to tell their pitchers not to go to their lips.

Potter continued to do it. "I'm sure," Hubbard said, "that Sewell told Potter to go to his mouth with an exaggerated motion, which he did. Nellie was a nice guy, but I ran him."

He developed a problem with Yogi during a game when Tommy Byrne was pitching for us. Tommy was as wild as ever, and Berra kept trying to pull Byrne's pitches back into the strike zone. While doing this, he also kept complaining about Hubbard's calls behind the plate.

When Hubbard had his fill of Berra, he leaned over him and said, "It's too much responsibility for you to umpire and catch too, Yog. One more word out of you and you're gone."

Berra said, "Well, bear down."

Hubbard told him, "That's it. You're gone."

Cal once had a two-part run-in with Jimmy Dykes, the colorful manager of the Chicago White Sox. Bert Shepard, the war hero who lost a leg as a P-38 pilot when he was shot down over Germany and made it to the big leagues anyhow while pitching on an artificial leg, remembers it.

Part one happened in Boston. It was a long game, and darkness became a factor. The White Sox were leading in the late innings, and Dykes went into several stalling tactics so Hubbard, the home-plate umpire that day, would call the game and Chicago would get the win.

With his goal getting closer, Dykes decided to change pitchers, thus using more time. When his new man reached the mound at Fenway Park, Dykes said that was the wrong pitcher. He wanted someone else, which would have taken up still more time while the darkness grew worse.

Hubbard wouldn't let him do it. He told Dykes, "Oh, no, Jimmy. I'm not letting you get away with that. This is the man you called for, and he's pitching."

Dykes argued—as only he could. Some of his arguments with umpires were classics. He said, "You're not satisfied with just umpiring the game. Now you want to manage my team, too. You're making my pitching decisions for me."

Hubbard just said, "Play ball."

Part two: The next week, the White Sox are in Washington to

start a three-game series. Ossie Bluege, Washington's manager, brings his lineup card to home plate before the game to present it to Hubbard, who is umpiring behind the plate again. Mule Haas, one of Jimmy's coaches, stands in for Dykes, a practice that some managers follow because they prefer to stay in the dugout and take care of more pressing matters while one of their coaches handles the routine business of presenting the lineup and going over the ground rules.

Hubbard takes Bluege's card, looks at it briefly, and accepts it. Under baseball rules, that officially sets the starting lineup for the Senators that day. Then Haas hands him the lineup for the White Sox made up by Dykes.

Hubbard routinely glances at the White Sox lineup. Then he says to Haas, "Wait a minute, Mule. There are only eight names here."

Haas says, "That's right, Cal. Dykes says you chose his pitcher in Boston and now you can do the same thing in Washington."

Hubbard goes over in front of the visitors' dugout on the third-base side at Griffith Stadium and throws Dykes out of the game before it even starts. It's one of the few times anyone ever was thrown out of a game before it started, and it must be the only time it happened when the one ejected never spoke to the umpire before getting the thumb.

Hubbard and Bill Summers were two of the most popular umpires, and for the same reasons. They ran their games well, they were decisive as well as accurate in their calls, they were always in position, and they didn't try to cover up their mistakes by flaunting their power. Nestor Chylak came along later and was a favorite among the American League players because he possessed those same abilities and attitudes.

Charlie Berry was my least favorite umpire because I considered him a "homer," an umpire who favors the home team in his decisions either because he is a performer playing to his audience or he is intimidated by the home fans and calls anything close their way.

I got into an argument with Berry one day and called him a homer as he was walking away from me. He whipped around and yelled, "What did you say?"

I didn't repeat it. I knew he wanted me to say it again to make sure he heard me right, and then he could throw me out of the game because calling an umpire a homer is about the worst insult you can make against him. Discretion is more than just the better part of valor—it's a way to keep from getting thrown out of a baseball game, too. I kept quiet and got to stay in the game.

Bill McGowan was never a big favorite of mine even though he enjoyed a great reputation, especially as the best balls and strikes umpire in baseball. I always found him autocratic, the kind of umpire you couldn't approach if you had a question about one of his calls.

When I was a rookie, several of the veterans around the league asked me, "Had any run-ins with McGowan yet?" In each case, when I said no, they said, "You will."

They warned me that McGowan would "get" me, and when I asked what for, they told me he would figure something out.

Red Rolfe and I had a set-to with him. Red grounded out, and on his way back to the dugout he called over to me and told me to get a look at the ball in case it was doing funny things because of a spot or a scratch. When I asked McGowan, he said, "What? You want to see the ball?"

I said, "Yes. I'd like to take a look at it."

With that McGowan sticks his finger in my face and starts to wave it like a first grade teacher lecturing one of her six-year-olds. "*You* can't look at the ball. Only *I* look at the ball."

So I said, "Well, then, would you take a look at it?"

He finally did. But it took that much of a discussion to get him to respond to a routine question, one that is an accepted request that umpires hear and grant every day of their lives.

Despite my reservations about McGowan, I credit him for giving some of the best advice for young umpires I've heard: "Make the players and managers respect you by your hustling. Keep on top of the plays. Always try to give a manager or a player a civil answer. Then walk away tough."

Like most veterans, McGowan couldn't be fooled. Joe McCarthy found that out when he tried to pull a fast one on him after the umpire threw Jake Powell out of the game when we were playing the Red Sox in Fenway.

McCarthy, always thinking, didn't want to lose Powell for the game, so he turned to one of our pitchers, Marius Russo, and said, "You go. Maybe he'll be satisfied."

As Russo was walking near the plate, going through the motions of leaving the game, McGowan said, "Where are you going? I want Powell, not you."

Russo comes back to our bench, but McCarthy says, "Try it again."

This time Russo makes it all the way to the plate on his way across the infield, but McGowan grabs him by the arm and leads him all the way back to our dugout. Then he hollers at McCarthy: "When I want Powell, don't give me Russo. Powell, get out of here!"

McGowan placed a certain amount of importance on displaying his authority through his gestures, and that's not a bad idea. Being emphatic and decisive is part of being a good umpire, and in that phase of his job, McGowan was one of the best.

The story was told that after he made it to the big leagues as an American League umpire in 1925 he practiced his calls in his hotel room with another umpire, Roy Van Graflan. The two would jerk their thumbs into the air in the gesture used then to call runners out and bellow at the top of their lungs, "Yer out!"

They'd keep repeating the gesture and the yell to improve their umpiring form. At one hotel, after more calls of "Yer out!" than the guests in the other rooms could count, someone hollered up from the hotel courtyard, "Hey! Don't you guys ever call anybody safe?"

When he was a rookie umpire, McGowan was told by one of the veterans that he could improve his wardrobe considerably by becoming friends with the traveling salesmen that umpires would run into in their hotel lobbies around the league.

"Just butter them up, entertain them a bit," he was told, "and you'll be able to get shirts, shoes, and everything you need for wholesale prices. Sometimes they'll even give you free samples."

Just such an opportunity arose shortly after. McGowan saw a man who looked as if he might be a traveling salesman in the hotel lobby, struck up a conversation with him, and found out that, sure enough, that's what he was.

So McGowan proceeded to suggest dinner and picked up the check. Then they had a couple of drinks, and McGowan picked up that check, too. Then as the evening came to a close, his stranger-turned-friend said to McGowan, "It's been a wonderful evening, Bill." He thanked him for such a good time.

McGowan said, "By the way. You never did mention what firm you're a salesman for."

The answer: "The Baldwin Locomotive Company."

In the National League, one of the best was Augie Donatelli. He told a writer, Larry Gerlach, "Umpiring is more than applying the rules and handling situations. You must be alert mechanically, be in the right position. That's important . . . If you're not in the right position and you guess at it, that is not good and you'll really catch hell."

He also talked about the mechanics involved in making a call: "You have to be decisive, and I always made a simple but very decisive motion. But no gestures, no dancing or jumping around. Toward the end of my career, some of the boys started 'showboating.' To me, showboating is out because you start taking your eyes off the ball and thinking more about how you make a particular call than the play itself."

Today's umpires, in this age of television, should take note.

Another sadness crept into the lives of the Yankees and baseball fans all over the world in 1948 when Babe Ruth died on the evening of August 16, seven years after our other beloved Yankee, Lou Gehrig, passed away.

Ruth died of cancer, and apparently he was the only one in New York who didn't know he had it. He had been sick off and on for two years, but members of his family believed that he never realized the nature of his illness, and they didn't tell him.

The New York writers and broadcasters, who were aware of his cancer, never reported it. Jack Lait, who was then editor of the *New York Daily Mirror*, wrote a column called "Broadway and Elsewhere." In his column after Babe died, Lait wrote, "Every newspaperman in New York knew for years that Babe Ruth had cancer of the throat. Yet that was never written. We knew he did not suspect and feared that the dread word would break him down."

Babe's body lay in state in the rotunda of Yankee Stadium from five o'clock the next afternoon until seven o'clock the following morning, before the funeral at St. Patrick's Cathedral on Fifth Avenue.

No more appropriate place could have been selected for the viewing than Yankee Stadium. After all, it has always been called "the House That Ruth Built" with his home runs that attracted all those fans and their dollars and made the Yankee organization successful. And it was his three-run homer that won the first game ever played there, on April 18, 1923.

In Japan, every baseball game in the country was halted for one minute in silent tribute to the man they called "Babu Russu." The gesture was proof that World War II was indeed over. Only four years earlier, Japanese soldiers were yelling "To hell with Babe Ruth!" from their sniper positions in the Pacific Islands to sucker American soldiers and marines out of their foxholes.

Former President Herbert Hoover joined in the thousands of tributes to the most famous athlete in the world, and an anecdote he told to reporters may have summed up the Babe Ruth story better than all the eulogies printed or spoken.

He said that during a visit to Los Angleles while he was president and Ruth was at his peak, a little boy asked Hoover for three autographs. When the president asked why he needed to sign his name for the kid three times, the boy said he wanted to keep one— and trade the other two for one of the Babe.

The Greatest Season of All

For the Yankees, 1949 was a year that had everything: high drama, deep disappointment, extremes in winning and losing, alarming injuries and exhilarating comebacks—and a pennant race so exciting that one of America's most prominent authors, David Halberstam, felt moved to write a book about it and *The Summer of '49* became a best-seller.

The season began with genuine cause for concern for two reasons: One, we were playing lousy baseball. Two, Joe DiMaggio was recovering from surgery for bone spurs on his right heel. No one knew when he would be able to play again, only that he might miss months, maybe the whole season.

On top of that, we had more adversity to overcome, which pennant winners must do. Charlie Keller was trying to return to his normal level of excellence after missing seventy-one games in '48 because of his back problems. Joe Page was a question mark after his off year in '48. Including Joe D., that's three essential players who were the subject of serious questions.

And we had Casey Stengel as our new manager.

Stengel came to us after fourteen years in the National League as a player and nine more as a manager—plus a reputation as a clown. He had an impish sense of humor, and some of the teams he was associated with, especially as a manager, were so bad he was driven to his antics just to preserve his own sanity and everyone else's.

In the minors, while playing for Maysville, Kentucky, in the Blue Grass League, he used to practice his sliding when going to his position in the outfield at the start of every inning.

There was an asylum for the insane across from the center-field fence, and its residents always cheered when they saw him slide into his outfield position. But Casey's manager used to tap his forehead and point at the asylum and say to him, "It's only a matter of time, Stengel."

He started playing pro ball in 1910 at the age of twenty, after discovering in his hometown of Kansas City that a left-handed person who wanted to be a dentist was in for a whole career of difficulty because the schools and the equipment were aimed at right-handers. So he signed a contract for $75 a month as an outfielder with Kankakee, Illinois, and then moved to Maysville after the folding of the league that Kankakee was in.

He made it to the majors in 1912 as Charles Dillon Stengel, but his teammates started calling him "K.C.," the original form of the nickname that stayed with him the rest of his life.

Casey was as much of a character in the majors as he was in the minors. He broke in with the Brooklyn Dodgers, and one of his first managers was the colorful Wilbert Robinson, known as "Uncle Robbie." During a dull moment in their spring training season of 1916, Stengel talked Uncle Robbie into trying to catch a baseball from one of those new inventions, an aeroplane, from four-hundred feet up.

Only Casey substituted a grapefruit. As the plane passed low over Daytona Beach, Robinson, never suspecting a thing, tried to catch what he assumed would be a baseball. The grapefruit sailed right through his hands and exploded against his chest. Uncle Robbie thought he had had a heart attack. Stengel said Robinson yelled, "I'm killed! I'm blind! It broke open my chest! I'm covered with blood! Somebody help me!"

Stengel isn't the only player who could have tried that against

Robinson, but he might have been the only one who could do it and live to tell about it. He played for Robinson for four of the first six seasons of his career, including two more after the grapefruit episode.

The Dodgers traded him to the Pirates in 1918, and on his first trip back to Brooklyn, he gave the Dodger fans another show. The Ebbets Field crowd greeted his return with a good-natured razzing. When he went to the outfield in the first inning, he saw a chance to get even. One of the members of the Dodgers' bullpen had captured a small sparrow, and Stengel went over and borrowed it. Then he slipped the bird under his cap.

"I could feel it breathing as I hustled to bat," he used to tell his audiences in later years. Stengel walked toward the batter's box while swinging five bats, acting as if he were going to hit one over the fence just to show up those Dodger fans. They responded with a loud round of boos.

Casey stepped up to the plate, waited until the pitcher was ready to throw, then asked for time out and stepped out of the box. Then he went through the motions of trying to get a piece of dirt out of his eye. The Dodger fans booed even louder.

Now he had his audience in just the right mood for his act. He turned toward the crowd, bowed low, and removed his cap with a wide sweep of his hand. The little bird, catching his first breath of fresh air after being held hostage on top of Casey's head, flew away to his regained freedom.

For the first few seconds, the crowd reacted in the way you would least expect: Silence. Then the stands almost collapsed in laughter.

Stengel was a .284 hitter for his career with a reputation for also being an excellent outfielder. He was a World Series hero, too, just as much as any of the Series heroes he managed for the Yankees. He hit an inside-the-park home run with two outs in the ninth inning to win the first game of the 1923 Series against the Yankees in brand-new Yankee Stadium.

Then he won the third game with a homer into the right-field seats in the seventh inning. In all he played in the World Series three times, with the 1922 and '23 Giants and the 1916 Dodgers, and hit a combined .393. The man could play.

He could teach, too. Mickey Mantle said that when he was a rookie with the Yankees, "I was just a kid shortstop, nineteen years old, and Stengel made me into an outfielder in a month."

His mangled statements to the news media became known as "Stengelese." Casey never ended a sentence. I think he used the word *which* to take the place of a period. But Casey knew precisely what he was saying—and doing. If he could confuse the reporters with his oral hocus-pocus, he could avoid giving them a direct answer.

He established his lingo as an art form with answers like this one in the mid-1950s:

> I guess the best guy I got is Berra who catches every day and then Mantle. Skowron maybe, but Skowron played a month only and then he got hurt so he can't count. Rest of our infield is pretty good, hard to pick out the best.
>
> I got that fella in left, and he can't field now, somebody else could use him, but I can't. So I wait, and then my big fella gets hurt because he's going at half-speed and he's got to bunt once in a while because he can't always swing from his heels. Especially when he hits the ball to the other side of the other fella he's sure to get on because nobody can catch him. But he wants to hit now and I give him his chance to play center and he does me a good job because he's a strong fella. But some fellas don't know about getting a thick handle like that Chicago fella does. He knows when you get it on the fists your muscle ain't worth a damn.
>
> But do you think these fellas understand that?

Translation: The "fella" in left field who "can't field now" was Bob Cerv. "My big fella" was Mickey Mantle. "The other fella" was the opposing pitcher. The one who "wants to hit now" is Cerv again. "That Chicago fella" is Nellie Fox.

Stengel raised Stengelese to a classic level with a virtuoso performance before the world's most skilled group in the art of oral confusion—Congress. It happened when he appeared before the Senate Subcommittee on Antitrust and Monopoly, chaired by Senator Estes Kefauver of Tennessee, on July 9, 1958.

The subcommittee was considering a bill requested by major-league baseball to solidify its exemption from antitrust laws, which had been granted in the 1920s, so it could operate the way it always had in matters like the reserve clause in our player contracts. Casey brought Mickey Mantle with him.

Senator Kefauver asked Casey if he supported the legislation before the subcommittee. In his answer, Casey was at the top of his game:

Well, I would have to say at the present time, I think that baseball has advanced in this respect for the player help. That is an amazing statement for me to make because you can retire with an annuity at fifty and what organization in America allows you to retire at fifty and receive money? I want to further state that I am not a ball player, that is, put into the pension fund committee. At my age, and I have been in baseball, well, I will say that I am possibly the oldest man who is working in baseball. I would say that when they start an annuity for the ball players to better their conditions, it should have been done, and I think it has been done. I think it should be the way they have done it, which is a very good thing. The reason why they possibly did not take the managers at that time was because radio and television or the income to ball clubs was not large enough that you could have put in a pension plan. Now I am not a member of the pension plan. You have young men here who are, who represent the ball clubs, they represent the players. And since I am not a member and don't receive pension from a fund which you think, my goodness, he ought to be declared in that, too, but I would say that is a great thing for the ball players. That is one thing I will say for the ball players, they have an advanced pension fund. I should think it was gained by radio and television or you could not have enough money to pay anything of that type.

In that thoroughly confused atmosphere, Senator Kefauver said, "Mr. Stengel, I am not sure that I made my question clear."

Casey answered, "Yes, sir. Well, that's all right. I'm not sure I'm going to answer yours perfectly either."

Kefauver kept trying: "I am asking you, sir, why it is that baseball wants this bill passed?"
Stengel elaborated:

I would say I would not know, but I would say the reason they want it passed is to keep baseball going as the highest-paid ball sport that has gone into baseball, and from the baseball angle—I am not going to speak of any other sport. I am not in here to argue about these other sports. I am in the baseball business. It has been run cleaner than any business that was ever put out in the one hundred years at the present time. I am not speaking about television or I am not speaking about income that comes into ballparks. You have to take that off. I don't know too much about it. I say the ball players have a better advancement at the present time.

By this time, Kefauver was becoming desperate for an answer to his question, so he turned to Mickey. "Mr. Mantle," he said, "do you have any observations with reference to the applicability of the antitrust laws to baseball?"
Mickey leaned into the microphone and said, "My views are just about the same as Casey's."

But Casey was no clown. He was a rich man thanks to highly successful investments in oil and banking. Jimmy Dykes, the manager of the Chicago White Sox, said, "Stengel's greatest asset as a manager is that he's independently wealthy." And when Casey got the Yankee job, he knew he didn't have to be a clown any more, so he became a serious, successful manager of men.
Casey couldn't have started his Yankee years in a clowning way anyhow. In a very real sense, he was a man with serious troubles. He was getting the chance of a lifetime as manager of the greatest team in baseball, but he was starting with the greatest player in the world out of action, recovering from more surgery for bone spurs on his heel.
Casey knew Bucky was fired simply because he didn't win the pennant both years. Winning it his first year and then coming within two and a half games in his second wasn't good enough by Yankee standards. You were expected to win every year. Casey

found that out after the 1960 World Series. In 1949, he suspected as much.

As he looked out at us at Al Lang Field in St. Petersburg that spring, he must have been asking himself, "Win the pennant with what? What do I see that makes anybody think we're going to win the pennant this year without DiMaggio when we couldn't win it last year—with DiMaggio playing 153 out of 154 games?"

Casey avoided clowning and concentrated on baseball. He wanted us to do the same in view of the obstacles we faced in hoping to regain the pennant, but there are always distractions that can creep into your life if you let them. Stengel was strict on that point, and he was never reluctant to let us know it, like the time he overheard several players talking about the stock market.

He came over to the conversation and said, "I've got a good tip for you guys. Buy all the railroad stock you can get."

One of the players said, "No fooling, Casey? How do you know?"

Stengel said, "Because when we start shipping you fellows back to the bush leagues next week, the railroads are going to get rich."

Beginning with his first year as our manager in 1949, Casey proved once more the truism that no manager can win without good players. When Stengel managed in the National League *without* good players, his teams lost. When he managed the Yankees *with* good players, his teams won.

He knew that as well as anyone. That's why I think he deserves far more credit than he ever received for agreeing to manage the Mets in their first four seasons.

Stengle knew the Mets would be bad, although he didn't know they would set the record for losses by losing 120 games in their first year. The Mets were an expansion team, and we already had proof how bad such teams are after being formed with nothing but the rejects from the rest of the teams.

The first two expansion teams in baseball history, the second generation of the Washington Senators and the Los Angeles Angels, who later moved to Anaheim and began calling themselves the California Angels, lost 100 games and 91 games respectively in 1961. The Mets were formed the following season, so the information on just how bad expansion teams are was fresh in his mind when he took the Mets job after being forced into retirement by the Yankees after the 1960 season.

He took the job anyhow. Why did he do it, knowing that he would be exposed to ridicule as the manager of a team that couldn't possibly win or even look respectable? He didn't need the money, and he certainly didn't need any more glory after managing the Yankees to ten pennants in his twelve seasons with them.

I'm sure he felt loyal to George Weiss, the Mets' general manager, who gave Casey his chance with us in '49, but Casey took the Mets job for a reason that I've always admired him for: He was loyal to baseball.

Stengel knew that baseball in New York needed somebody like him, especially four years after the Dodgers and Giants wounded their fans so deeply by moving to California. So he agreed to serve his sport.

The day after Casey died, the governor of New York, Hugh Carey, paid him one of the highest tributes anyone ever received, and no one deserved it more than Casey Stengel as player, manager, and human being. Governor Carey said:

Casey Stengel had the baseball mind of a genius, the heart of Santa Claus and St. Francis, and the face of a clown. Something very good has gone from our lives.

A man who later managed the Mets himself, Yogi Berra, spoke volumes in only two words about every manager's record. He was asked what it takes to be a good manager. His answer: "Good players."

In Casey's years as a National League manager, he obviously didn't have enough good players. In three years of managing the Dodgers and six years as the skipper of the Boston Bees, Casey never finished higher than fifth, and his teams were seventh, which was next to last in those years, five times in those nine years.

With the Yankees in 1949, the biggest question facing him was whether he had the players to win the pennant.

Our primary problem when the season began was to overcome the absence of DiMaggio, put some of those individual off seasons of 1948 behind us, get used to our new manager, and go out and win the pennant. From the start, we were a team dedicated to a common goal, and the most serious one of all was Stengel himself.

The reporters covering us didn't have any new stories for their readers and listeners in '49 about Stengel the clown because there weren't any. We believed in ourselves, and we believed in Stengel.

When the season started, there was no reason to believe that we would succeed in our determination. If anything, the evidence pointed in the opposite direction, and not just because we didn't have Joe D. As our schedule of spring training games came to an end, we were miserable. Not only were we losing, we were looking bad while we were doing it. Our problem was more than just who wasn't playing. It was how the rest of us *were* playing.

We ended our schedule of preseason games in a perfectly terrible way. We traditionally closed our schedule of spring exhibition games by playing a weekend series against the Dodgers for the Mayor's Cup. That year we lost all three games to Brooklyn and looked bad in every game.

That's when teams reveal their character or the lack of it. It is a time when one or more players have to step forward and lead their teammates in some way or another—by what they say and do.

The first to come forward and provide the leadership that we needed so badly was Charlie Keller. We were starting our season at home against Washington, and Stengel had the usual opening-the-season meeting, then asked if anyone had anything to say. That's when Keller spoke up.

It wasn't the most logical time for him to assert himself as one of our leaders, not after missing so many games in '48 and hitting only .267 with 6 home runs and 44 runs batted in. But Charlie, the strong, silent type if there ever was one, felt compelled to say something. He told us bluntly and briefly, "If we don't start bearing down, we're going to be an embarrassment to the New York Yankees."

That must have hit home with every man in our home clubhouse at Yankee Stadium because of the extra warning it carried: Not only would we fail to win the pennant, we would be an embarrassment to the Yankee tradition of Ruth, Gehrig, DiMaggio, and McCarthy. None of us wanted to be a part of that. Maybe the Yankees of the 1990s feel that way, too—and maybe they don't—

but the Yankees of 1949 cared about Yankee pride. Keller's warning was an alarm bell going off for all of us.

Keller was telling us that we would have to get tough on ourselves. We knew that the Red Sox were a better team than we were, with Ted Williams, Dom DiMaggio, Johnny Pesky, Junior Stephens, Bobby Doerr, Mel Parnell, and a strong lineup from top to bottom. And we weren't forgetting that their manager was Joe McCarthy.

We knew that the Indians were the world champions, so they weren't going to be pushovers, either.

With DiMag missing, Keller recovering, and Page struggling, we had to fill those voids the only way possible—by playing together as a team now more than we ever had before, even more than we did under McCarthy.

I didn't know how many years I had left. I turned thirty-six just before spring training began, and my knee felt older than that, but I was as determined as any man on that club to do my part in the absence of the Yankee Clipper and in the midst of the uncertainty that confronted us at the start of the American League season. That determination made my performance during Joe's absence even more satisfying.

We were the Senators' second game of 1949, after the Presidential Opener in Washington when President Truman, having shocked the world with his upset victory over Tom Dewey the previous November, got to exercise his presidential privilege again by throwing out the first ball. The Senators beat the Philadelphia A's, 3–2, and headed for New York to help us open our season.

In the paper the next morning, two stories had special significance in view of later developments. One said that a poll of Associated Press baseball writers picked the Red Sox and the Boston Braves to be in the World Series. Out of 206 votes cast, the Yankees got only 6. The other item, on the front page, appeared under a headline that said:

U. S. PREPARES TO WITHDRAW ALL TROOPS FROM KOREA

Even though the Berlin airlift was still in full swing, with American C-54 cargo planes flying food and supplies into the city every

day to keep its people alive during a blockade by Russian troops
that lasted over a year, the adjustment in the United States to a
peacetime mentality was deep-rooted by now.

We were more interested in the pleasant things in life, like the
new cars that Americans were buying in greater numbers every
year. You could get a new Packard for $2,357, one with a 130-
horsepower engine, eight cylinders, and overdrive. Its ads in the
papers said it featured a "free-breathing engine design—born of
Packard's wartime experience producing all the PT boats and
America's fastest planes." The ads also boasted, "Of all the Packards built during the last 49 years, over 50% are still in service.
Countless Packards have rolled up individual records of more than
400,000 miles."

Another big ad in the paper in those days showed two of our
most popular actors, Don Ameche and Brian Donlevy, announcing
the arrival of Blatz beer in New York. Crosley refrigerators were
advertised for sale for only three-dollars a week and up to ninety-
one weeks to pay. And the Sunday night after we opened our
season, you could turn on the newest national craze, your television set—or go to your neighbor's if they had the only one on
the block—and watch Shakespeare's *Macbeth*.

Sid Hudson of the Senators was going against Ed Lopat of the
Yankees when our 1949 season got underway at Yankee Stadium
before a crowd of 40,075 fans. Governor Dewey and Mayor
O'Dwyer were there, along with Babe Ruth's wife, Claire. All of
us, including every member of both teams, marched to center field,
where the Yankees had erected monuments to Miller Huggins,
their manager in the 1920s, and Lou Gehrig in earlier years. There,
Mrs. Ruth unveiled a plaque on a new monument, which read:

George Herman "Babe" Ruth. 1895–1948. A great ball
player. A great man. A great American. Erected by the Yankees and the New York Baseball Writers. April 19, 1949.

None of those dignitaries got to throw out the first ball, not even
Joe DiMaggio, who was wearing a blue suit and a camel's hair
overcoat instead of Yankee pinstripes as he continued his recovery
from his heel surgery. The honor went to a teenage boy from St.

Mary's Industrial School in Baltimore, where Babe's parents sent him when he became too difficult for them to handle.

Hudson and Lopat battled to a 2–2 tie through eight and a half innings. In the bottom of the ninth, I came up with two outs and the bases empty. With a count of one ball and one strike, I hit Hudson's next pitch over the right-field wall near the foul line. It gave me a feeling of elation to know I had helped my team start off the season with an exciting win, a feeling that happily returned in October.

James Dawson of the *New York Times* wrote in the paper the next morning that my home run was hit "by the man who is regarded as baseball's current greatest outfielder," the kind of praise from a writer that can help you start your season in the proper frame of mind.

George Weiss was also in the proper frame of mind. He predicted to the writers after our Opening Day victory that the Yankees were going to be tough despite our many injuries. "We'll surprise a lot of people," he said, "because we're stronger in reserves than the others are in regulars."

The next day, I hit another home run, this one into the bleachers in right-center field next to the bullpen. The homer came in the fourth inning off the Senators' Paul Calvert and was the first run of the game. We won again, this time 3–0, behind Vic Raschi, who was just as outstanding as ever. He pitched a three-hitter and did not allow a Washington runner to reach third base.

The injury bug continued to bite us, adding still more players to its list of victims. George Stirnweiss, "Snuffy," our backup second baseman behind Jerry Coleman, showed up with a sprained ankle. One of our pitchers, Cuddles Marshall, had a throat infection. Another pitcher, Bob Porterfield, had arm problems. Our substitute catcher behind Yogi Berra, Charlie Silvera, was hit in the mouth by a ball during practice. Not even the owners were safe. Del Webb was stuck in his hotel room with a heavy cold.

Another opportunity to win one for my team came ten days later, on April 30, and I was able to cash in on that one, too. I hit a home run in the ninth inning with a man on base to beat the Red Sox, 4–3.

Two weeks later, I had another back-to-back success story, this time against the Cleveland Indians. I hit a homer in the seventh inning to beat the Indians, 4–3, on May 17. The next day, I got two hits off Bob Feller and helped the team to a 6–0 win. Nine days later my two-run homer in the first inning started the scoring in the game as we defeated the A's, 3–0.

Stengel told reporters, "Henrich is one of the greatest players I ever saw to get the pitch he wants." I caught some needling about that from players around the league, because it was well known that I laid off the curveball except in the most critical emergencies. When I caught some ribbing for what Stengel said and for refusing to swing at the curveball, I told my tormentors, "There ain't a rule in the book that says I have to swing at it."

Except for one disastrous series when we let the lowly A's sweep us in three games, the good times continued into June. On the first day of the month, I broke a 0–0 tie against the White Sox with a home run and we went on to win the game, 3–0. On June 26, with Joe D. still out of our lineup, I hit a two-run single in the eighth inning to break a 2–2 tie and help us beat the Tigers, 6–2, in the first game of a doubleheader. In the second game, I hit a two-run homer, but the Tigers won.

Milton Gross of the *New York Post* calculated that during DiMag's absence from our lineup, which lasted sixty-five games, I was able to drive in the winning run in eighteen of our victories.

We were winning because of a strong team attitude on the part of every one of our players. Two questions were foremost in the mind of each of us after every game: How did our *team* do? And what did I do to help? There were teams in the league with better individual players, but in 1949 there was not a better *team*. With that attitude, we were in first place until the last Monday of the season. And we were there again when it counts the most: after the last day.

Players can tell when the members of the opposition have a team attitude. When a hitter is willing to "give himself up" by hitting a ball on the ground to the right side when his team has a runner on second and nobody out, you know that player has a good team attitude. He knows he's going to get charged with a time at bat and not get credit for a hit or a sacrifice, but he does it anyhow because he knows if he gets his teammate to third with only one out, the runner can score on a flyball, a wild pitch, a passed ball, a balk, an error, and maybe a few other ways.

When a hitter is willing to "take one for the team" by getting hit by a pitch because he knows his team needs him on base, the way Frank Crosetti did so often, you can tell that player has a good team attitude. He's passing up the opportunity to get some glory with a big hit when he knows it's more important to his team for him to get on base so they can start a rally or keep one going.

Averages won't conceal a player's attitude on this subject. One of my pet peeves is to see a good hitter come up in a situation that calls for a sacrifice bunt after he's gotten a base hit on an earlier trip to the plate. He's up for the third time, and it's the sixth inning. He knows he's going to get a fourth trip to the plate. His team has a man on first and no outs.

The player lays down a bunt. Only he's not bunting for a sacrifice—he's bunting to get another hit. You can tell that by where he's trying to place the ball. Here's the rub: In trying for a bunt hit instead of making sure he gets down a good sacrifice that will advance his teammate to second base, he knows that if he doesn't get a hit out of it, he will at least avoid getting charged with a time at bat. He'll be 1-for-3 on the day, and if the bunt rolls for a hit, he's 2-for-4.

That's a selfish attitude, one that hurts his team—but it helps his batting average. A well-known player in the American League told me once that he was hitting .315, but I said to myself, "That's the softest .315 I've ever seen in my life." He knew his average, but I knew something more important: With that attitude, his team was destined to finish in the second division.

While we were playing like champions, Stengel was managing like one. He handled us players with skill and just the right touch, realizing that every player is different and therefore has to be approached in a different way, not with different rules or different standards but with a different approach after success or failure. McCarthy was a strict disciplinarian at all times. Casey wasn't a stickler for rules 100 percent of the time if you were producing for him.

Vic Raschi was talking about Stengel's methods to a reporter years later. "He started the platoon system," Vic said. "Some of the guys might not have liked it, but Casey made a lot of ball players a lot of money by platooning them. He got mad at you more when you were winning than losing. It would really upset him if the other team made mistakes and that's why we won . . . but he never chewed anybody out when we were losing."

Stengle also learned in his earlier managerial jobs and in private business about the value of delegating authority. He had Jim Turner run his pitching staff. Frank Crosetti coached the infielders. Bill Dickey was in charge of the catchers, and Stengel himself worked with the outfielders. He operated like an executive supervising his staff—and succeeded in the job for twelve years.

George Weiss estimated that it cost the organization $400,000 to develop each young player during the late 1940s and into the '50s, a serious amount of money for player development in any era. He made an interesting additional point: Through the emphasis on proper development of our young players in the minor leagues, the Yankees were also developing good coaches and managers.

Casey also introduced what he called "instructual schools," classes at St. Petersburg before and during spring training when he would go over the most fundamental elements of how to play the game. Everyone's attendance was required, from the oldest veterans to the youngest prospects in camp.

In addition, he and Weiss emphasized teaching a player how to play more than one position. "It's no accident," Weiss said, "that defense has probably been the most consistent factor in our success, notwithstanding our great slugging reputation."

Casey was also more of an experimenter than McCarthy. Joe played percentages in his personnel decisions, but Casey wasn't afraid to move a man to a new position, or to platoon two players at the same position, especially if one was a right-handed hitter and the other left-handed. He was a real pioneer in platooning, and today it is an established part of managing.

He platooned me at first base early in the season, with Dick Kryhoski, who contributed his share to our success with a .294 batting average in 51 games at first base. He did the same thing in left field with Keller, whose back still bothered him, and Gene

Woodling, who took over the job during the season, playing 98 games in the outfield and hitting .270.

Charlie was giving everything his very best effort, but his back let him play in only 60 games, and many of them were as a pinch-hitter. He played only 31 games in the outfield. And his back bothered him so much he hit only .250 with only 3 home runs and 16 runs batted in.

I haven't met a player yet who liked platooning if he had the job at the start, and I'm no exception. I didn't really like being platooned early in the season, but Stengel knew what he was doing, and the truth is that yes, my left knee was bothering me so I could use some relief from time to time. In that way I could stay fresh and strong and thus help my team more over the long haul of 154 games—and a World Series if we got there.

Hank Bauer and Gene Woodling fought Stengel all the time on his practice of platooning them. Stengel knew which hitters could handle certain pitchers and which pitchers gave them trouble. It wasn't a simple case of playing a right-handed hitter against a left-handed pitcher or vice versa. It didn't make any difference which hand the pitcher threw with, Casey knew whether you were usually successful against that guy or not. If you were, you were in the lineup. If you had trouble against him, you started the game on the bench.

It worked, but you didn't tell that to a tough cookie like Bauer. He and Casey had more than one disagreement on the subject. In the long run, though, Hank felt he benefited from having Casey as his manager in other ways, such as his instructions and tips to him. In later years Hank said Stengel "made a better ballplayer out of me."

Stengel was smart enough to think of platooning in the first place and to know that he had his critics. He began the strategy as far back as the late 1920s when he was managing in Toledo, where he had a mixture of young hopefuls and some over-the-hill ex–major leaguers. He became known for it especially while managing at Oakland, just before Weiss tapped him for the Yankee job.

Some players and writers criticized the techniques as disruptive and "overmanaging." Paul Richards, who joined the managerial profession two years later as the skipper of the Chicago White Sox and later managed the Baltimore Orioles, said, "Stengel doesn't do anything different from anybody else. He just has to make a bigger act out of it." And Richards wasn't the only one who felt that way.

Stengel had the courage and wisdom to stick to his convictions, even though he knew full well what his critics were saying. "I know a lot of players never understood my platoon system," he said years later, "and neither did a lot of other people. They say that now that I'm out of baseball there won't be much platooning. Well, I'll say this—I don't think the Yankees would have won ten pennants in my twelve years in New York without it."

He was right. And the fact is, platooning has long since been an established managerial technique and is used now more than ever.

Stengel had his own simple technique for managing the twenty-five players on a major-league team: "Keep the twenty guys who hate you from the five guys who are undecided."

On June 28, every Yankee player's prayers were answered. Joe DiMaggio returned to our lineup. No athlete ever performed more superbly immediately after coming back from an injury.

Our record at that stage of the season was 41 wins and 24 defeats. We were in first place by four and a half games over the Philadelphia A's, who were surprising everyone that year. The Tigers and Red Sox both trailed us by five games, and the Indians were six out. In the National League, the Dodgers were in first place, but that league was having its usual dog fight. Brooklyn's lead over the St. Louis Cardinals was only one game.

We had just split a Sunday doubleheader with the Tigers in Yankee Stadium before 62,382 fans. We won the first game but lost the second. I hit my sixteenth home run in the first two and a half months of the season in the second game, but when it's in a losing cause, too much of the fun goes out of it.

We played an exhibition game on Monday against the Giants, and Joe D. was in the lineup. He was giving us no reason to expect any immediate results from him, though. He popped up to the infield four times.

We moved up the East Coast to Boston for three games beginning on Tuesday, the 28th. What Joe did there is now a part of baseball lore. He hit four home runs and a single in eleven trips to the plate in those three days—that's a .455 average—and drove in nine runs. In center field, he caught thirteen fly balls. He was doing it while wearing a special shoe on his right foot, one with no spikes on the heel.

In the first game of the series, Joe singled in his first at-bat of the season in the second inning, a line drive to left-center field. Hank Bauer came through for us with a three-run homer in the second inning, and in the third Joe D. hit a home run into the screen above Fenway Park's legendary "Green Monster" wall in left field with Rizzuto on base. Both hits came off one of the brightest young pitching prospects in the American League that year, Mickey McDermott, a nineteen-year-old left-hander.

Joe McCarthy was tempting fate by starting a left-hander in Fenway Park, where there is an unwritten rule of managing that says left-handed pitchers are a dangerous choice because the right-handed hitters will be able to pull the ball over the Monster, which is only 315 feet from the plate.

McCarthy, of course, knew this better than anyone, but he gambled with McDermott, even against a team with power like us. He knew something else, too: that most of our power was from the left side with Berra, Woodling, Keller, Brown, and me. He was gambling that the percentages of throwing a left-hander against our left-handed power would offset the risk that one of our right-handed hitters, especially DiMaggio, might make him pay for the chance he was taking. After all, Joe hadn't played a game since the year before and this was almost July.

Joe got the job done in the outfield, too. He pulled in six fly balls and fielded three base hits with no trouble. His performance in every aspect of his game was an adrenaline shot for every Yankee. We didn't much care what the experts said, or how those writers in the Associated Press voted at the start of the season. We were headed for the World Series again after missing it in 1948, and with Joe DiMaggio back and first place all to ourselves, we knew we were in the driver's seat.

The win in that opening game of the series gave us a lead of four and a half games over the A's and six games over the other three teams in the race, all of them now virtually tied for third place—the Indians, Tigers, and Red Sox. The headline in the *New*

York Times the next morning was a thing of beauty for all of us players and our fans:

DIMAGGIO'S 2-RUN HOMER HELPS YANKS WIN

That headline looked like old times, and it seemed to say it all.

Back home in California, in the home Joe bought for the family in the Marina district of San Francisco, his mother had her maternal priorities in order. In the days when a long-distance telephone call was still something to get excited about, DiMag called to share his good news with Mom. She was seventy-one and a widow by then, and her boys meant everything to her.

"I spoke to her in my bad Italian," Joe said, "and she understood it all right, but homers and singles didn't mean a thing to her. She asked me about my foot and then kept repeating: 'Grazie a Dio. Grazie a Dio.' " His mother was saying "Thanks be to God."

Joe said, "Mom has been saying the Rosary every night since I can remember, and when I went into that game, she wasn't praying for homers or singles. She was praying for my foot. You can't buy things like that."

In the second game, Joe topped his performance of the day before. He hit two homers and drove in four runs, leading us to a 9–7 victory over Boston in a game that had to hurt the Sox. They had a 7–1 lead over us after four innings, which looked as safe as a lead in Fenway Park can look the way Ellis Kinder was pitching for them. But while they had Kinder, we had DiMaggio.

With two outs in the fifth, Rizzuto and I drew walks off Kinder, and Joe jumped all over that opportunity. You never want to walk the man in front of a hitter of DiMaggio's ability, and you certainly don't want to walk the two men in front of him. But that's what Kinder did, and Joe D. did what all great hitters do. He made Kinder pay for his mistake, with a home run to left field. The blow put us back into the game. Instead of trailing 7–1, suddenly we're in a 7–4 game, on one hit, and Joe wasn't finished.

In the eighth inning, he hit another homer off another Boston left-hander, Earl Johnson. This one came with the bases empty and tied the score, 7–7. It was a thing of beauty that sailed high and mighty over Fenway's forty-foot wall and the twenty-foot net on top of it and landed in the street behind the ballpark. We added two runs after that to get the win and knock the starch out of the Red Sox.

Joe Page won the game for us in relief. It gave him a record of six wins and only three losses, a reassuring improvement over his 1948 performances. With both Joes producing—DiMag with his big bat and Page with his late-inning heroics coming out of the bullpen—we were looking more and more like the Yankees of 1947.

In the final game of the series, Joe hit his fourth home run in his first three games to power us to another win over the Sox, 6–3. This one was just as majestic as his second the day before, and I had another good view of it, from first base. Snuffy Stirnweiss, recovering from his sprained ankle, and I singled. Then Joe jumped on a Boston left-hander again, this time Mel Parnell, one of the best pitchers in either league.

DiMag hit a 3–2 pitch high over the net. The ball hit a light tower and bounced back onto the field, and the Ladies Day crowd of 25,237 fans had to admire this man's performance, even if he was the opposition.

Joe's home run made a winner out of Raschi for the twelfth time. Our Springfield Rifle had only two losses. Parnell lost his fourth game against ten wins. Mel was to play a key role in our fate in the last week of the season, not once but twice. We hadn't heard the last of the rest of his team, either.

When we left Boston, we had a lead of five and a half games over the A's. The Red Sox were in fifth, now trailing us by eight games.

When we got back to New York, we found plenty of entertainment for those valuable afternoons or evenings when we could take our mind off the pressure of the pennant race for a few hours of relaxation. There was a bumper crop of all-time great plays in the legitimate theaters of New York, and Eileen and I saw as many of them as my playing schedule permitted.

It was a blockbuster lineup that included *A Streetcar Named Desire*, *Kiss Me Kate* with Alfred Drake and Patricia Morison, Henry Fonda in *Mister Roberts*, Mary Martin and Ezio Pinza co-starring in *South Pacific*, Lee J. Cobb in *Death of a Salesman*, *Detective Story* starring Ralph Bellamy, *Born Yesterday*, and Ray Bolger almost dancing his shoes off in *Where's Charley?* The 1949 season was as exciting on Broadway as it was at Yankee Stadium.

And if I wanted to see a musical kind of baseball, I could go to the movies at the Lane Theater on 181st Street at St. Nicholas Avenue or the Plaza at 58th and Madison and see Gene Kelly, Frank Sinatra, and Esther Williams in *Take Me Out to the Ball Game*.

The list of leaders in the American League the morning after we completed our sweep of the Red Sox showed you how much our team attitude was doing for us. There wasn't a Yankee among the top five batting averages. George Kell of Detroit was leading the league in hitting, and Dom DiMaggio of the Red Sox was second. We didn't have a player listed among the leaders in runs batted in, either.

It would have been even more un-Yankee not to have any of us on the list of home-run leaders as well, but I showed up there with my 16, good enough to tie for third place in the league with Eddie Joost of the A's behind Ted Williams and Vern Stephens, the Red Sox shortstop.

We were doing it with team play, the McCarthy way, while McCarthy was trying to win with the Red Sox, who on paper were a stronger team than we were. We had something else the Red Sox didn't have: Joe Page back in his 1947 form. He made 60 appearances for us in 1949, the most in the major leagues. One statistic in particular shows you how superior he was in his specialty: Ted Wilks of the St. Louis Cardinals led the National League in saves that year with 9. Joe led both leagues with 27. That wasn't all. He won 13 other games, giving him a direct role in 40 of our 97 victories.

Joe was the most confident man I ever saw coming out of a bullpen. When he walked onto the field at Yankee Stadium from the bullpen in right-center field, he didn't unlock the gate on the chain-link fence. He jumped over it. John Wayne never swaggered onto a battlefield with more confidence than Fireman Joe showed when he entered a baseball game for us.

Red Rolfe, our old third baseman, was managing the Tigers in

1949. He knew from his years of watching Johnny Murphy save games for us how valuable a relief pitcher like Murphy or Page is to a team. He was talking about it to the writers one day in 1949 when he said, "I wonder if you fellows realize what it means for the Yankees to know they have Page in the bullpen. Stengel calls. Out Page comes to strike out everybody in sight—and there goes your rally. He's Stengel's most valuable pitcher, and maybe his most valuable player."

Red wouldn't get any arguments about that from anyone in the American League, player or manager. It was common knowledge that if you were going to beat us, you had to score your runs early, by the fifth or sixth inning at the latest. After that, you would have Page to contend with, and that was no formula for winning a game.

Stengel said, "He has more confidence than anyone else in the world, and the opposing teams know it."

Page kept coming through for us as we headed toward the climactic weeks of the season. We were trying to fight off a red hot Boston team, which caught fire right after we swept them at the end of June on DiMaggio's dramatic comeback, and Page was helping us to keep winning in the face of the increasing pressure from the Red Sox.

He gave us another big shot in the arm under pressure when we faced Boston in a night game at Yankee Stadium on September 7. Allie Reynolds started the game by walking the first three hitters, and Bobby Doerr singled in two runs, but we overcame that and had a 3–2 lead with one out in the eighth inning.

Doerr caused us more trouble by hitting a triple. Stengel made a quick decision and called for Page. Our fireman was ready again, maybe more ready than ever because now he had a chance not only to help his team once more in a pressure situation but to do it against his old enemy, Joe McCarthy, and deal McCarthy's team a serious setback to their hopes of winning the pennant.

The Red Sox were a loaded lineup that year. Every man in their batting order was a tough out, including the one facing Page at that point, Al Zarilla. But Joe was able to meet the challenge, and he did it with style. He got Zarilla on a popup. Then he struck out the next four hitters in a row—Billy Goodman, Birdie Tebbetts, Matt Batts, and Dom DiMaggio.

Once again, Fireman Joe saved the day. Over the course of baseball's long season, you can always look back at several different games and say that this one or that one would have changed the course of history if it turned out the other way. That could be said of this game. Page saved that game for us. It gave us another victory and the Red Sox another loss. And we won the pennant by one game over the Red Sox.

Page relieved Reynolds seventeen times, saving ten wins for Allie and us that season and picking up three for himself. Some of the writers referred to the combination of Reynolds-Page as our "two-headed pitcher." They were becoming our generation's version of the Lefty Gomez–Johnny Murphy tandem of earlier years.

Our bullpen coach, Jim Turner, thought at least a part of Page's success was in the way he warmed up before coming into a game, lobbing the ball at first and not bearing down until he reached the mound and took his final warmups.

"Then he burns them over," Turner said. "I never saw this type of warming up until I came to the Yankees. In the National League, the relief pitchers burn them over in the bullpen."

You get an idea of how hard Page used to bear down—literally—when you learn that he used to come home from our games with aching jaws and never understood why. Then his wife, Kay, asked him if he gritted his teeth while he was pitching.

"As soon as the words came out of her mouth," he said, "I knew she had hit on the reason. I used to bear down so hard on everything, including my jaws, that I guess I must have forced my teeth back deeper in their sockets."

The fact is that we wouldn't have had Page for the 1949 season if it hadn't been for George Weiss, who continued to make all the right decisions as our general manager after taking over following Larry MacPhail's explosion at our 1947 victory party.

After Page's off season in '48, Weiss received overtures from some of the other teams in the American League about his availability. Clark Griffith of the Washington Senators said he might be talked into trading Early Wynn, the future Hall of Famer and 300-game winner, plus some minor-league players. Bill Veeck, never one to stand pat even though his Indians were the 1948 world champions, mentioned Johnny Berardino and Hank Edwards.

Weiss was displeased with Page's performance in '48, but his baseball instincts took over and he decided to hold on to him. He did something else that was smart, too, and fair. Instead of cutting Page's salary, he gave him a contract for the same amount— $20,000—for 1949.

When the bell rang to start our season, Joe was ready to regain his 1947 form, and that's exactly what he did. In the process, he was making believers out of all those cynics who said Casey Stengel was nothing but a clown.

George Weiss made another decision in 1949 that helped us immediately and for four seasons after that. He went out and got one of the greatest hitters in the game, Johnny Mize.

He was a six-foot-two, 225-pound slugger and first baseman from Demorest, Georgia, who was called "the Big Cat" and "Big Jawn." He could hit a baseball into the next county, and for a high average, too. He's in the Hall of Fame now after fifteen years—he lost three of his best years in the navy during the war— for a career that included 359 home runs, 2,011 hits, and a .312 lifetime batting average.

Frankie Frisch, "the Fordham Flash" who was Mize's manager when Johnny was a star with the St. Louis Cardinals before the war, could offer testimony to Mize's greatness as a hitter. "I'm glad I never had to pitch against him," he said. "A guy could get hurt that way. He had me scared even when I would be out behind the pitcher during batting practice, picking up the balls as they were thrown in from the outfield.

"If you want a chance to really gauge a hitter's power, stand out there some day. I remember my first impression of Mize at our spring training camp was that he could hit a ball as hard as anybody I ever saw."

Mize was a star with the Cardinals right from the start. He hit 19 home runs as a rookie in 1936, the same year that DiMaggio and Feller were rookies in the American League, and then had home run years of 25, 27, 28, and 43, leading the National League with the last two figures in 1939 and '40. Those 28 league-leading homers in 1939 were accompanied by a league-leading batting average, .349. In his first five years in the majors, he hit 142 home runs for the Cardinals.

But then things went sour for him. His 43 home runs in 1940 were accompanied by a .314 batting average and tied Chuck Klein's National League record for left-handed hitters, which Mize broke with 51 homers in 1947. "The sports pages were full of Mize," he said. "I somehow got the impression that I was quite a hitter. However, when it came time to talk contract with Branch Rickey for 1941, I discovered that hitting home runs was nothing at all."

He still remembers what Rickey told him: "John, it is true that you hit a few home runs, but your average dropped to .314. I believe you should take a cut in salary."

Mize says, "That must have been the only time in the history of the major leagues that a man hitting forty-three home runs was asked to take a pay cut."

After one more year of that kind of a relationship, Mize was traded to the Giants, where he continued to star, and when he came back from his navy service in the Pacific, it was obvious to everyone that not even the war had stopped him. He reported to the Giants' spring training camp in 1946 in superb condition, leaner and more dangerous than ever.

For all of his power, Mize was also a contact hitter, much like Joe D. and Ted Williams. Even with all those home runs, he didn't strike out much, the way most power hitters do when they take those big swings. He struck out more than fifty times in only one season, 57 in 1937, his second year. The rest of the time, including his biggest home-run years, his strikeouts were running in the thirties and forties.

Mize was a serious student of hitting, also like Ted and Joe. He remembers that he had a set routine to prepare himself for each game: "Every night before I went to bed, I'd look in the paper to see who was pitching the next day. Then I'd lie awake half an hour or so just imagining I was standing at the plate. I'd try to visualize how I might be thrown to, what to look for."

He changed bats, and even stances, depending on the pitcher and the situation. "The problem with a lot of batters," he says, "is that they just get in there, dig a foothold, and swing away. I say this: If you get in there and just dig yourself a hole without thinking first, you'll bury yourself in the same hole."

By 1949, Johnny was supposedly slowing down. At least that's what his manager, Leo Durocher, thought. He was quoted in the papers as saying that he wanted a team with more speed, and Mize was too slow. He said he thought the Giants might be able to get only one more season out of him, maybe not even that.

He was thirty-six years old, but the comments seemed strange. Durocher was talking about the National League's home-run king. He had won the championship the year before with 40, the fourth time he led the league in homers.

It seemed like unique logic. Weiss must have thought so, too. On August 22, he bought Mize from the Giants in a straight cash transaction for $40,000. The purchase paid immediate dividends, including two big ones in the World Series.

Mize's arrival underlined the George Weiss philosophy of giving the Yankees the strongest bench in the league, what Earl Weaver of the Orioles in later years called "deep depth." In 1949, we were deep.

It was a good year to be in contention for the pennant and a World Series check. Prices weren't getting any lower, not with all the inflation after the war. Gabardine slacks by Hart, Schaffner & Marx were up to $17.50 at Wallach's, and even Towertown's cost $8.50 at any of its ten stores. At Saks on 34th Street, Koolano suits of pure wool and mohair were all the way up to $42.50, and bathing suits to wear at Coney Island and Atlantic City cost $6.98.

On the family side, with kids coming along, Eileen and I were always interested in preserving our memories with plenty of pictures, sometimes even in color. Kodak's Duraflex camera cost as much as $13.50 in some stores, but if you were on a tight budget you could pick up a brownie for $2.75. If you wanted to have enough soft drinks at those family get-togethers where you'd be taking a lot of pictures, you had to be prepared to spend a dollar for a case of twenty-four bottles of Coke. You didn't get a choice of bottles or cans. They weren't putting soft drinks in cans then.

You had to do your shopping during the week, though. Most department stores and clothiers were closed on Saturdays and Sundays during July and August. The major exception was Gimbel's. That store seemed to have an ad on every page of the paper telling us that it was open on Saturdays during the summer.

If we had any money left over from our living expenses, we

could always invest it at the Knickerbocker Federal Savings and Loan Association on Lexington Avenue at 58th Street. Knicker-bocker ran an ad that summer saying, "There's no need to journey to the outskirts of the city to earn a good return on your savings!" It offered "a generous dividend which has never been less than 2 percent!"

Head to Head

Throughout the season, our commitment to each other was being tested because of the incredible streak of injuries. We had seventy-two in all, but all of us kept helping each other out, and if we happened to be one of the injured, we got back in there as soon as we could.

I was put in that spot several times myself. I broke a toe in batting practice before a game against the Indians at Yankee Stadium, but I played anyhow. The papers the next day said I would be out at least three or four days. I didn't know where they got that information, but I knew where they *didn't* get it—from me. I played that afternoon. I also hurt both knees and banged up some ribs during the course of the season.

On August 28, I crashed into the right-field wall at Comiskey Park in Chicago and broke the second and third lumbar vertebrae in my back. I was put in a plaster cast at St. Luke's Hospital back in New York, and the reports in the press and on the air were that I would be out of action for the rest of the season and the World Series, too, if we got that far.

I never believed that for one minute. I told the same reporters

244

who wrote that stuff that I would be back before the season was over, which was only another month, and that we would win the American League pennant—"if nothing happens to Rizzuto."

After three weeks I was back in the lineup, playing with a brace on my back. With the injuries to my thumb, my knees, my ribs, and my back, I still managed to play in 115 games—61 in the outfield and 52 at first base plus two pinchhitting appearances—and come to bat 411 times. A story in one of the papers quoted DiMaggio as saying, "Tommy Henrich is the steadiest ball player I've ever seen."

Maybe he was talking about another Tommy Henrich.

Right after we swept them in Boston, the Red Sox caught fire. They stayed hot through the entire second half of the season. We were still winning, but the Red Sox were winning even more. By simply refusing to lose, they erased our lead of twelve games over them. People remember the Giants' comeback in 1951 when they wiped out the Dodgers' lead of thirteen and a half games, but the same thing almost happened two years before with us, and just because Boston would not allow itself to cool off.

Together the Yankees and the Red Sox created one of the richest legends in the whole baseball lore of nail-biting pennant races. It came down to the last week of the season, then to the last day, and then to the last inning.

On September 26, a Monday, the Yankees and the Red Sox made up a game that had been rained out earlier in the month. The Sox beat us, 7–6, in front of 66,156 screaming fans at Yankee Stadium, and how it happened ignited a fire that generated even more tension and drive for both teams.

The Sox scored the winning run in the eighth inning when Johnny Pesky slid across home plate on a bunt by Bobby Doerr. The "safe" call by the home-plate umpire, Bill Grieve, led to a near-riot on the field and harsh statements and actions off the field.

Doerr's bunt came to me. I wanted to be on the alert against the possibility of a squeeze play, when the hitter lays down a bunt so he can "squeeze" his teammate on third base home with a run. I crept in on the infield grass and was only thirty-five feet from home plate when I scooped up Bobby's bunt.

My throw to Ralph Houk, our catcher, was in plenty of time.

I didn't want to throw it hard; that might have handcuffed Houk because of the short distance between us. The important thing, instead, was to make sure my throw was accurate. I did, and it was. Houk caught it in plenty of time to tag Pesky, and he was blocking the plate to make sure Johnny couldn't get through. Johnny seemed to get a late start on the play, and there was speculation that he missed the sign for the squeeze play.

Houk tagged Pesky out in the minds and eyes of everyone in the ball park that afternoon except one: Bill Grieve.

After the game, Doerr set the record straight where Peksy was concerned. "Pesky didn't get the squeeze sign because I didn't give any," he said. "He didn't know I was going to bunt. It was something I thought up all of a sudden. The only two persons in the Stadium who suspected I would bunt were myself and that smart guy, Tommy Henrich."

Houk said Pesky couldn't have been safe because he had the plate blocked, which is the way it looked to the rest of us in the infield. Pesky disagreed, saying the plate was not blocked and he was able to slide under Houk's catcher's mitt and touch the plate with his foot before Houk tagged him on the hip.

Grieve's decision ignited an uproar on the field and around the entire American League. In Washington, Shirley Povich of the *Post* described us as "the Grieve-stricken Yankees" and said the Red Sox "ought to cut umpire Bill Grieve in for a full World Series share, if they win the pennant."

Cliff Mapes, our outfielder, who wasn't in the game, caught up with Grieve on the field as both teams and all the umpires headed for their dressing rooms. Cliff yelled ahead to Grieve and asked him how much he had bet on the game. Grieve whirled around and started toward Mapes, but other players and the other umpires, Charley Berry and Cal Hubbard, stepped in and prevented either man from doing something that might end his career right there.

Grieve reported the incident to the league office in Chicago immediately. The next day, the president of the American League, Will Harridge, lowered the boom on the Yankees.

He fined Mapes $200 and Stengel and Houk $150 each, but he did more than that. He gave us a stern warning about severe punishments that would follow any repeat of our actions.

Harridge told the Yankees, "In our opinion, Clifford Mapes is guiltier than anyone else for his verbal attack on Grieve during and after the ball game. Mapes was the only player who deliberately waited for the umpire and followed him to his dressing room despite being repeatedly cautioned against it by Umpire Berry."

Harridge said he fined Houk for "his conduct in charging and pushing Umpire Grieve and putting on an uncalled-for demonstration over the decision." Stengel was fined for "your conduct in pushing the umpire and whirling him around."

Harridge told our organization, "Never before to my knowledge has a player or manager been permitted to remain in the game after a demonstration of this kind. We are making every honest effort to keep intact the clubs contending for the pennant. In this endeavor we assumed, of course, we would have the full cooperation of the players and managers."

Then he dropped the other shoe: "Any recurrence by any member of your club of yesterday's conduct will result in automatic suspension for the balance of the season."

Weiss sent back his immediate protest that the Yankees never had an opportunity to tell our side of the story before Harridge, sitting as judge and jury but listening only to his umpires, found us guilty and imposed the sentences.

The response by Weiss was right on the mark. He reminded Harridge that no Yankee had been fined for anything all through the season and the tension-filled pennant race, and a New York player had been thrown out of a game only once all year.

Mapes responded to Harridge by issuing a statement in which he did not deny asking Grieve how much he had bet on the game. Cliff pointed out that "such a remark is almost as old as baseball itself and is made often in bench jockeying. If Umpire Grieve really believes I meant an attack on his honesty, I would like to take this occasion to apologize."

Weiss applied the zinger. He told Harridge that the fines "were as hasty and erroneous as the umpire's decision."

The next day, Raschi defeated the A's, 3–1, on a four-hitter at Yankee Stadium for his twentieth victory. At the same time, the Red Sox beat the Senators in Washington, 6–4.

In the National League, things were almost as close. The

Dodgers were leading the league by one game over the Cardinals, and those two teams also had four games each left to play. Not only did we not know yet if we would be in the World Series, we also didn't know who our opponents would be if we got there.

More drama unfolded in the games of both the Yankees and the Red Sox on the following day. In our game, we took a 4–0 lead over the Philadelphia A's into the seventh inning on home runs by Bobby Brown and Jim Delsing, a rookie outfielder for us, but the A's came up with five runs to take the lead. Tommy Byrne, our starter, was relieved by Fred Sanford, who later gave way to Joe Page. For once, Page wasn't effective either, and Stengel, still making all the right moves, pulled a switch by replacing Page with Reynolds instead of the usual Page-for-Reynolds substitution.

In the seventh, we went to work again and scored three runs with some of our "five o'clock lightning." Reynolds was as good a relief pitcher that day as Page was the rest of the season. Superchief mowed down six men in two innings, striking out four and holding the A's to one run. Allie won 17 games for us that year, and two of his wins were in relief. He produced more Page-like dramatics out of the bullpen for us in the World Series.

There was more good news at Yankee Stadium that afternoon. Joe DiMaggio had been out of our lineup again, this time with a stubborn virus that knocked him out of action on September 18. Before this win over the A's, he worked out for the first time. Still too weak to play, he took two turns in the batting cage. He managed to hit one into the left-field stands.

Mel Allen went down to Washington to broadcast the Red Sox game that night with the Senators because the pennant race was in its last week and everyone in New York was going crazy. I was one of Mel's listeners that night—when lightning struck again.

The Senators were completing a Jekyll-Hyde season. They won nine games in a row on their first western swing and were welcomed home with a parade down Pennsylvania Avenue on their return. But then they reverted to form. They lost eleven in a row and were dead last, headed for 104 defeats, when the Red Sox opened their series against them.

Boston's one-game lead had been cut in half by our win that

afternoon, so the pressure was on the Red Sox. They had to win so they could go back up by a full game. If they lost, both teams would be tied for first place in the American League.

Chuck Stobbs, a young left-hander, was taking things into his own hands for the Red Sox. They were going for their twelfth straight win. He was shutting out the Senators after eight innings, 1–0, and even scored the only run after he doubled to left and Dom DiMaggio singled him home.

In the bottom of the ninth, Al Kozar singled home Gil Coan to tie the game, 1–1. My excitement was growing on each pitch as I listened to Mel Allen on my radio in New York, especially when Joe McCarthy brought in Mel Parnell, his ace left-handed starting pitcher, to face Buddy Lewis with Kozar on third and two outs.

Then disaster struck the Red Sox. Parnell's 0–1 pitch to Lewis hit the dirt in front of the plate and bounced past Birdie Tebbetts for a wild pitch. Kozar scored the run that won the game for Washington, 2–1, and dropped the Red Sox back into a tie with us for the league lead.

Shirley Povich's article in the Washington Post the next morning began:"Into the same dirt where he rubbed their noses three times this season, Mel Parnell of the Red Sox uncorked a wild pitch last night."

Both teams were rained out on Thursday, and on Friday we suffered another setback. We lost to the A's, 4–1, on a three-run homer by Ferris Fain off Ed Lopat. At the same time, the Red Sox beat the Senators, 11–9. Washington once again took with one hand and gave away with the other. The Senators outhit Boston, 18–5, but their pitchers gave Boston's hitters thirteen walks.

The Red Sox had reason to think the gods were shining on them as they headed into Yankee Stadium for the last two days of the season. They were back on top in the American League standings, leading us by one game.

It was Saturday, October 1, when the Red Sox and Yankees took the field for the start of a two-game showdown that couldn't have been written any better in Hollywood. The pitching matchup was Mel Parnell against Allie Reynolds. The same teams that had been going at each other the entire second half of the season in a real dogfight were playing each other to decide the pennant. No-body was going to back into this pennant by having a day off while the other team won or lost.

This was going to be head-to-head for everything. And with the Red Sox one game ahead when we started, there wasn't going to be any tie.

In the National League, things were still just as close. Brooklyn was one game ahead of St. Louis, with the Dodgers playing two games in Philadelphia and the Cardinals meeting the Cubs twice in Chicago. Burt Shotton was turning to his aces, Don Newcombe, his twenty-three-year-old rookie right-hander, and Ralph Branca, his 13-game winner who faced us in the 1947 World Series.

We were leading the season's series against Red Sox, but it was close, eleven wins for New York and nine for Boston. Casey Stengel was confident. After our loss the day before, he was blunt in his remarks to the writers: "That puts it up to us to show if we're a good ball club . . . I feel that now we're going out and beat the tar out of the Red Sox tomorrow and Sunday. I really feel it."

We had the emotional edge over the Red Sox as we took the field to practice before our Saturday game. It was Joe DiMaggio Day at Yankee Stadium.

The Yankee Clipper was still trying to fight off the effects of his virus, but he was going to play anyway, and before the game he was the toast of the town. He was honored with a shower of gifts that may still be a record for that kind of thing, if such records were kept. He was given everything from a new car, a speedboat, and cash awards down to three-hundred quarts of ice cream and lemonade to go with it. Even his mother got a new car, and his son got a bike.

The array of gifts made the infield at Yankee Stadium look like a going-out-of-business sale for the entire island of Manhattan: money, food, two watches, a trophy, two TV sets, a rifle, a bronze plaque, and more. There was a cocker spaniel puppy, too, and a four-year college scholarship for a deserving New York high school student.

The outpouring of people, affection, and presents was proof once again of the magnetic hold on New York City enjoyed by this heroic figure. I don't know that Babe Ruth himself could have generated the enormous affection, loyalty, and even worship that

Joe Dimaggio enjoyed in New York that day. As David Halberstam wrote in *The Summer of '49*, Joe was "the last great hero of the radio era."

Joe donated the food to various institutions around town, and he gave the cash to two of his favorite charities, the New York Heart Fund and the Damon Runyon Memorial Cancer Fund. Then, after being introduced to the crowd by Mel Allen, he gave what must have been the longest speech of his life. It was a revealing one, too, because it told the 69,551 fans how all of us on that team felt about being a New York Yankee:

> When I was in San Francisco, Lefty O'Doul told me, "Joe, don't let the big city scare you. New York is the friendliest town in the world." This day proves it. I want to thank the fans, my friends, my manager, Casey Stengel, and my teammates, the gamest, fightingest bunch that ever lived.
>
> And I want to thank the good Lord for making me a Yankee.

The score of the game was as close as the pennant race. The Sox jumped out to a 4–0 lead in the early innings. After the fourth inning, Rizzuto came back into our dugout and said that Birdie Tebbetts, while he was standing on second as a base runner, said to him, "Looks like we'll throw our batting practice pitcher tomorrow."

With that incentive relayed to us by Rizzuto, we were able to break a 4–4 tie when Johnny Lindell hit a home run into the lower left-field seats in the eighth inning with two outs and nobody on base, on the first pitch to him from Joe Dobson. Lindell was a hero, but he had to share that honor with our man of the hour throughout 1949, Joe Page.

Page came into the game early, with no outs in the third inning, and held the Red Sox to only one hit. Thanks to Johnny and Joe, we won the game, 5–4. After each of the two teams had played 154 games, including a tie game for each, we were dead even.

Casey Stengel was earning his salary just in the way he handled Page. He told him at the start of the season that he didn't care what Joe's training habits were as long as he was ready when

Casey called him into a game. The first time Joe saved a game for us, Stengel made sure to thank him in our dressing room.

That was a far cry from Page's experiences with the manager across the field from us, Joe McCarthy. Stengel's skilled touch with Page, contrasted with McCarthy's strict attitude, paid off with Joe's consistently successful performances throughout the season, and by that pressure-packed final weekend, with every man on the spot, it was still paying major dividends. Fireman Joe, with Lindell's help, got us where we needed to be. A loss in that game would have clinched the pennant for the Red Sox. Instead, we had just as good a chance to win the pennant on Sunday as they did. And we had Vic Raschi.

The matchup for the last game of the season was Raschi against Ellis Kinder, one of the pitchers I hated to hit against most because his pitches seemed to have nine different speeds. Joltin' Joe, eighteen pounds thinner and still so weak that he probably shouldn't have been playing, gave us a huge lift by starting the game. Raschi was going for his twenty-first win, and Kinder already had won twenty-three. We were going up against the team that many people considered the most talented in the American League, and certainly we were opposing one of the best managers in either league—and the best one I ever played for.

The Red Sox were an offensive powerhouse. Ted Williams won the Most Valuable Player Award that season with a .343 batting average, a fraction of a point behind George Kell. Ted also led the league in home runs and tied for the RBI title with his teammate, Vern Stephens, at 159 each. With only a fraction of a point more on his average, Ted would have won another triple crown.

He led the league in bases on balls, too, plus doubles, runs scored, total bases, slugging average, and home-run percentage, finishing ahead of Vern Stephens and me in that department. You couldn't pitch around Williams on that team, walking him because you knew that the man behind him wasn't a threat. Every man in that lineup was dangerous, from top to bottom.

With all that offense making them such a scoring machine, there was also the Boston defense to contend with. The Sox team fielding average was .980, only three points behind the Indians, who had the league's best, and three points better than we were. Goodman had the best average of the league's first baseman, and Stephens and Pesky, who was playing third now, both led their positions in double plays.

Aside from my finish with the third most home runs and the third highest slugging average and home-run percentage, the only other Yankees to finish in the running in any offensive category were Yogi, who had the fourth highest home-run percentage and the fifth best slugging average, and Phil Rizzuto, who was second in stolen bases. On defense we matched up better. Coleman and Rizzuto led their positions in fielding average, and Berra led the catchers in making the most double plays.

In pitching, the Red Sox had the upper hand, too, at least in statistics, although nobody was ever better at winning big games than Raschi among starting pitchers and Page among relievers. Even so, Parnell had the most wins, the best earned run average, and the most innings pitched, Page led the league in games pitched and saves.

Rizzuto, who was a contender for the Most Valuable Player Award himself—and he won it the next year—got us started immediately after Raschi shut out the Red Sox in the first inning. The Scooter tripled down the left-field line and into the corner. When I came to bat, my job was to score him. Never mind getting a hit, necessarily; just get him home and forget about your average.

I looked around at the Boston defense against me. McCarthy had the right side of his infield—Doerr at second and Goodman at first—playing back. They were willing to give up the run to get an out in the first inning. Their thinking was to avoid a big inning by the Yankees at the start of the game and worry about getting the run back later.

I thought to myself, "Okay, you got a deal. Maybe I can't hit Kinder that well, but I know I can at least hit a ground ball off him to the right side that will score Rizzuto and get us the lead right away." I was always a good contact hitter even though I also hit the long ball. I never struck out more than 63 times, and this year I did it only 34 times. I was confident I could get the Scooter home by just hitting the ball somewhere, agreeing with Williams that "when you make contact, things start to happen."

I did, with a fourteen-hopper to Doerr at second base. We were winning, 1–0, after one inning.

The game rocked along that way until McCarthy lifted Kinder

for a pinch-hitter in the eighth inning. Some of his players said later they thought he should have left Kinder in there, because there was reason to believe that we weren't going to score any more runs off him if we played until midnight. But I don't know where they got the idea that they would score even one run. They told me they thought Raschi might get tired, but I don't know why they thought so. Vic was one of the great pressure pitchers of all time. He wasn't about to get tired. He was thriving on that stuff.

That's one of the fascinations about baseball, though. Boston could not afford to let us score any more runs, not with only two more innings to play and us in the lead already, 1–0. On the other hand, the Sox needed a run to stay alive. McCarthy took the gamble and lifted Kinder. It didn't work, because Boston didn't score, and now we didn't have to worry about Kinder, a pitcher who always gave most of us trouble.

In comes Mel Parnell, again, just after pitching the day before. I was the leadoff hitter, left-hander vs. left-hander, a matchup that usually favors the pitcher because so many left-handed hitters have trouble hitting left-handed pitchers. You don't see them that often since most pitchers are right-handed.

I decided not to pull the ball into right field against Parnell. He had a good slider, which broke away from a left-handed hitter. If you try to pull that pitch, you'll usually hit a grounder for an out. My idea simply was to get on base somehow.

I fouled off one of Parnell's pitches, just protecting the plate and shortening my stroke so I could have better bat control and dump the ball into left field for a hit.

After the foul ball, I heard DiMaggio say in a low voice from his spot in the on-deck circle behind me, "No, Tom. Go for it."

Joe's remark prompted me to change my thinking. I decided to try to pull one of Parnell's pitches, if I got the right one. Sure enough, Mel curved me inside, so I pulled the ball—five rows into the seats in right field. It was my twenty-fourth home run of the season.

Then, with the bases loaded a few minutes later, Jerry Coleman hit a soft fly ball off Tex Hughson that fell in for a three-run double. It's a good thing, too, because we needed those extra runs in the ninth.

As I trotted from our dugout to first base for the start of the

Boston ninth, I said to Raschi when I passed him, "Don't walk anybody, Vic." He didn't need to hear that. He knew full well that he didn't want to walk anybody, but I felt compelled to say it anyhow. If it didn't help Vic to hear it, maybe it at least helped me to say it.

With one out and two on—one of them on a walk to Williams, but that's no crime because it prevented him from hitting a home run—Doerr hit a two-run triple that went over DiMaggio's head, much to the surprise of everyone including Joe himself. It scared all of us, because all of a sudden we knew we didn't have enough protection in center field, even with the great DiMaggio out there.

Joe was just too weak from his virus to make that play, to be able to run back and catch up with the ball. That wasn't Joe DiMaggio out there at all. It was just a man who was sick and didn't have the strength to do anything, much less compete for the pennant in the last game of the season. He was playing on guts alone, but he knew his team needed more than guts at this critical point. We needed people at every position who could handle anything hit in their vicinity.

So Joe did one of the most unselfish things I've ever seen on a field in any sport. He took himself out of the game. He knew he was putting his team in danger of losing the pennant that we could feel in our hand. When he came off the field with that graceful, gliding stride of his, head cocked slightly to one side, he received a thunderous ovation and deserved every decibel of it.

Now Stengel had to make some of his patented managerial moves, and that's where our depth, compliments of George Weiss, helped us to win. What could have been a serious problem for other teams was no difficulty at all for the Yankees. Casey moved Cliff Mapes from right field to center and Bauer from left to right, then inserted Gene Woodling into the game to play left field.

Mapes immediately caught a fly ball, then threw a strike to Berra at the plate to hold the runner at third base. As the first baseman, I was the cutoff man in the infield, responsible for leaving my position at first and stationing myself between the mound and home plate, ready to cut off the throw from the outfield if I heard Yogi yell "cut!" and then throw to one of the bases to get one of the runners who might be trying to take an extra base on the throw home.

Mapes was exactly the kind of outfielder who could make that throw. He had the straightest, most accurate throwing arm of any outfielder I ever saw. The Red Sox obviously knew this, too. Doerr did not try to score after the catch.

Two outs and we were still winning, 5–2. Then Billy Goodman singled home Bobby Doerr to make it 5–3.

The way Raschi was pitching, we weren't going to need any outfielders anyhow. Vic was pitching a five-hitter, and now he was down to needing only one more out.

Berra, who was becoming one of the smartest catchers in the game, called for time out, then trotted out toward the mound to make sure all these goings-on plus the pressure turned up to the maximum setting were not beginning to affect Raschi's composure. I trotted over from first base, and the three of us gathered near the mound to make sure Vic was still in control of things.

Yogi and I are going to give our buddy Vic a pep talk. Yogi asks him if he's okay, and Vic snaps at him, "Just give me the damn ball and get the hell out of here."

I went back to my position fully as confident as Vic was, and I'm sure Yogi did, too. That kind of an attitude is contagious. As I was trotting back to first, I was thinking to myself, "We're in."

At that point, Birdie Tebbetts, Boston's catcher, lofted a high pop fly into foul territory behind first base. Tebbetts was a good right-handed hitter with a lifetime .270 average for fourteen seasons who got an even 1,000 hits in his career. He was a long way from an automatic out up there, but this time he wasn't able to get the bat around against Raschi, which probably contradicted the speculation by some of Birdie's teammates later that Raschi might have started tiring by the ninth. Not this day.

Jerry Coleman, playing second for us, called for it, but I called him off by yelling "I got it! I got it! I got it!" I squeezed that baby. I wasn't going to let Jerry or anybody else catch that ball.

I'd been waiting for it all season. I still have it.

My heart went out to my old manager, Joe McCarthy, and all of his players. It was their second crushing disappointment in a row, coming the year after they lost the first playoff game in the history of the American League to the Cleveland Indians in '48.

The Dodgers experienced the same kind of back-to-back devastation when they lost to the Phillies on the last day of the 1950 season and then to the Giants on Bobby Thomson's "shot heard 'round the world" the next year. I can't imagine a harder one-two punch to take than what the Red Sox had to survive in 1948–49 and the Dodgers in 1950–51.

The Dodgers didn't have that burden yet. In 1949, success was theirs. They won the pennant by beating the Phillies in ten innings, 9–7, on a hard-hit ground ball through the middle and into center field by Duke Snider that scored Pee Wee Reese. Jack Banta won the game in relief. Banta was a six-foot-two-inch right-hander from Hutchinson, Kansas, who won 10 games for the Dodgers that year. He developed arm trouble and dropped out of the big leagues after being able to pitch only one full season, 1949.

Now we had the Brooklyn Dodgers in front of us, the only obstacle left between us and baseball's world championship. We were in an uncertain position. The oddsmakers made us 5-to-8 favorites to win the World Series and 5-to-7 choices to win the first game, but those were calculations based on our performance. The question that they didn't know the answer to—and neither did anyone else—was whether we would be able to maintain our winning ways long enough to win four more games or whether the season-long strain of winning in the face of so much adversity would leave us drained of any emotion or strength to survive the heat of the Series against one of baseball's most formidable opponents.

It was a great time for the inevitable scalpers. They were asking $100 for tickets. What they didn't know, and wouldn't want anyone else to know, was that if you stepped around to the bleacher window, you could get a ticket for a dollar—and there wasn't any line. For that first game, that's exactly what 9,727 fans did.

Mayor O'Dwyer was sitting squarely on the horns of a political dilemma. He wasn't just the mayor of Manhattan, where the Yankees played. He was the mayor of the entire city including Brooklyn, where the Dodgers played. When the reporters asked him which team he would be rooting for, he ducked it. He didn't duck the game, though. He was there, along with Ty Cobb and Trygve Lie, the first secretary general of the new United Nations.

The city's transportation officials expanded the subway service every way they could for the latest Subway Series. They increased the number of cars on the trains from six to eight, reduced the "headway" between trains from eight minutes to six, and operated five special ten-car trains between Brooklyn and the Yankee Stadium station at 161st Street.

A representative of the Hotel Association of New York said rooms were at a premium. He called our World Series "the biggest thing since the war." The New York Telephone Company felt the same way, establishing an answering service that would give the inning-by-inning score of each game every fifteen seconds. Call MEridian 7-1212.

The person who may have been the most excited one of all in New York that week wasn't even a New Yorker. He was from St. Louis, a thirty-seven-year-old cab driver named William Julian. When the borough president of Brooklyn, John Cashmore, returned to his office after a victory celebration for the Dodgers' pennant, there was this cab driver waiting for him.

He had a ready explanation for his presence. He told Cashmore, "You rode in my cab out in St. Louis during the crucial series in September, and you said if the Dodgers won the pennant I could come out here as your guest to see the World Series. Remember?"

Cashmore said, "I remember that bet. I'm delighted to pay it." He did, too, and he put the cab driver up at the St. George Hotel in Brooklyn, where the Dodgers' families stayed on their visits.

Sixteen _____

Top of the World!

Burt Shotton's pitching selection was Don Newcombe, a hulking twenty-three-year-old from New Jersey, a six-foot-four-inch right-hander who threw hard and got all of his 220 pounds into his fastball. He was a rookie and a 17-game winner, for which he received the National League's Rookie of the Year Award.

Newk was one of Brooklyn's rich crop of good black athletes. Unlike some of their first black players like Jackie Robinson, Roy Campanella, and Dan Bankead, who were in their middle to late twenties when Branch Rickey broke the color barrier two years earlier, Newcombe was only twenty-two when the season started. With that much size and youth, he was the kind of pitcher who could give you nine strong innings, more if necessary. Reynolds was eleven years older.

The Dodgers were loaded with talent. They had the same record we did—97 wins and 57 losses—and they had survived a long and tense battle for their league's pennant. They had four future Hall of Famers in their starting lineup—Campanella, Reese, Robinson, and Snider—and a fifth player who should be, Gil Hodges.

In pitching, Newcombe tied for the most shutouts in the league and had the second most strikeouts, the third most complete games, the most strikeouts for every nine innings pitched, the fewest hits per nine innings, and the third highest won-lost percentage. His 17 wins tied for fourth place.

Elwin "Preacher" Roe, who earned his nickname by telling so many stories in the down-home delivery that he developed back in Ashflat, Arkansas, led the league that year in winning percentage with .714 thanks to a record of 15 wins and only 6 losses. He also had the third best earned run average, the fourth most strikeouts, the third most strikeouts per nine innings, and the second fewest walks over nine innings.

The weather forecast said it would be cloudy with a chance of showers and a high of 77 degrees expected. It turned out that both pitchers needed every ounce of strength at their command. It was a battle of zeroes, with both pitchers throwing shutouts for eight innings. Allie received a big helping hand from Joe D. in the sixth when he made a great catch of a ball hit by Robinson.

Going into the ninth, Reynolds had a two-hitter and Newcombe a four-hitter. Superchief set the Dodgers down without a run again in the ninth. There were 66,224 fans jammed into Yankee Stadium that afternoon, and they had no idea of how long they'd be there.

I had an opportunity to answer that question. I was the first hitter for the Yankees in the ninth, with the score still 0–0. I knew one thing for sure: I was going to have to hit my way on. Newcombe hadn't walked a man yet.

The first two pitches to me were balls. Now I was in the driver's seat. Newcombe had to throw a strike—he just *had* to. He didn't want to miss again and be within one pitch of walking the leadoff hitter. You never want to do that anyhow, because it changes the complexion of the whole inning for the defense. And to do it in the last half of the ninth inning of a 0–0 game is one of the cardinal sins of pitching.

Something else made that possibility even more frightening for Newcombe. The man on deck to hit after me was Yogi Berra, followed by Joe DiMaggio. Newcombe knew all of these things as well as I did, maybe better, as he began his windup.

He came in to me with his curveball. His curve did not usually break a whole lot. It was a fast curve, and that was to my advantage, too, because the hitter doesn't have to adjust as much to the difference in speed between that pitch and a fastball. With a slow, roundhouse curve, the difference in speed is much greater, and your timing as a hitter is thrown off that much more. That's why I hated those things—but the fast curve I was able to handle some times.

This was one of those times. The pitch was in the strike zone, and I was ready for it. I swung and hit a long fly ball to right field. As I was running down the first-base line, I was watching Brooklyn's right fielder, Carl Furillo, who was running to his left toward the foul line.

While I was running as hard as I could, I was trying to see if it would drop in for an extra base hit, which would give us the potential winning run in scoring position at second base and nobody out with DiMag coming up, or if it would stay in the air long enough to clear the wall for a home run.

Furillo continued running to his left. Then he lifted his head to follow the flight of the ball, and the second that he did, I said to myself, "This game is over!" I knew I had a home run—another bolt of our Yankee five o'clock lightning—and we had won the opening game.

Bill Dickey was our first-base coach, and he almost tackled me with joy as I went around the bag. I avoided him as much as I could. I didn't want him to touch me because of the possibility that the umpires could rule he had assisted me as a runner, which is against the rules. I didn't want to be paranoid, but I was determined not to have anything mess us up now, even something as freakish as that would have been.

Some of my teammates told me I had a companion as I rounded the bases. They said Jackie Robinson picked up my journey as I neared his second baseman's position and followed me around the bases, making sure I didn't miss one and give him the opportunity to have me called out.

As I rounded third, Dickey's elation became unrestrained again. He dashed down to the plate from his first-base coach's box and formed a "Welcome Home" committee with Yogi and our bat boy. He made another attempt to tackle me. Then he kissed me, much to the delight of the photographers who were snapping away.

In our dressing room, Stengel was as hopped-up as Dickey. He kept hollering, "How that Henrich hit it! What a blast! The touch of the master!" Joe Page said he vaulted over the bullpen fence and onto the outfield grass as soon as I hit it. He told me, "I knew as soon as I heard the crack where that pitch was going."

Dickey explained his two attempted tackles by saying, "I just had to leap all over Tommy for that one." Somebody asked Joe D. if he thought Reynolds might be called upon to pitch three games in this World Series, and Joe's answer was a classic of confidence: "Not if we win four in a row."

In the Brooklyn dressing room, Newcombe was as subdued as you would expect any athlete to be in that kind of situation. He confirmed to reporters that I hit a low curveball.

Three thousand miles away in San Francisco, Paul Brown, the coach of the Cleveland Browns who was winning the championship of the All-America Conference every year, was sitting with his quarterback, Otto Graham. Paul and I were friends from back home in Massillon.

Brown predicted to Graham before the game that I would win the game for the Yankees. He told me later that as I came to bat in the ninth inning, Graham said, "Well, your Massillon friend has his chance right here."

Years later, after his career as one of the greatest quarterbacks in history, Otto told me that he hated to see Paul right again.

I got my picture on the top half of the first page of the *New York Times* the next morning, which I attributed to superior news judgment until I heard what one reporter asked Stengel in the dressing room moments after my home run: "Casey, in your opinion, what was the turning point in the game?"

Preacher Roe picked up his whole Brooklyn team the next day. It was a 1–0 game again, only this time we were the ones on the short end. Preach held us to six hits, and Raschi, followed by Page in the ninth, allowed Brooklyn only seven. In the first two games, all four starting pitchers had been sensational. The only run of the game was scored in the second inning by Robinson on a single by Hodges.

On the next day, October 7, Tommy Byrne opposed Brooklyn's Ralph Branca in the third game after the Series moved to Ebbets Field. Casey and our pitching coach, Jim Turner, decided to get

Byrne out of there in the fourth inning after he allowed two hits and a run—a homer by Reese—and had loaded the bases. Joe Page came to our rescue again.

We got out of it with the Dodgers scoring only the Reese run, and with a run of our own in the third, we had a 1–1 game. Things rocked along like that into the ninth inning, the third tense, low-scoring game in a row where a mistake by anyone had the potential to cost your team the game.

The man keeping us in the game was our Fireman Joe. In our ninth, we rallied for three huge runs, and we had two men to thank for that: Johnny Mize and George Weiss, the man who got Mize for us. Big Jawn wasn't starting for us because he came down with a sore right shoulder shortly after he joined us. During our to-the-wire battle against the Red Sox, Mize was available only for pinch-hitting. He delivered for us twice in eight trips.

Mize hadn't pinch-hit more than seven times in any season since his rookie year thirteen seasons before, when he did it fifteen times. Over the years, as a student of hitting, he was a knowledgeable man on the specialty of pinch-hitting. He said the big difference between pinch-hitting and playing every day is that you get to see the pitcher only once as a pinch-hitter instead of the three or four looks you get as a starter. You have to make all of your calculations and adjustments in that one time at bat instead of getting three or four chances.

The Big Cat came up with the bases loaded, as always looking even bigger as he stood in the left-handed side of the batter's box and held that powerful bat of his, ready to pull the trigger. He singled in two runs off Ralph Branca. We added a third, and it's a good thing we did. We won, 4–3.

Our bullpen depth was the difference again in the fourth game, and this time our hero was Reynolds. We built an early 6–0 lead, but Ed Lopat dug a hole for himself in the sixth and the Dodgers came up with four runs.

Stengel called for Reynolds, who started 31 games for us that year. On this day, as a relief pitcher, Allie faced ten men and got them all.

When we took the field for the fifth game, we stood on the threshold of accomplishing something great. Finishing third the year before, being saddled with injuries all during this season, and missing DiMaggio for the first half of the season and then again over most of the last two weeks because of that virus, all while getting used to playing for a new manager, we stood within one game of becoming the champions of the baseball world again.

The town was alive with excitement. Our fans were filled with anticipation. The Dodgers' fans were keeping their fingers crossed, hoping that their heroes could survive one game at a time through the sixth game and then beat us in seven.

Even without our help, New York was an electrifying town in 1949. It was big and crowded and hustle-bustle, with men all dressed alike dashing up and down Madison Avenue carrying attaché cases and women shopping along Fifth Avenue. Except for the government in Washington, New York was the capital of the United States.

There was plenty of entertainment. Larry Parks was starring in *Jolson Sings Again* at Loew's State on Broadway. One of the other hit movies of the late 1940s was a Jimmy Cagney film called *White Heat*. In the climax, Cagney, a crazed escaped prisoner who always promised his mother he'd make it to the top, stands atop one of those huge white oil storage tanks that look like giant baseballs along what is now I-95 in New Jersey. Flames are licking at him from every side as he screams toward his deceased mother in the skies above something that could have been our battle cry that year: "Top of the world, Ma! Top of the world!"

The radio networks were competing hard against each other and against the newest threat facing them—television. Many of the shows, both radio and TV, originated in New York. The networks had large display ads in the papers that week beating the drum about their lineup of coming attractions.

There was an ad announcing the CBS radio lineup for Sunday of that week—"all on CBS tonight!" The list was a galaxy of 1949 talent featuring Jack Benny, Amos 'n' Andy, Edgar Bergen with Charlie McCarthy and Mortimer Snerd, Red Skelton, Horace Heidt and His Musical Knights, and Eve Arden as "Our Miss Brooks."

NBC took on CBS with its own array of attractions: "Radio City Playhouse," "The Harvest of Stars" with James Melton,

"Hollywood Calling" with John Lund and Ann Blyth, the Phil Harris and Alice Faye show, "The Adventures of Sam Spade," "The Theatre Guild of the Air" with Jimmy Cagney, and "Take It or Leave It," with no less than Eddie Cantor asking the $64 question.

The 33,711 fans who crowded into Ebbets Field, including Governor Dewey and Mayor O'Dwyer again, hardly had a chance to find their seats before we jumped off to a 2–0 lead in the first inning. With Cal Hubbard calling balls and strikes, Rex Barney walked Rizzuto and me on nine pitches to start the game. Then he made a wild throw trying to pick the Scooter off second base, enabling Phil to move over to third and me to second.

In that spot, Joe D. came through for us again, as he did so often, heel or no heel, virus or no virus, bruised legs or no bruised legs. He hit a long fly ball to center field, which Duke Snider caught up with at the 399-foot sign. It was good enough to score Rizzuto and move me over to third after the catch. Then Bobby Brown singled me home, and we had the first two runs of the game.

The game erupted into a slugout. The same World Series that began with two 1–0 games ended with 33 runs being scored in its final three games. We scored three more times in the third inning, single runs in the fourth and fifth, and three more in the sixth.

By the time the Dodgers came to bat in the home half of the sixth, we had a lead of 10–1. Some of our younger players began laughing it up on the bench, and that upset me. I didn't holler criticism at my teammates often, but I did that day.

I told them, "Knock it off! We're never going to have a better chance to win the World Series than right now. This is no time to rejoice. Bear down!"

Then Vic Raschi ran into trouble. Brooklyn chipped away with a run in its sixth and then exploded for four more in the seventh, three of them on a home run by Gil Hodges. All of a sudden, the Dodgers were back in the game.

Casey brought Page into the game with two outs in the seventh. He exuded that same supreme confidence that he always showed. When he walked to the mound to take the ball, he brought with him his uncanny ability to excel under pressure and his unique philosophy that helped to make him a winner in his specialty as a relief pitcher:

> After all, why should a relief pitcher go looking for trouble when he knows it will come looking for him? If there was no trouble, there wouldn't be any relief pitchers. So, in a way, trouble is our best friend.

Fireman Joe came in and cut the Dodgers off. He got us out of the inning without any more runs by Brooklyn. Then he shut them out in the eighth. He ended the game, the World Series, and the season with a flourish in the ninth inning. With two men on base for the Dodgers, Fireman Joe struck out Snider on nothing but fast balls. Then he struck out Robinson with one curveball. Everything else was his "heater," as the players call a pitcher's fastball. After a walk to Gene Hermanski, he struck out Hodges—all fastballs.

We were the world champions again.

In our dressing room, the atmosphere was pandemonium. Page, who gave up only two hits and no runs in two and two-thirds innings while striking out four and walking only one, gave Stengel the baseball that he struck out Hodges with, and Casey wasn't parting with it. Someone asked him if he could have it, and Stengel hollered, "Not this—no, no, no! I'm keeping this for myself!"

I felt there was significance to Page's generosity in giving that ball to Stengel. He was showing his appreciation to his manager for giving him another chance after his off season in '48. The gesture was proof of the skill and wisdom with which Stengel managed Page in 1949. He helped a man to believe in himself again. In doing so, Casey was helping his whole team.

The press wanted to know if this was Casey's greatest thrill in baseball. He said no—winning the pennant was. Then he talked to the reporters about us:

> This has been one happy family from the time spring training started. There has never been a sour note in this clubhouse, on the dugout bench or on the field. A really great bunch of

fellows, and I'm indebted to every one of them for the way they came through for me. They won it—not me.

When the noise died down to a mere roar, the photographers posed Casey with some of his players. Then one of them, ready to click his shutter, said, "All right, Casey—let's have a victory yell."

Stengel screamed out, "Happy New Year!"

In the Brooklyn dressing room, Jackie Robinson, the National League batting champion and eventual winner of the league's Most Valuable Player Award, was talking quietly to reporters. Jackie was only a .188 hitter in the Series with two singles and a double in 16 times at bat. He offered no excuses, even though the Dodgers were without Carl Furillo, a .322 hitter during the season and one of the best outfielders in baseball, for most of the Series after the first game.

Jackie told the press, "They really knocked us down and stepped on us."

In addition to the team championship, individual recognition came our way, too. Phil Rizzuto and Joe Page finished second and third behind Ted Williams in the voting for the American League's Most Valuable Player Award. *Sport* magazine voted me its Athlete of the Year for all sports. Casey was voted Manager of the Year.

With all the glory for the team and the individual honors and the hundreds of thousands of words written and spoken about the New York Yankees of 1949, Vic Raschi, our 21-game winner, told the story best in one sentence: "There was a love on that club that you could find only on a championship team."

Seventeen

The Last Time

Our 1949 dream season was the capstone of our careers as Yankees for Joe DiMaggio and me. Nothing before or after was quite so grand. In my case, it came with only one year to spare. By the time the 1950 season arrived, the years and 1,211 games were just plain wearing out my left knee. I played in 73 games, but 39 of them were as a pinch-hitter. My times at bat dropped to 151 after running in the 400s and 500s for six straight years. The only alternative to my knee problem was surgery, and at age thirty-seven there was no guarantee of the results, so I rejected the option.

For Joe, the future was much brighter. None of us had any reason to suspect that it would also be short. He tore up the American League's pitchers again in 1950, playing 139 games on two healthy heels instead of one. He hit .301, the eleventh time in his career—and the last—that he topped .300, drove in 122 runs, and hit 32 homers. There was not the slightest hint in his performance that 1950 would be his last great year, and the next to last season of his brilliant career.

For the DiMaggio brothers, 1950 was a banner year. Joe was third in the league in home runs, fifth in RBIs, tops in slugging average, and fifth in total bases. Up the coast in Boston, Dom DiMaggio was doing at least as well as Joe: third in the league in hitting with a .328 batting average, third in hits, and first in stolen bases, triples, and runs scored.

As always, George Weiss kept good young blood flowing into the parent club from our minor-league system, and he continued to acquire proven players from other major-league teams. Three of the new faces of 1950 included two kids who were future stars, Whitey Ford and Billy Martin, plus an established veteran, Tom Ferrick.

Weiss called Ford up from our farm team at Kansas City, the Blues, in the middle of the 1950 season. Whitey immediately stood the league on its ear by winning his first nine games. He finished at 9–1 with an earned run average of 2.81 and topped that off by starting and winning our final game in the World Series, going all the way to two outs in the ninth before Stengel lifted him.

Then he was grabbed away from the Yankees for the next two years. The Communist army of North Korea charged across the 38th Parallel on June 25 and invaded South Korea. All those troops and planes that we had pulled out of Korea the year before had to be sent right back in there. President Truman declared a state of national emergency, and the Selective Service began drafting 80,000 men a month. We were scared all over gain, wondering if the rest of us would have to go to war for the second time in only five years. People began calling it "World War Two and a Half."

In some ways, Whitey was an Ed Lopat clone. They were both native New Yorkers, short and stocky, left-handed "cutie" pitchers who got you out on slow, breaking pitches that drove you crazy instead of trying to overpower you with a fastball. They talked with the same New York accent and even walked the same way. On top of all that, they became good friends, the thirty-two-year-old veteran and the twenty-three-year-old rookie, "Steady Eddie" and the kid who became known as "the Chairman of the Board."

Whitey was an independent cuss, and he sometimes drove the Yankee management crazy. One front-office member complained to a writer, "He never runs away from a party." He was a holdout almost every year, haggling with Weiss from the time he was a rookie. He played winter ball when he was still a minor leaguer, against orders from the Yankee front office, but management never complained about him when he stood on that hill sixty feet and six inches from home plate.

He won 236 games over sixteen years even with those two years lost because of the Korean War, broke Babe Ruth's pitching record for the most consecutive scoreless innings in World Series play, and was a 20-game winner twice, a winner in double digits eleven other times, earned run champion twice, and the pitcher with the most wins three times.

Tom Ferrick may not have been as good, but he wasn't as lucky either. He was still another New Yorker, but he never had the luxury of pitching for a team like the Yankees except for 30 games in 1950 and 9 in '51 before being traded to the Senators. The rest of his career was spent laboring—and it *was* labor—for the A's, Indians, and Browns.

His career totals show only 40 wins against 40 losses, plus a win in our 1950 World Series, but in Tom's own way, he was as much of a success story as Whitey, although he'd never tell you the story behind his baseball career. It's a rare story, one he never talked about much, of inspiration that should motivate anyone.

His mother wanted him to be a priest, so after he graduated from high school he entered Glenclyffe Seminary at Garrison, New York, across the Hudson River from West Point.

He told us that he wasn't excited about the place at the start, but then he discovered he liked it. "I didn't want to return home," he said. "I stayed four years and would have become a member of the Franciscan Order, but my stepfather died suddenly and I became the sole support of my mother and younger brother."

He said he hated to leave the seminary, "especially after working so hard. But everything can't turn out the way you'd like. I simply had to go out and find a job."

He found it as a pipefitter in the shipyards at Jersey City. He picked up a few extra dollars so badly needed at home by pitching for a semi-pro team in his spare time.

That's when he came to the attention of the New York Giants, who signed him to a contract with their minor-league system in 1936. He worked his way up to Richmond, Virginia, in two years, but fate interfered again, this time in the form of a sore shoulder.

A transfer to the Giants' team at Jersey City at the start of the 1939 season was no help. He couldn't throw a baseball any more.

But Ferrick was just as determined as the rest of us in those days that he was going to be a big-league ball player. That was his dream. It wasn't the money back then. Young ball players weren't making any more than young people in any other field, but all of us had a love for baseball that was genuine and deep. With us, it wasn't just a job, it was a calling. All of us felt that we were meant to be major-league baseball players because we loved our sport and had a certain amount of ability to play it. With that combination, we weren't going to make anything less than a 100 percent effort to reach the big leagues, and all the money problems and injuries and skimping by in small towns on starvation wages—even a death in the family—weren't going to stop us from trying our damndest to make it in baseball.

That's why Tom went back to New York and began to make the rounds of doctors and chiropractors to see if anybody could solve his mystery. Eventually the problem was discovered: two muscles "that were twisted and rubbing against each other like two pieces of rope. That caused all the soreness. When the muscles were worked back into their normal positions, I started throwing again, without pain."

That got him to the Philadelphia A's in 1941 as a twenty-six-year-old rookie, only to lose three more years because of military service in the war. When the war was over, he was with the Cleveland Indians, a six-foot-two-inch right-hander hoping—and probably praying—to stick around enough years to enjoy what he had endured so much to achieve.

He did, too. He was a major-league pitcher for nine years. Nobody ever had more reason to be proud of 40 wins than Tom Ferrick.

Billy Martin was still another story. He had a father-son relationship with Casey Stengel dating back two years, when Stengel was Martin's manager at Oakland in the Pacific Coast League. He was a firebrand of a player who would tear the uniform off your back to beat you, and he was a complicated human being who suffered through deep disappointments, depression, and a series of brawls in back alleys and bars that became a long-running show, lasting as long as he was in a baseball uniform as player, coach, or manager.

His father was a Portuguese crop hand from Hawaii who abandoned Billy's mother when Billy was eight months old. In their hometown of Oakland, the man closest to him in his early years was Father Dennis Moore of St. Ambrose's Church.

Father Moore remembered how poor the family was. At eight years old, Billy "was a solemn little fellow," the priest said. He remembered that the family was "very poor." Martin swept out the church in exchange for food packages for his mother and younger sister.

He even had a close call with death at the tender age of ten. "They ate some tainted meat," Father Moore remembered, "and it was thought Billy would die. The church even made plans to bury him."

Frank Lane said he thought the Yankees let Martin get away with too much in his first years with them, thus contributing to his combativeness. Lane was an executive with the Indians and White Sox in our league and observed Martin closely. "They've encouraged a jittery kid to play the tough little mug," he said. "You can see why Martin is the Rocky Graziano of baseball."

In spring training, he didn't act like a rookie; he acted as if he owned the place. A perfect example was the time that he needled Johnny Mize on our train coming north from Florida when Johnny started to say something. Billy interrupted him and blurted out, "Go ahead, Johnny. Give us a few thousand well-chosen words."

When we played the Dodgers in New York before the season started for the Mayor's Cup, Jackie Robinson grounded out. He turned and trotted past our dugout on his way to the Dodgers' side of the field. Martin was standing with his foot on the top step of our dugout. As Jackie was trotting past us, well within earshot, Billy said to him, "You big busher! It's a good thing you're not in my league. I'd have your job in a week!"

He was a kid yelling that stuff to the man voted the National League's Most Valuable Player the year before. With performances like that, Martin brought new meaning to the term "brash rookie."

But the kid could also play the game. We opened the season in

Boston in 1950, and in his first game in the major leagues he hit a double and a single in the same inning, something no rookie in the American League ever did before.

Then, in one of those decisions that players never agree with—and shouldn't—he was given the word: We had Jerry Coleman and Snuffy Stirnweiss, proven veterans, available to play second base. Martin was being farmed out to Kansas City temporarily.

After he finished packing, Martin confronted George Weiss, and that competitive fire in his gut that made him so valuable as a player for eleven seasons exploded. He hollered at Weiss, "I'll make you pay for this! I'll get even!" He said he would come back and be a star, and that when he did, it would cost Weiss plenty in salary.

Martin made good on everything. The Yankees recalled him after only twenty-nine games at Kansas City. He hit an even .250 in thirty-four games with us as a utility second baseman. But his real value was on our bench. I spent some time there with him that season, and I saw him—and heard him—as he got on every team in the league while we were trying to repeat as champions. He didn't back away from anybody.

Stengel, who was behaving himself so well because he wanted to secure his reputation as a serious and successful manager, delighted in Billy's antics. He referred to Martin as "that fresh kid who's always sassing everybody and getting away with it."

He roomed with Mickey Mantle for a while, and neither of them believed in retiring with the chickens at night. New York's bright lights appealed to both of them, the kid from the small town in Oklahoma and the one who endured all that poverty as a boy. The word went around at one point that the Yankees were going to split up Martin and Mantel in an effort to get both of them to behave a little better with new roomies.

Billy had a quick response to that suggestion: "Why bother? We'll just keep two other guys out late."

While we were gaining talented players to strengthen our chances of repeating as champions in 1950, we lost another man who was a champion by himself—Charlie Keller.

His back was hindering him too much to let him play regularly for us, but there was another manager in the American League who was anxious to have him on his team. Our old teammate and Charlie's close pal, Red Rolfe, was managing the Detroit Tigers. He signed Charlie as soon as the Yankees let him go.

Everyone knew that Charlie's bad back kept him from swinging the bat with the authority he used to have, but hitting wasn't the only thing about Charlie that Rolfe respected. He said he got Charlie "because I wanted to add a little class to my ball club."

It was a happy reunion for both men. They enjoyed each other's company when they were teammates on our ball club because they were so much alike. Neither of them liked to do a lot of hell-raising. Both were serious, quiet men. Red's idea of a wonderful evening was to play bridge with three other guys who didn't talk. Charlie felt the same way.

They were both intelligent, classy men. We old-timers who were still playing for the Yankees were delighted to see our old buddy Charlie get to play for such a close friend. But it was bittersweet news to us. We missed Charlie. I thought the world of the man, and when he hit .314 as the Tigers almost won the pennant, I rejoiced for my two old friends and their friendship with each other.

Casey Stengel always placed great emphasis on teaching, and in 1950 he stepped it up to a new level. He began his "instructual school" for our young players. They came two weeks before the start of spring training, and they were put through every aspect of the game. Later in the decade he told people that his school was "the best reason why the Yankees keep winning year after year."

In his emphasis on instruction, Casey was the exact opposite of Joe McCarthy. Whereas McCarthy would only tell you to lay off the low, inside curveball or get rid of the ball quicker, Casey would stand out there on the field and show you how. He was a master teacher, and he taught every phase of the game. He even showed pitchers how to keep runners from taking big leads against them, even though he was not a pitcher himself.

I helped at his 1951 school, when the Yankees trained in Phoenix, the first year of my retirement from playing. My special student was a kid who had just set the record for most errors by a shortstop in his minor league year at Joplin, Missouri: Mickey Mantle.

The Yankees were grooming him as DiMag's successor, and my job was to teach him how to throw from the outfield with men on base. I showed him how to get set before the catch, getting your footwork down pat so you're taking your last step or two just as you're catching the ball. That enables you to have the maximum amount of momentum going toward your target. I showed him how to make the catch off the shoulder of your throwing arm and told him why that's important: so you don't have to bring the ball all the way across your chest before you can throw it. I showed him how to make his throws "over the top," overhand instead of a three-quarters motion, to get more velocity.

For days on end I lobbed the ball into the air and helped Mantle to get everything coordinated into consistently strong—and quick—throws from the outfield.

Mickey was an excellent and willing student. I knew he was going to be a great one just because of the combination of his enormous talent and his good attitude in working hard so he would be even better. My first evidence of his potential as an outfielder came on an alert, crisp play in one of our early exhibition games.

Jim Busby, one of the fastest runners in either league, was on third base for the Chicago White Sox when the hitter sent a fly ball to center field. It was the kind of fly that Busby scored on almost every time. But not this time. Mickey threw a strike—a quick one—to Yogi on the fly. Busby put his brakes on and scrambled back toward third. Yogi whipped the ball to Bobby Brown, and Busby was out.

I knew then that Mickey, who could already hit and run and catch anything near him, was learning how to throw, too.

Today I see outfielders who get paid $3 million a year and are not fundamentally sound in their jobs. Players can talk all they want to about how much stronger they are then we were, or faster, or able to do other things, but too many of them today are not complete, sound baseball players.

Too many of the outfielders don't get to balls they should reach, because they were playing the hitter wrong in the first place or didn't bother to notice where their pitcher was pitching this particular hitter or didn't try to remember what kind of a sequence of pitches he has used on this hitter in the past. Many of them take far too long to release the ball on their throws. And how many times over the course of a season do you see outfielders who don't care about other fine points of their jobs such as hustling to cut off balls hit up the alley or hitting the cutoff man?

At the plate, too many of them swing the bat one way and one way only—for the fence—regardless of what the pitcher is doing. The pitcher is certainly not throwing the same pitch every time, . but the hitter is taking the same swing.

José Canseco is a perfect example. He's going to swing hard enough to put that ball into the next county whether it's a fastball inside, a slider outside, a knuckleball, or anything else. He's going to take the same from-the-heels cut whether the count is 3–0 or 0–2.

A three-run homer is nice, but you can help your team just as much by punching a ground ball to the opposite field in the late innings on a hit-and-run play that gives your team a man on third with only one out and makes it possible for you to win the game on a fly ball. But too many of today's players don't play the game that way.

It's a shame. And this much the men who used to play big-league baseball know: With the attitudes that so many players have today, they never would have lasted in our time. It's the difference between being selfish and having a good team attitude. One wins fat contracts for yourself. The other wins championships for your team.

At Casey's instructual school, the accent was on being smart. He used to ask, "Why miss a hundred signs a year? Why run the bases with your head down? There aren't any ditches out there, no bumps, and the bag won't move. You look around at what's going on, and you think."

He gave his own personal instructions, conducting a lecture at each of the nine positions on how to play that position and what to look for the man playing it when you're a base runner. And he didn't miss a thing.

He'd stand there making all sorts of gestures with his body English and waving his arms, and he'd say, "Here's first base.

When you get his far, you got eight things to think about. You read the pitcher. You look around and check the outfield. How can they throw? Don't get halfway to second and say, 'Oops, I forgot if that fellow can throw.' Don't get suckered into being caught off base. Keep your foot on the bag until you're ready to do something. Watch where the ball's hit and get a fast start. Watch for signs, and don't run when there aren't any outs unless you're positive of what's going on.''

He even lectured on the proper use of sunglasses. ''Keep your hand up like this and then flip them down,'' he told our young players. ''It eliminates an extra move.''

Casey emphasized teaching because he was aware of what others had taught him. He remembered his lessons well, what happened to teach him certain things, who taught him, and the reasons for doing things in a certain way depending on the situation. One lesson he learned came from the great John McGraw, the legendary manager of the Baltimore Orioles for three years the first time they were a major-league team at the turn of the century who then spent thirty years managing the Giants.

Stengel told the story of chasing down a long fly ball to deep center field with Rogers Hornsby on base and then throwing it to George ''Highpockets'' Kelly, the first baseman who was in the middle of the infield to cut off Stengel's throw. But the throw was low, and Kelly had to lean down for it, using more time. Hornsby beat the throw home with the run that won the game.

This was when Stengel and McGraw were with the Giants after Casey played a year and a half in Philadelphia. After the game, McGraw got hold of Stengel and said sternly, ''From now on, young man, when you pick up that ball in the outfield, be sure you look at the relay man. And throw it up high around his head and shoulders, where he can catch the ball and throw it home without taking a hop, skip and jump.

''You lost that game for me, and if you don't do better, you'll be back in Philadelphia with those tail-end bums.''

What was the lesson learned? ''After that,'' said Casey, ''I remembered to throw the ball high.''

The guiding genius behind all of this, and behind Stengel himself, was George Weiss, the man fired by Larry MacPhail at our victory party in 1947 and hired the next day as general manager after Dan Topping and Del Webb bought out MacPhail.

He was getting us the players we needed, and in Stengel he got us the onetime clown who with the Yankees became the most successful manager of his time. That, Weiss said, was "the best decision I ever made."

Weiss came to the Yankees as the director of their farm system in 1932, at a time when the Yankees' offices were in three rooms overlooking Bryant Park at 42nd Street. Colonel Ruppert said he wanted a first-rate farm system like the one the Cardinals had and he was willing to pay Weiss top dollar—$12,000 a year.

He demanded excellence in all things, from himself and everyone else. "This includes," he said, "everything from operating a good restaurant for members of the Stadium Club to two-platooning on the field when the circumstances demand it."

His favorite Yankee team was mine, too—1949. He said, "A couple of players I had confidence in came through that year, and our winning spoiled the fun for a lot of people who had picked us to finish in the second division."

With all of his intelligence and shrewdness, George was also superstitious. He would never watch a game in the ninth inning if we were winning. He said he left when we were ahead because he hated to see us lose.

His greatest single transaction had to be getting Joe DiMaggio from the San Francisco Seals for $25,000 and five players who were never heard from again in the major leagues. One became a dentist. The others won the Pacific Coast League championship for the Seals the next year, so it was a good deal for both teams.

For the Yankees, it was an absolute steal. Weiss knew that other teams were prepared to bid high for Joe. But he also knew that the Seals wanted players because they might be able to win the championship with the right combination. That's what he gave them from our minor-league system, plus what was a bargain-basement amount of cash for the man considered by many, including me, to be the greatest all-around player in the history of baseball.

DiMag almost became half of the biggest baseball deal ever made. In 1950, Weiss and Dan Topping talked to Boston's owner, Tom Yawkey, about a one-for-one trade, DiMaggio for Ted Wil-

liams. Both men would have broken every home-run record Babe
Ruth ever set, with Joe hitting into that screen above Fenway
Park's Green Monster and Ted taking dead aim at the "short
porch" in Yankee Stadium, only 296 feet down the right-field line
from home plate.

The word we got was that the deal had been proposed late in
the evening, or maybe into the early morning, after at least several
rounds of liquid refreshments, and that in the cold light of morning, all parties involved decided to return to a more sober line of
thought.

Weiss, however, was quoted later as saying that Yawkey backed
out of the deal. But if you want an intriguing thought to bring
some entertainment to a boring evening in February, just think of
what would have happened if that deal had been made.

As the summer of 1950 unfolded and Americans were singing
along with Gordon Jenkins and the Weavers on "Goodnight, Ir-
ene," we found ourselves in another knock-down, drag-out fight
in the American League, and the Dodgers were in the same spot
in the National League. Once again, we were battling the Red
Sox, plus the Detroit Tigers, managed by our old teammate, Red
Rolfe, while the Dodgers were trying to fight off the Phillies again.

In Brooklyn's case, it came down once more to the last day of
the season. It also came down to Duke Snider. And again, "the
Duke of Flatbush" came through, but this time the outcome was
different. Snider singled in the ninth inning, as he did in 1949
when he scored Reese with the pennant-winning run, but this time
his teammate, Cal Abrams, was thrown out at the plate trying to
score from second on Duke's hit to the outfield. Then Dick Sisler
hit a home run, and the Phillies were the National League champions.

We managed to fight off the challenges of Detroit and Boston,
beating out the Tigers by three games and our old tormentors, the
Red Sox, by four. Except for Joe D., Rizzuto, and Berra, we did
it without any Yankees among the top five players in the league's
hitting departments. The leaders were almost all from Detroit,
Boston, and Cleveland.

Maybe we didn't have individual statistical leaders, but we were
following the Yankee formula of winning as a team. Some of our

averages weren't enough to win the league batting title by themselves, but together they were enough to win the pennant for our
team. Rizzuto at .324 was the league's MVP; Berra came into his
own as a star at .322; Bauer did the same at .320; and DiMag hit
.301.

Our averages below the magical .300 mark weren't that bad
either: Coleman .287, Woodling .283, Mize .277, and me at .272,
followed by Billy Johnson and Joe Collins, plus contributions from
Brown and Mapes. I was pleased that I was able to keep my
batting average respectable, and I was proud that I was still able
to leg out 8 triples, only three behind the league leaders, Dom
DiMaggio, Bobby Doerr, and Hoot Evers.

Vic Raschi was becoming our meal ticket on the mound. He
was a 21-game winner again, and this time he had the best won-
lost percentage in the league with only 8 losses for a percentage of
.724. Pitching and defense kept us in the running all year long,
another reflection of Stengel's emphasis on teaching fundamentals.

Lopat finished second behind Raschi in won-lost percentage,
Raschi had the second most wins behind Cleveland's Bob Lemon,
Reynolds and Raschi were two-three in strikeouts, Lopat was
fourth in ERA, and Page had the second most saves, 13, behind
Mickey Harris of Washington.

Raschi was finishing among the league's leading pitchers again
even though more games were being played at night. Our Springfield Rifle would have preferred a trend in the opposite direction.
He didn't like night games.

"There may be pitchers who prefer to work at night," he said,
"but I'm not one of them. Pitching at night develops extra problems. Your reactions are speeded up. The plate looks closer, so
you think you can blow the ball by the hitters. At night your
curveball is slowed up. The hitter sees it better. Your fast ball is
speeded up. I just don't feel at home under the lights. I feel as if
I'm pitching in a make-believe world."

To give us more late-inning strength and provide Casey with as
much maneuverability as possible for our stretch drive and a potential spot in the World Series, Weiss bought Johnny Hopp from
the Pirates on September 5. Most American Leaguers knew Hopp

only by reputation from his twelve years as an outfielder-first baseman in "the other league," seven with the Cardinals. Weiss was
making one of his patented moves, like getting Johnny Mize from
the Giants late in the previous year.

I never quite understood the Hopp transaction, even though
Weiss said he thought my knee made it necessary. The word was
that we got Hopp for defensive purposes, yet Joe Collins, Johnny
Mize, and I teamed up to handle first base and did an adequate
job. Johnny had a fielding average of .996, and Joe and I each
had a .987, which was even with or only one point below four
starting first basemen in the league.

We were also told that his bat would be a valuable addition to
our attack if we made it to the World Series. The only trouble
with that reasoning was that Hopp never hit well in World Series
games. He had an average of .176 in 1942 against the Yankees,
an 0-for-4 Series against the Yanks the next year, and .185 against
the Browns in '44. For the record, he came to bat twice for us in
our 1950 Series against the Phillies and went hitless. He was a
consistently good hitter over a fourteen-year career with a lifetime
average of .296, but his career Series average was only .160.

With Mize hitting 25 home runs, he and Collins and I produced
39 homers and 134 runs batted in. As far as the World Series was
concerned, the whole thing didn't make any difference anyhow. I
was declared ineligible, to make room for Hopp in the Series, and
Mize had two singles in fifteen trips, Hopp was 0-for-2, and Collins
didn't have an official at-bat.

I was steamed about the whole thing. First Weiss insulted me
by taking me off the roster; he obviously felt I wasn't going to be
able to produce anything. Then he put Hopp in there expecting
him to do something. But Hopp didn't do anything that I wasn't
already doing and hadn't been doing since 1937.

My biggest consolation in the midst of my unhappiness over
what I considered a stupid move and an act of disloyalty on the
part of George Weiss was in a comment made by Joe DiMaggio.
He was spending the evening with his friend Toots Shor in the
cocktail lounge of the Warwick Hotel in New York the night before the first game of the 1950 World Series.

When they started talking about what Weiss had done in removing me from the team roster, Joe told Toots, "I'd rather lose with Tom than win without him."

When Weiss got Hopp, I thought it was only the latest piece of evidence that the Yankees still had not solved their first-base problem, eleven years after the retirement of Lou Gehrig. I never minded playing there to help the team—I played 189 games there for us, plus another 5 in the '49 World Series—but there never was any doubt in my mind that I could help the team more in the outfield, where I played 1,017 games.

The acquisition of Johnny Hopp was an admission that we still had problems at that position. The fact is that the Yankees had trouble of several kinds as the 1950s began. In addition to their fruitless search for a solid, all-around first baseman, they had looked for years for a good Jewish player to appeal to the city's large Jewish population. They wanted Hank Greenberg, a native New Yorker, at the start of his career, but Hank was an outfielder–first baseman who began his major-league career in 1930. In those years, the Yankees had some of their strongest teams. Greenberg chose Detroit.

The Yankees actually had a Jewish player on the team at the time, but they didn't know it. He was Jimmy Reese, an infielder with New York—and Babe Ruth's roommate—in 1930 and '31. Reese's religious preference turned out to be irrelevant. He had trouble breaking into the New York infield and was gone from the Yankees after the '31 season. He wasn't gone from the majors, though. He's still a big leaguer as a coach with the California Angels at age eighty-six.

The Yankees were also beginning to feel pressure to sign a black player. In 1950, it had been three years since the Dodgers integrated major-league baseball with Jackie Robinson. In the meantime, they added Roy Campanella, Don Newcombe, and Dan Bankhead. Our other rivals in New York, the Giants, had Monte Irvin in the second year of his Hall of Fame career.

In the American League, the Indians already had played Larry Doby, Satchel Paige, Minnie Minoso, and Luke Easter. It wasn't until 1955, when Elston Howard appeared in 97 games as an outfielder, catcher, and pinch-hitter, that the Yankees became an integrated baseball team.

The Yankee players never talked among ourselves about signing black players, for the simple reason that we never discussed what the front office was doing unless it affected one of us directly, as the Johnny Hopp decision did.

None of us had any fear about losing his job to a black player. Yankees never thought in such negative terms. My own attitude, and I'm confident that my teammates felt the same way, was that any player who could help us would be welcomed by us.

The Yankees had an excellent black player in their farm system in those years: a first baseman, Vic Power. He was playing for our farm team in Kansas City in the last few years before the Philadelphia A's moved there and made it a major-league city.

Power was a fancy-fielding right-handed first baseman and an aggressive hitter who made it to the big leagues with the A's in 1954. He enjoyed a big-league career of twelve years and achieved a lifetime batting average of .284. He was an excellent all-around player throughout his career, including his years in the Yankee organization. Besides his ability as a hitter, he was the best fielding first baseman I ever saw.

It wasn't that George Weiss and the rest of the Yankee management didn't want a black player on our team in 1950. It was that they didn't want *that* black player. Not Vic Power. He was considered too much of a troublemaker and a showboat. Before he could play a game with the Yankees, he was traded to the A's in a ten-player transaction.

In 1955, after I left the organization, the Yankees brought up Elston Howard, and everyone in the organization welcomed him with open arms. Why? Because he was such a beautiful man, cast in the image the Yankees wanted—a talented athlete who could help the team to win and conduct himself like the distinguished individual he always was.

People in the organization told me at the time how happy they were that Ellie was perfect for the team and for his role as its first black star. He and I became close friends in the years that followed. Every summer when I returned to Yankee Stadium to play in the annual Old Timers Game, he went out of his way to visit with me. I grew to admire him enormously, just as I admired Willie Randolph for so many of the same reasons when he broke in twenty years after Ellie.

We beat out Detroit by only three games, and it was another dogfight, with Boston only one game behind the Tigers. I was agonizing that I wasn't able to see more action, but I was grateful that I was at least able to contribute as what today we would call "a role player." I was filling in at first base, pinch-hitting in pressure situations and teaming up with Joe D. and others to give the younger players as much leadership as possible and trying to instill in them the same pride in the Yankees that we felt.

I remember two hits at the end of the 1950 season, wondering after each, "Was this my last one?"

The first came in Washington, when Casey sent me up to pinch-hit against Mickey Harris, a left-handed relief pitcher. We had two men on base. The first three pitches from Harris were balls. When I looked down to the third-base coach's box, Frankie Crosetti was relaying the "hit" sign to me from Stengel.

I felt like stepping out and rubbing my hands in glee. Any hitter loves to get the green light on 3–0, especially a fastball hitter like me, because you know that's what it's going to be.

It was a fastball, all right. I parked it on top of the Griffith Stadium scoreboard in deep right-center field. I got a triple out of it, plus those two RBIs. After I slid into third, Casey kindly sent in a pinch-runner and I hobbled to our dugout on the third base side, my left knee hurting worse than ever. As I approached the dugout steps, I thought to myself, "That might be it."

But a few days later, in Philadelphia, I was facing Joe Coleman, a right-hander. He gave me a fastball on a 1–2 pitch and I hit it to right-center field in Shibe Park for a double.

That was my last hit—number 1,297.

Not only did we not lead the league in any individual offensive category, we didn't do it in any of the defensive departments, either. Our hitters as a group led the league only in triples. Our pitchers, as a staff, led the league in shutouts, saves, and strike-outs.

In the National League, after the Phillies won the pennant on the home run by Sisler, the Yankee management requested permission to waive the usual requirement that a player be on a team's major-league roster on September 1 to be eligible for the World Series. Hopp was ineligible by five days, and Weiss and Stengel wanted him available in the Series. To clear a spot for him on our roster, they would make me and my bum knee ineligible.

The Phillies said okay in a sportsmanlike gesture. Later I found out that they were being a little *too* sportsmanlike. Their manager, Eddie Sawyer, one of the classy men in baseball, told me years later that the Phillies jumped at the opportunity that Weiss and Stengel were giving them. Sawyer said, "We didn't want you sitting over there on the Yankee bench ready to come in and beat us."

I was prepared for life after my playing career. I was a coach with the Yankees in 1951, but Casey didn't seem to care whether I was there or not. I respected Casey and liked him, but I was never one of the boys in his inner circle. I wasn't even the first-base coach. After a year of looking for something to do, I left the Yankees. I worked as a television sports reporter on the CBS morning news—where our anchor was Walter Cronkite—in 1952 and '53 before accepting the presidency of Red Top Brewery in Cincinnati.

I returned to baseball and New York as a coach with the Giants in 1957, but when Walter O'Malley and Horace Stoneham conspired to move the Dodgers and Giants to California, I didn't feel like going that far with them. John McHale hired me as a coach with Detroit for 1958 and '59, the coaching job I enjoyed the most.

Then a baseball fan back home in Ohio who hated the Yankees and rooted for the Senators made me an offer I couldn't refuse. Ray Koontz of Canton, the chief executive officer of Deibold, manufacturers of bank and security equipment, hired me to do public relations work at conventions and sports events. I was happy in that job until I retired into what I call "gainful unemployment" and moved to Arizona in the 1980s.

All of that was still ahead of me when the 1950 World Series began. It was a strange Series. People today remember that we won it in four straight, which we did, and the tendency is to think we blew the Phillies away. Just the opposite was the case. Our first three victories were by scores of 1–0, 2–1, and 3–2. The only game decided by more than one run was the fourth and last, and that was no blowout either, only 5–2.

The team batting averages sounded more like the weights of the players: .222 for us and .203 for the Phillies. The Philadelphia pitchers, led by Robin Roberts, Ken Heintzelman, and Jim Konstanty, compiled an earned run average of 2.27. That might have been good enough to pitch their team to the championship of baseball except for one thing: Our pitchers—Reynolds, Raschi, Lopat, Ford, and Ferrick—had an ERA of 0.73.

The victories required hard work by my teammates. Raschi pitched a two-hitter in the first game, and the only run by either team came on a double by Brown and back-to-back long fly balls by Bauer and Coleman. In the second game, DiMaggio won it for us with a home run in the tenth inning. Reynolds pitched all ten innings for us, and Roberts did the same for the Phils.

The Series moved to Yankee Stadium for the next three games, if all three were going to be necessary. After your team wins the first two games of the World Series, speculation immediately sets in about the possibility of a sweep. That was the question in 1950, too, after New York won the two Philadelphia games. Coleman won the third game with a single in the ninth inning that scored Woodling and made a winning pitcher out of Tom Ferrick, who relieved Lopat at the start of the ninth.

The fourth game may have been decided by three runs, but it was as much of a nail-biter as those three one-run games. A homer by Berra and a triple by Brown powered us to a three-run sixth inning, and we entered their ninth with a 5–0 lead. Ford was pitching a five-hitter, but he got into a serious jam, giving up two runs, then putting two men on base.

Reynolds, always ready to start or relieve, whatever his team needed him for, came in from the bullpen and struck out Stan Lopata to seal our second straight World Series championship, our third in four seasons, and the second in what turned out to be a record five straight Series victories by Casey Stengel's Yankees. They broke the record of four straight that we set while having such fun under Joe McCarthy in 1939.

I was proud to have been a member of the last three of those four McCarthy teams, the clubs of 1937, '38, and '39, and to have been a part of the first two of those Stengel teams. Joe DiMaggio and I were the only ones. And then only Joe was left.

Eighteen

Yankee Pride Then—and Now?

I was a loyal and enthusiastic Yankee supporter at those World Series games in Yankee Stadium, but I felt out of place in street clothes while my teammates—I still considered them that—were wearing the Yankee pinstripes with the NY on the front that I loved so much to put on every day of my career.

After Reynolds saved the championship game for us—I was still saying "we" and "us"—I walked away from Yankee Stadium, my favorite spot on this earth from 1937 through 1950. I didn't cry about it. I looked forward to my new career. And golf was going to be a whole lot easier on my knee than barreling into second base to break up a double play.

But I wouldn't be a Yankee player any more.

That special pride that we had—born with Babe Ruth, exemplified by Lou Gehrig and Joe DiMaggio, and displayed by all of us from my days as a pumped-up rookie to my final day as a gimpy veteran—was something all of us from those teams felt then and still feel today.

You can talk to any of us about it: Joe DiMaggio, Phil Rizzuto, Bill Dickey, and the rest from my early Yankee years to those on my last team in 1950 like Allie Reynolds, Bobby Brown, Whitey Ford, Yogi Berra, Ed Lopat, and Tom Ferrick.

Our substitute catcher who went on to bigger things, Ralph Houk, can tell you about it, plus our ex-marine in the outfield, Hank Bauer, and the one with the sweet .300 swing, Gene Woodling. So can Johnny Mize and Jerry Coleman and our left-hander who never was as flaky as he wanted you to believe, Tommy Byrne. So can Cliff Mapes, Billy Johnson, and Bill Bevens from our teams of the late 1940s, or Atley Donald, Marius Russo, and Spud Chandler from our teams of earlier in that decade, or Frank Crosetti, "the Crow," who was on all of our teams as player or coach, beginning in 1932.

The rookie who came up the year after I retired, Mickey Mantle, can tell you about Yankee pride, too. So can "the voice of the New York Yankees," Mel Allen, and Red Barber, who joined the Yankee announcing team after broadcasting for the Brooklyn Dodgers.

Dan Daniel was interviewing me in April of 1949 for an article he was writing for the *Sporting News,* and he was asking me why I thought we would do well in that pennant-race-turned-legend, especially in view of DiMaggio's absence. Dan made the point that so many others also made that year and in other seasons, too: that the Red Sox had better players than we did, and in some years so did the Indians and the Tigers.

All of us on the Yankees knew that. But we also knew that those clubs with better *players* weren't better *teams.* I told Daniel in that interview, "I hope the pride a player has in being a Yankee doesn't die out. It's more than a tradition. It's a mental, almost physical, lift for a player to put on a Yankee uniform."

DiMag, Charlie Keller, and I used to sit around the clubhouse and talk about it and about the history and prestige that was the New York Yankees. DiMag and I used to tell our younger players, "Go out on the field like a Yankee."

I told Daniel for his article, "This spirit which was born here with Ruth should never die. It won't."

The sad truth, of course, is that Yankee pride, if it isn't dead, is at least in a deep freeze. Two things put it there: big bucks and

George Steinbrenner. Steinbrenner may not have been any more of a villain in the front office than some of those who were there when we played, but there's a big difference—the ones who were there with us were competent. Ed Barrow, Larry MacPhail, and George Weiss knew what they were doing.

Steinbrenner did not, certainly not after his early successes. In the 1980s he badly mismanaged the Yankee organization. By the time Commissioner Fay Vincent forced him out of baseball in 1990, he had ruined more than just an organization that had been successful for as long as the oldest senior citizen could remember. He had done something even worse—he had ruined a tradition.

Steinbrenner transformed the New York Yankees from the most successful organization in the history of baseball into a circus sideshow of arguments, fights, and buffoonery that looked more like "Saturday Night Live." They won games—more than any other team in baseball in the 1980s—but they won only one pennant and no world championships, the worst record for Yankee teams since before World War I.

That tells you something about the Steinbrenner way, and why it didn't work. He proved that you can't *buy* a championship, any more than you can buy a player's strong commitment to his team, fondness for his teammates, or loyalty to them. Those are three essential ingredients for the success of a *team*—any team in any sport or business—and Steinbrenner's Yankee teams never had any of them.

I feel sorry for George, because away from baseball, he is a thoroughly decent, enjoyable man. He's kind, he's charitable, a nice guy to be around socially. But when he was in his baseball job with total authority over the New York Yankees, he would become an egomaniac.

In his last several seasons as their chief executive officer, Steinbrenner destroyed the image of the Yankees, and the brutal misfortune about it is that he will admit no blame for it. I believe that in his own heart, he truly wanted to add to the Yankees' prestige. But that ego seemed to get in his way everytime. Sad.

The other culprit is the money in the game today. Steinbrenner bears a major part of the blame for that, too, in his silly efforts to peel off large amounts of dollars from his bankroll and hand out multiyear contracts to buy a pennant instead of earning one through hard work and intelligent management.

As one who played when we had to beg and scream and hold out for even a livable wage, and as a former player representative of the Yankees, I'm delighted to see that today's players are getting what they're worth—and more, in some cases. Many of them will tell you that they're not really worth two or three million dollars a year, but if the owners are crazy enough to put it on the table, the players are smart enough to pick it up.

That was the Steinbrenner way. It did not breed consistent success for him or loyalty to him. Dave Winfield certainly doesn't express any undying affection for good old George, and neither does Don Mattingly. For that matter, how many of today's players feel that much loyalty to their teams and their fans in today's big-bucks environment, established more than a decade ago by Steinbrenner and a few others?

There is reason to wonder if today's players will speak of their teams and their teammates twenty or thirty years from now the way Joe DiMaggio, Phil Rizzuto, and I speak of our Yankee teams. Or the way Pee Wee Reese, Duke Snider, and Carl Erskine speak of the Dodgers of their era. Or the way Dom DiMaggio and Ted Williams talk about the Red Sox. Or even the way former players still on the younger side, like Jim Palmer and Brooks Robinson, speak with such loyalty and enthusiasm about their old buddies on the Orioles and their fondness for the good folks of Baltimore.

Those of us who played major-league baseball in the 1930s, '40s, and '50s are in our sixties and seventies now, but there are still plenty of us around to bear witness to those days and those values, to the way baseball used to be, and should be again.

And there are those lucky ones of us from that time who are able to say, "I was a Yankee."

Index